PUBLIC SOCIOLOGY

Public Sociology
Fifteen Eminent Sociologists Debate
Politics and the Profession in the
Twenty-first Century

EDITED BY
Dan Clawson, Robert Zussman, Joya Misra, Naomi Gerstel,
Randall Stokes, Douglas L. Anderton, and Michael Burawoy

UNIVERSITY OF CALIFORNIA PRESS Berkeley   Los Angeles   London

All royalties from the sale of this book are donated to the American Sociological Association Minority Fellowship Fund.

University of California Press, one of the most distinguished university presses in the United States, enriches lives around the world by advancing scholarship in the humanities, social sciences, and natural sciences. Its activities are supported by the UC Press Foundation and by philanthropic contributions from individuals and institutions. For more information, visit www.ucpress.edu.

University of California Press
Berkeley and Los Angeles, California

University of California Press, Ltd.
London, England

Library of Congress Cataloging-in-Publication Data

Public sociology : fifteen eminent sociologists debate politics and the profession in the twenty-first century / edited by Dan Clawson . . . [et al.].
   p.   cm.
Includes bibliographical references and index.
ISBN-13: 978-0-520-25137-3 (cloth : alk. paper)
ISBN-10: 0-520-25137-7 (cloth : alk. paper)
ISBN-13: 978-0-520-25138-0 (pbk. : alk. paper)
ISBN-10: 0-520-25138-5 (pbk. : alk. paper)
   1. Sociology—Methodology.   2. Sociology—Philosophy.   3. Applied sociology.   I. Clawson, Dan.

HM511.P83   2007
301—dc22   2006023163

Manufactured in the United States of America

15 14 13 12 11 10 09 08 07
10 9 8 7 6 5 4 3 2 1

This book is printed on New Leaf EcoBook 50, a 100% recycled fiber of which 50% is de-inked post-consumer waste, processed chlorine-free. EcoBook 50 is acid-free and meets the minimum requirements of ANSI/ASTM D5634-01 (*Permanence of Paper*).

Contents

Acknowledgments / vii

INTRODUCTORY

Introduction
ROBERT ZUSSMAN AND JOYA MISRA / 3

For Public Sociology
MICHAEL BURAWOY 23

INSTITUTIONALIZING PUBLIC SOCIOLOGY

Public Sociology and the End of Society
ALAIN TOURAINE / 67

Stalled at the Altar? Conflict, Hierarchy, and
Compartmentalization in Burawoy's Public Sociology
SHARON HAYS / 79

If I Were the Goddess of Sociological Things
JUDITH STACEY / 91

Going Public: Doing the Sociology That Had No Name
PATRICIA HILL COLLINS / 101

POLITICS AND THE PROFESSION

Speaking to Publics
WILLIAM JULIUS WILSON / 117

Do We Need a Public Sociology? It Depends on What
You Mean by *Sociology*
LYNN SMITH-LOVIN / 124

Speaking Truth to the Public, and Indirectly to Power
ARTHUR L. STINCHCOMBE / 135

The Strength of Weak Politics
DOUGLAS S. MASSEY / 145

From Public Sociology to Politicized Sociologist
FRANCES FOX PIVEN / 158

FALSE DISTINCTIONS: CONCEPTUAL RESERVATIONS

The Sociologist and the Public Sphere
IMMANUEL WALLERSTEIN / 169

About Public Sociology
ORLANDO PATTERSON / 176

For Humanist Sociology
ANDREW ABBOTT / 195

INTERDISCIPLINARITY

Whose Public Sociology? The Subaltern Speaks,
but Who Is Listening?
EVELYN NAKANO GLENN / 213

A Journalist's Plea
BARBARA EHRENREICH / 231

REJOINDER

The Field of Sociology: Its Power and Its Promise
MICHAEL BURAWOY / 241

Editors and Contributors / 259
Index / 263

Acknowledgments

We would like to thank Karen Mason, Brittnie Aiello, and Jason Rodriquez for their help in preparation of this manuscript. We would also like to thank the American Sociological Association for its endorsement of this project, and Naomi Schneider, Justin Hunter, and Valerie Witte at the University of California Press for their enthusiasm and skill in guiding the manuscript to publication, and Mary Ray Worley for her excellent copyediting.

INTRODUCTORY

ROBERT ZUSSMAN AND JOYA MISRA

Introduction

The 2004 meeting of the American Sociological Association was among the most successful in the organization's hundred-year history. Overflow crowds packed the ballrooms of the San Francisco Hilton to hear a glittering array of speakers, including economist Paul Krugman, Indian novelist Arundhati Roy, and former president of Brazil Fernando Henrique Cardoso (himself a sociologist). The centerpiece of the meetings, however, was Michael Burawoy's presidential address. In that address, published in the *American Sociological Review* and reprinted in this volume, Burawoy issued an impassioned call for a revitalization of sociology in a turn to a "public sociology," distinguished by its use of reflexive knowledge and its appeal beyond the university. Although by no means incompatible with other forms of sociology, only public sociology, Burawoy argues, can restore sociology to its calling as an "angel of history, searching for order in the broken fragments of modernity, seeking to salvage the promise of progress."

There is a long tradition in presidential addresses to the American Sociological Association (ASA) of reflections on the discipline and its direction. Burawoy's address is very much a part of this tradition. In his reflections on the character of sociological knowledge, Burawoy situates himself in a perennial controversy that runs all the way from William Ogburn's 1929 call for scientific sociology through Lewis Coser's 1975 attack on methods without substance. In his reflections on the public role of sociology, he situates himself within a tradition of political activism and social engagement earlier articulated by Alfred McClung Lee in 1976, Herb Gans in 1989, and, most recently, Joe Feagin in 2001. But if Burawoy's address is part of a long tradition, it also breaks with that tradition. Burawoy's call is not just for a reconceptualization of sociological thought but for a reformation of sociological practice. His address challenges us not just to think differently but also to act differently.

Burawoy's ASA presidency itself emerged out of a moment of intense controversy within the discipline. On one front, Burawoy himself played a leading part in a bitter controversy over the appointment of the new editors of the discipline's leading journal, the *American Sociological Review,* a controversy that, in the eyes of many, raised fundamental questions about sociology's willingness to acknowledge its own diversity of perspectives and demographics and, in the eyes of others, raised equally fundamental questions about the character of and commitment to standards of scientific rigor. On another front, two-thirds of the voting members of the ASA supported an official association resolution opposing the war in Iraq—much to the despair of many of the remaining third, who thought the resolution a dangerous politicization of a primarily scientific organization. In a discipline unsure of its internal direction and divided about its political engagements, Burawoy's call for public sociology has become the focal point of battles over the discipline's future.

Never lacking energy, Burawoy has crisscrossed the United States and has visited England, Canada, Norway, Taiwan, Lebanon, and South Africa to promote his vision of public sociology. The response has been variously enthusiastic and critical, but always intense. *Social Problems, Social Forces, Critical Sociology,* the *British Journal of Sociology,* and *American Sociologist* (among others) have all published special issues addressing public sociology. The ASA itself has established a column on public sociology in its newsletter, *Footnotes,* and has also created a special task force and Web site on public sociology. But the controversies continue.

In the fall of 2004, Burawoy approached the editors of the ASA's Rose Monograph Series (Doug Anderton, Dan Clawson, Naomi Gerstel, Joya Misra, Randall Stokes, and Robert Zussman), the only book series that is an official part of the ASA, to edit a book on public sociology. Although we decided, after much discussion, that the book was not appropriate to the Rose Series, which specializes in policy-oriented research monographs, we do believe that a book on public sociology will be of wide interest, both within sociology and beyond. This book is the product of that belief, a belief affirmed as well by the American Sociological Association, which has endorsed this volume as an official ASA publication.

WHAT IS PUBLIC SOCIOLOGY?

Public sociology, in Burawoy's rendition, is a sociology that engages with diverse publics, reaching beyond the university, to enter into an ongoing dialogue with these publics about fundamental values. Public sociology includes what Burawoy calls "traditional" public sociology, sociology written for an audience that, while often atomized, is far wider than the discipline. This is the sociology of op-ed pages, of widely read books like David Riesman's *The Lonely Crowd* (1950) and Robert Bellah and colleagues' *Habits of the Heart* (1985), and of (at least by original intent) the American Sociological Association's new journal, *Contexts*. Public sociology also includes teaching, especially teaching that engages with students' own lives and experiences, helping them develop a "deeper self-understanding of the historical and social contexts that have made them who they are." Most important, though, is "organic public sociology." This is sociology in which "the sociologist works in close connection with a visible, thick, active, local" public. The project of this sociology—played out in engagement with the labor movement, neighborhood associations, communities of faith, immigrant rights groups, and much else—is to "make visible the invisible, to make the private public."

Burawoy is proposing not that public sociology supplant other sociologies but that it find a place within a disciplinary division of labor that includes professional sociology, critical sociology, and policy sociology as well as public sociology. Professional sociology, Burawoy acknowledges, is the sine qua non of other sociologies, supplying "true and tested methods, accumulated bodies of knowledge, orienting questions, and conceptual frameworks." In contrast, critical sociology is the "conscience of professional sociology," constantly questioning the foundations, both normative and descriptive, of professional research programs. Critical sociology insists that sociology "confront the pressing cultural and institutional problems of the time" rather than lapsing into obsessive attention to issues of "technique and specialization." Yet critical sociology, as Burawoy understands it, is also marked by its unrepentant academic character, a preoccupation with abstract research programs rather than the common sense and actual experiences of those for whom it purports to speak. Policy sociology, unlike either professional sociology or critical sociology, does speak to audiences beyond the university. But it does so, Burawoy argues, "in the service of a goal defined by a client" and provides "solutions to problems" formulated elsewhere or, particularly in its pathological forms, legitimates "solutions that have already been reached."

Public sociology, then, is distinctive. Unlike professional sociology and policy sociology, public sociology is "reflexive" rather than "instrumental," addressing issues of value and purpose rather than matters of technique. Unlike professional sociology and critical sociology, public sociology addresses—and even helps create—publics beyond the university. Where economics addresses markets (and, Burawoy argues, tends to develop an interest in their expansion) and political science addresses the state (and, Burawoy argues, tends to develop an interest in its stability), public sociology is bound to civil society—that vast array of associations and movements that stand apart from both the state and the economy. And in this sense, Burawoy argues, sociology—and particularly public sociology—"represents the interests of humanity . . . keeping at bay both state despotism and market tyranny."

Burawoy's tone is elegant, respectful, and conciliatory. He insists that his four types of sociology are complementary, even synergistic, rather than contradictory. He insists also that public sociology has "no intrinsic normative valence," that it can "as well support Christian fundamentalism as it can liberation sociology." His plea for public sociology, then, seems to be little more than a polite request, deeply liberal in spirit, to find a place at the table (metaphorical as well as fourfold) for a variety of different types of sociology. As Lynn Smith-Lovin remarks in her highly critical essay included in this volume, when she first heard Burawoy's arguments for public sociology, she had "no argument with his simple message: that all four sociological activities are interrelated, mutually reinforcing, and mutually dependent. . . . Who could argue with that?" Second readings (Smith-Lovin's included), however, have been very different.

Burawoy's case for public sociology, we would like to suggest, proceeds at two levels. At a conceptual level, Burawoy's case rests on a variety of distinctions, one between types of audiences, another between types of knowledge, and yet another (among state, economy, and civil society) meant to locate sociology in a distinctive intellectual space. Although even Burawoy's harshest critics seem willing to accept his distinction between academic and extra-academic audiences, his distinction between "reflexive" and "instrumental" knowledge has met with considerable criticism, as has his effort to defend sociology as a distinctive discipline.

But Burawoy's essay, although theoretically sophisticated, operates as much at the level of practice as at the level of theory. And at this level—the level of practical implications—the response has been even more heated. If Burawoy's intention is simply to set a place at the table for public sociology along with the other sociologies already there, his critics have argued that this is anything but a simple task—that the table is already crowded, that the addition of a new guest will fundamentally change the character of the dinner party already in progress. As a practical matter, then, Burawoy's polite request turns out to be a virtually revolutionary demand. As both his sympathizers and critics acknowledge, taking Burawoy's plea for public sociology seriously would require rethinking and remaking our relationship to the university, our relationship to other disciplines, the ways we train graduate students, the ways we reward and honor colleagues, and (not least) the way we practice politics. And these are no small matters.

INSTITUTIONALIZING PUBLIC SOCIOLOGY

Beyond specifying different types of public sociology, Burawoy is vague as to what public sociology would involve. This vagueness is, we suspect, intentional, an expression of long-standing utopian traditions meant to set free the imagination. Others, though, have been far more specific. These specifications have included calls for sociologists to write better—a call likely to inspire as little controversy as it would be hard to realize. Specifications have also included testimonials about service learning, accounts by sociologists of their efforts in various programs to join the teaching of sociology with community activism.[1] These testimonials are also likely to provoke little controversy: so long as public sociology, whether in the form of service learning or small institutes, is kept insulated from a putative disciplinary core, few would object to the struggles of a hardy few to do good works.

But can there be such a thing as public sociology in one course or public sociology in one institute? Writing from the perspective of French sociology, Alain Touraine, in his essay included in this volume, argues quite the reverse. For Touraine, public sociology is in no sense peripheral to the sociological enterprise but is central to the theoretical and practical restoration of agency within the discipline. Writing from the different perspective of American sociology, Sharon Hays and Judith Stacey also argue that public sociology, if we are to take it seriously, cannot be insulated. As they suggest, a serious public sociology would require far-reaching reforms of the ways we all teach and practice. Although also sympathetic to the agenda of public sociology, Patricia Hill Collins is concerned that the institutionalization of public sociology within the discipline may, paradoxically, make it harder to practice effectively.

Alain Touraine approaches public sociology from the standpoint of an outsider to American sociology but accepts Burawoy's main arguments. Touraine argues that the main task of public sociology is to study the "actors who try to link the global economy with specific cultures." As a result, for Touraine, public sociology occupies the central place in sociology in its search for actors. Public sociology, he argues, is in fact reshaping professional sociology, pushing it in the direction of studying institutions, not in terms of the social system, but in order to defend "individuals and groups against dominant forces." At the same time, Touraine shows how research is "strongly connected both with a national, cultural, and political history and with the division of intellectual labor, which influences the representation both of sociology and of its frontiers with neighboring social sciences," and urges public sociology to truly "address ourselves to publics that are exterior to our own society." By tracing where and when different forms of sociology have waxed and waned, Touraine contextualizes the current American emphasis on public sociology (an effort Burawoy himself returns to in his reply in the final essay of this volume).

Where Touraine, writing from France, sees public sociology as an already accomplished practice, Sharon Hays, writing from the perspective of the United States, has more doubts. What worries Hays in particular is "the tendency to accept existing hierarchies within the discipline and merely to insert public sociology among them." This, she argues, would do little to affect the conflicts and inequalities within sociology and would open up "the potential for simply *compartmentalizing* public sociology within the discipline—thereby reproducing its second-class status." Hays is guardedly optimistic about the possibilities for public sociology. As teachers, she argues, most of us are already engaged in at least one form of public sociology. Similarly, the significant autonomy that accompanies most academic positions allows ample opportunities for activism.

But a sociology that truly includes public sociology, Hays argues, would require "shifting the weight to another foot." In particular, departments and universities would have to encourage a style of teaching that engages with moral and political questions. They would have to acknowledge that public sociology is not an "extracurricular" activity, but a fundamental part of our jobs, as important as teaching, conducting research, and publishing. And, even more difficult, Hays argues, sociologists would have to broaden their ideas of what constitutes intellectually serious activity, acknowledging that essays addressed to wider publics or reports written for community groups are no less rigorous for being more accessible, so long as they offer depth and insight. And this is no small order.

Judith Stacey is even more specific. Addressing herself to "policies and practices in graduate admissions and curriculum; in hiring, teaching, assessment, and reward structures for faculty; and in the rhetoric and culture of sociological writing and discourse," Stacey offers a series of "not-so-modest proposals." What, she asks, would our departments look like if we really did try, as Burawoy advocates, to reconstruct sociology as a global discipline (Thesis IX) and to construct a field that allowed sociologists to realize their frustrated aspirations for public sociology?

Stacey's suggestions for remolding the global division of sociological labor are simple enough: establish "sister" relationships between U.S. departments and departments in other nations; establish permanent positions for the regular appointment of visiting faculty from other nations, particularly from the Global South; expand affirmative action to graduate admissions for international students, again particularly for those from the Global South; and require graduate students not only to master a second language but also to participate in at least one research project with an international component. Simple though Stacey's proposals may be, it is easy to imagine deans, department chairs, and even faculty members scoffing at them, insisting on their impracticality.

If Stacey's proposals for internationalizing sociology are modest, her suggestions for reforming graduate education would involve, in her words, nothing less than "a daunting, countercultural mission both within the discipline and far beyond." Horrified by the "Chaplinesque assembly-line model of scholarly productivity that has come to dominate academic hiring and promotion standards," Stacey challenges the very core of the discipline: declare a "rotational moratorium" on academic publishing that requires full-time faculty to refrain from publishing every third year; change the standards of tenure and promotion so that they "directly counter assembly-line standards of productivity"; and make our journals "literally and unapologetically more 'journalistic.'" Stacey's proposals, even if meant satirically (and it is our own suspicion that she is dead serious), would put public sociology in the center of nothing less than a revolution in how we reward and practice sociology. Burawoy's own caution notwithstanding, it is little wonder that the prospect of public sociology makes some sociologists very nervous.

Patricia Hill Collins identifies herself unabashedly as a practitioner of public sociology, as someone who was doing public sociology long before the category of public sociology was named and classified, and even long before she herself became a sociologist. She notes that those "who are most likely to commit to public sociology have had experiences that provide them with a distinctive view of social inequality." While she has no doubts that sociologists should continue to practice public sociology, like Hays, she worries whether institutionalizing public sociology will simply "foster a kind of sociological ghettoization, primarily because those who gravitate toward public sociology may already hold subordinate status within the discipline itself." Particularly at a moment when anything associated with the "public" has given ground to massive efforts at privatization, naming public sociology may merely "install a permanent and recognizable underclass" within sociology, burdened with a stigmatized term. For Collins, "naming public sociology, and thereby opening the doors to the valid question of defining its distinguishing features," may create a subtle shift "from doing an unnamed, messy, and thus incorrigible public sociology to talking about public sociology in ways that shrink its possibilities."

POLITICS AND THE PROFESSION

The deepest concern of those sociologists who are nervous about the prospects of public sociology is that public sociology will politicize sociology. *Politicization* is a complicated term, and it is important to understand what aspect of politicization makes Burawoy's critics nervous. First, it could refer to the activities of sociologists as individuals. Burawoy is altogether explicit that he imagines the public sociologist as a partisan, defending the "interests of humanity." But few if any would object to individual sociologists acting as partisans: even Burawoy's harshest critics are quick to testify that, as individuals, they have both deep political commitments and, in many cases, long and distinguished careers of acting on those commitments. Second, it could refer to a particular political position. Although Burawoy is himself unapologetically of the Left, he is insistent that public sociology is itself politically neutral in this sense. Some (for example, Smith-Lovin in her essay in this volume) are skeptical that Burawoy would be as enthusiastic about public sociology if it were to be turned to the purposes of the Right. Others (particularly Frances Fox Piven in her essay in this volume) think Burawoy is too cautious, that he should drop his ostensible political neutrality in favor of an explicitly leftist sociology. Yet, it is *politicization* in a third sense that has generated the strongest criticisms and the most heated controversies. *Politicization* in this sense, as it is used or implied by Lynn Smith-Lovin, Arthur Stinchcombe, and Douglas Massey, refers to the intrusion of political concerns into what they see as the intellectually rigorous core of the profession. At issue for them is Burawoy's view of the sociological division of labor. Where Burawoy imagines public sociology and professional sociology as complementary, even drawing strength from each other, his critics insist that this complementarity is an illusion. Their fear, then, is that a politicized sociology will distract from and eventually undermine the possibilities of the rigorous and disciplined pursuit of truth.

Of the essays in this book, William Julius Wilson's is the most sympathetic to Burawoy's position. Wilson argues that it is not just the findings of sociological research that contribute to "public discourse on issues such as persistent poverty, urban planning, and criminal justice." Even more important, Wilson argues, are sociological frameworks, concepts such as labeling and concentration effects, which have become staples of public discussion and policy processes. The key, Wilson argues, to extending the range of sociological influence is lucid writing.

Wilson also explicitly takes on the claim that public sociology will undermine professional sociology. Rather than challenging the legitimacy of professional sociology, public sociology will enhance that legitimacy: "The more sociology is ignored by the media and policy makers, the less attention it receives as an academic discipline and therefore the more removed it is from the decision-making arena, the fewer students it attracts, and the more difficulty it has in obtaining funding for research from private foundations and government agencies." For Wilson, then, the issue is not whether sociologists should enter into public debate but how they can do so most effectively.

Yet, Wilson's essay is marked as much by its silences as by what it says explicitly. Wilson limits his comments to what Burawoy has called "traditional" public sociology, the sociology of op-ed pages and books written for a mixture of lay and professional audiences. Does he believe that "organic" public sociologists who attach themselves to a social movement, who position themselves as activists rather than as scholars, can maintain the "expertise and legitimacy" necessary for public sociology to flourish?

If Wilson leaves this question unanswered, Smith-Lovin, Stinch-combe, and Massey do not. Each is explicit that public sociology is, at best, a distraction, at worst, an imminent threat to the core tasks of generating professional knowledge. While Smith-Lovin, Stinchcombe, and Massey clearly take a generally critical stance toward public sociology, each does so for somewhat different reasons.

Lynn Smith-Lovin's and Arthur Stinchcombe's primary concern is that public sociology will undermine the core task of professional sociology, that of cumulating knowledge for its own sake. While Smith-Lovin has no objection to "urging individual sociologists to become involved in civic life," she strongly opposes embracing "value-laden activity . . . within the disciplinary structure itself." She understands, to be sure, that universities and the disciplines within them are not and probably cannot be hermetically sealed from the outside world. But understanding that, she and Stinchcombe both argue that universities and disciplines should attempt to shield scholars from outside pressures (of granting agencies as well as political movements). If we do not, as Stinchcombe puts it, value "the idle curiosity" of our leading scholars and "stick them in ivory towers with tenure and without questions on the bottom line," we will not have "any truth" to speak to power.

Stinchcombe adds one more twist to this argument. Where Burawoy and most of his critics agree that sociology does have something important to say to various publics—and differ primarily over the right way of saying it—Stinchcombe is not so sure. The relevant truths of sociology are truths about the future, but such truths are elusive. And to get accepted, even the limited truths we have of most social processes would require an understanding of how different bureaucracies institutionalize their own views of the future. As a result, he suggests, "we have nothing to tell public audiences about how to free up money from Star Wars to close the race and class gaps in academic achievement test scores, even if we knew how to close them."

The danger of public sociology, for Smith-Lovin and Stinchcombe, is not simply that it distracts from knowledge for its own sake but that it represents an antithetical principle. To the public sociologist, Smith-Lovin argues, "truth value is not empirical, established through standards of peer review, but is established through the consensus that is formed as a result of dialogue with a public," while Stinchcombe worries that public sociology, in his terse formulation, will be "high in affect, low in competence." Only by maintaining self-consciously traditional and professional standards of evaluation, Smith-Lovin continues, will sociology be able to maintain "the legitimacy and internal consensus that allow us to sustain the discipline." And without that, she fears for the very fate of academic freedom.

Although Douglas Massey winds up in the same position as Smith-Lovin and Stinchcombe—sympathetic to individual political participation but critical of collective participation by the discipline—he gets to that position by a different route. Where Smith-Lovin and Stinchcombe worry that an engaged public sociology will erode professional standards, Massey worries that a disciplinary politics would erode the political effectiveness of individual activists. Drawing on his own experience consulting and testifying about issues of immigration policy, racial segregation, and human rights, Massey argues, first, that effective action requires an accurate understanding of the groups and structures one seeks to modify through political action. Like Smith-Lovin and Stinchcombe, he fears that public sociology will compromise that accuracy. Second, he argues that "a reputation for impartiality and objectivity greatly enhances the value of the statements that the association *does* choose to make on questions of public import." And third, he argues that by advancing scientific rather than political criteria of truth, the American Sociological Association helps build professional respect and scientific legitimacy, which are prerequisites for the effective engagement of individual sociologists. Having served as president of both, Massey compares the American Sociological Association to the much smaller, but less explicitly political, Population Association of America and concludes that "the political clout of the ASA on Capitol Hill is minuscule. Inside the Beltway, the sad reality is that few people pay any attention to the political stands collectively taken by sociologists."

For Frances Fox Piven, the issues lie far outside the Beltway. Where Massey, Stinchcombe, Smith-Lovin, and others worry about the politicization of sociology by public sociology, Piven worries about what kind of politics public sociology will encourage. Like Hays, who characterizes Burawoy's address as a "politician's speech—designed to . . . avoid ruffling too many feathers," Piven not only wants a politicized sociology but wants a politicized sociology that is unashamedly of the Left. In her reading, the problem is not too little influence in the Washington Beltway, but that the Beltway exercises too much influence inside of sociology: "Public sociologists of the policy science variant were for hire. We sought out patrons, and inevitably we fell under their influence. . . . All of this sophistication—our ever-more-careful research designs and our ever-larger research projects—was put to work investigating causal relations dictated by the interpretations, the story lines, advanced by our patrons."

Piven does not abandon the ivory tower. But she sees it as a fortress of a different sort than do Smith-Lovin and Stinchcombe. Rather than providing protection against a politicized public sociology, Piven sees the university as a protection against powerful political forces that have gathered on the right. Given the choices she sees, Piven is clear which publics she sides with: "If public sociology is to thrive, we have to recognize not one public but many publics, and once we acknowledge the sharp divisions in our society, we have to decide which publics we want to work with. I propose as a guideline that we strive to address the public and political problems of people at the lower end of the many hierarchies that define our society." For Piven (as for Touraine, and unlike for Burawoy), public sociology cannot be neutral. It is, of necessity, dissident and critical.

FALSE DISTINCTIONS: CONCEPTUAL RESERVATIONS

Burawoy's vision of public sociology is a vision of practice—of a way of doing (and rewarding) sociology. But it is not only a vision of practice. Indeed, the power of Burawoy's argument lies in the connections he makes between practice and a conception of sociological knowledge. Burawoy, then, is not simply interested in applying sociological knowledge: he also wants to rethink what that knowledge consists of. In particular, Burawoy distinguishes between instrumental knowledge and reflexive knowledge. Instrumental knowledge, he argues, focuses on means. In contrast, reflexive knowledge is focused on ends and "interrogates the value premises of society as well as our profession." While instrumental (or technical) knowledge is the core of professional and policy sociology, reflexive knowledge is central to critical and public sociology. But not all of Burawoy's critics agree. Orlando Patterson, Immanuel Wallerstein, and Andrew Abbott, in particular, argue that Burawoy has made a false distinction.

For Patterson, Burawoy's conception of public sociology and reflexive knowledge is, at the same time, overly categorical—imposing sharp distinctions on a social world which is "at best fuzzy"—and underelaborated—failing to recognize the range of forms that public sociology may take. Patterson distinguishes three types of public sociology. One he calls "discursive," roughly similar to Burawoy's traditional public sociology, where sociologists are actively involved in public conversations with various nonsociological audiences. While, Patterson argues, discursive public sociology is a flagging tradition in the United States, it retains its vitality elsewhere, most notably in Europe and India. A second type is characterized by "active, civic, especially political, engagement" of the sociologist, a rough parallel to Burawoy's organic public sociology. But Patterson departs from Burawoy in his conception of the third type, which he calls "professional," "the kind of public sociology in which the scholar remains largely committed to the work but becomes involved with publics and important public issues as an expert."

Drawing on his own experiences advising clients as diverse as Michael Manley, the radical prime minister of Jamaica (on globalization), or the newly installed President Gerald Ford (on ethnic revivals), or an audience of personnel executives from the top five hundred corporations assembled by *Forbes* magazine (on affirmative action), Patterson sharply challenges Burawoy's claim that a professional expert working for a client is not practicing public sociology. "The fact that one works for a client is an irrelevance," Patterson argues, "as is the question of whether one is paid." What matters, he continues, is "boldly presenting one's point of view" and that "what one does be of public interest." For Patterson, then, criminologists and demographers in the employ of government agencies and even market researchers working for private employers may count as public sociologists so long as their work "entails and engages a public." Indeed, Patterson notes that sociology has "committed a slow kind of disciplinary hari-kari" by "systematically shedding all those areas of the study of society that the public is most interested in."

More than Patterson, Immanuel Wallerstein acknowledges the tension between instrumental and reflexive knowledge, between the knowledge of professional sociology and the knowledge of the organic public intellectual. But where Burawoy emphasizes the strengths of each, Wallerstein emphasizes the dangers of both. Like Smith-Lovin, Stinchcombe, and Massey, Wallerstein sees the intellectual honesty of organic public sociologists compromised by political loyalties; unlike them, however, Wallerstein is no more optimistic about the possibilities of a value-free professional sociology as, he argues, "it is intrinsically impossible to keep one's values from entering one's scientific/scholarly work."

For Wallerstein, the answer to the dilemmas posed by different types of knowledge is that all sociologists should engage with both. All sociologists (and all social scientists), Wallerstein suggests, should perform three functions: an intellectual function, to develop plausible analyses of the empirical world; a moral function, to understand the moral implications of our work; and a political function, to consider the best way to realize a moral good as we understand it. These functions, he argues, are linked, sequential, and inevitable. If, for example, a scholar privileges the intellectual function, "one is burying (and thereby denying) the implicit moral and political choices that are in fact being made. But hiding them (from others and from oneself) does not mean that they are not being made." Similarly, Wallerstein claims that a scholar who attempts to privilege the political task will be unable to consider "the degree to which the political choices are affecting the validity of the intellectual and moral choices."

Wallerstein calls for all scholars to fulfill intellectual, moral, and political functions consciously and actively. As a result, Wallerstein rejects the notion of public sociology as something separate from the rest of sociology. As he argues, "all sociologists—living, dead, or yet to be born—are, and cannot be other than, public sociologists. The only distinction is between those who are willing to avow the mantle and those who are not."

Where Wallerstein argues that instrumental and reflexive knowledge should be deployed together, Andrew Abbott is more skeptical of the very distinction, arguing that the exclusion of reflexivity from any sociology would constitute a "disastrous error." As he argues, "There are no 'good' versions of purely instrumental or reflexive work." For Abbott, sociology is inevitably value-laden, not only because we are all embedded within our particular standpoints, but because "the social process is itself a process of values: not so much in the knower as in the known." All categories of analysis are shaped by values, and to pretend otherwise is to create bad sociology. Instead, Abbott argues, sociological research must always be both instrumental and reflexive, perhaps as "perpetually succeeding phases in the research process." In contrast to a distinctive public sociology, Abbott calls for a consistently humanist sociology which requires us to consider and "modify" our categories and analyses "continuously" in order to take a moral stance as sociologists.

Both Abbott and Wallerstein call into question the assumption some have made (although explicitly denied by Burawoy himself) that reflexivity is somehow equated with a particular political viewpoint. Reflexivity may appear at different places on the political spectrum: indeed, for Abbott, reflexive knowledge need not have any political valence at all. "One can be a heedless mainstream sociologist," Abbott argues, "and even a cowardly one. But one can also be in the mainstream for moral reasons as profound as those that put others in opposition."

INTERDISCIPLINARITY

Where Wallerstein and Abbott argue against what they see as false distinctions within sociology, Evelyn Nakano Glenn and Barbara Ehrenreich (as well as Judith Stacey in the essay discussed earlier) argue against distinctions between sociology and other disciplines. Burawoy is unapologetic in his defense of sociology. In his account, the social sciences differ from the natural sciences and the humanities in their combination of instrumental and reflexive knowledge. While natural scientists focus on instrumental knowledge, and those in the humanities focus on reflexive knowledge, social scientists combine both types of knowledge, making the social sciences central to public and policy interventions. And within the social sciences, Burawoy argues, sociology is uniquely suited to represent the "interests of humanity."

The special subject matter of economics, Burawoy argues, is markets and the special subject matter of political science, the state. Not only do practitioners in both disciplines emphasize instrumental knowledge to the exclusion of reflexivity, but they tend to develop an interest in the expansion and stability of that which they study. In contrast, sociologists not only study but also defend civil society, the only viable alternative to the tyranny of markets and the despotism of states. If the social sciences occupy a special location within all scholarly disciplines, sociology occupies a special position with the social sciences.

At the same time, Burawoy reacts strongly to the notion that disciplinary specialization is anachronistic, arguing that unified social science is a "positivist fantasy" and "all too easily dissolves reflexivity, that is, the critical and public moments of social science." Interdisciplinary knowledge does exist with cross-disciplinary borrowing that maintains professional sociology's distinctiveness, limited transdisciplinary infusion in critical sociology (from feminism, poststructuralism, and critical race theory), multidisciplinary collaboration around social issues in public sociology, and joint-disciplinary coordination in the policy world, which privileges knowledge produced by economists and political scientists. These forays into interdisciplinarity do not, however, rob sociologists of a distinct identity. As Burawoy argues, "The social sciences are not a melting pot of disciplines, because the disciplines represent different and opposed interests—first and foremost interests in the preservation of the grounds upon which their knowledge stands."

As Judith Stacey argues, Burawoy's focus on economics and political science as sociology's main "competitors" requires a "rhetorical sleight of hand that attributes his disciplinary selection criteria to space limitations" that exclude such fields as geography, history, and psychology that "could certainly mount robust competitive or, better, complementary claims to representing 'the interests of humanity.'"

Evelyn Nakano Glenn extends this argument. She notes that for many scholars, disciplinary boundaries are counterproductive. She argues that Burawoy's essay is marked by a bias "toward looking sideways at peers and upward at superiors, that is, to elaborate on sociology's relation to the 'peer' disciplines of economics and political science." Left out of Burawoy's essay are not only "lesser" fields like geography and anthropology, mentioned only in passing, but "subaltern" fields such as ethnic studies and women's studies, which are never even mentioned.

Glenn argues that academic sociology professionalized itself by pushing public sociology out of the discipline (particularly when done by women and racial and ethnic minorities). As she notes, "Historically, academic sociology 'professionalized' as did other fields, such as medicine, by redefining itself as rigorously 'scientific' and nonpolitical, by ejecting members of marginalized groups who might lower the prestige of the field, and by setting up barriers to new entrants from marginalized groups." More recently, activist and political debates around gender, race, ethnicity, and sexuality have been diverted to new departments or programs in ethnic studies, women's studies, and gay, lesbian, and bisexual studies—all without fundamentally restructuring sociology itself. Glenn recalls that W. E. B. DuBois's Black Reconstruction was reviewed in the *American Journal of Sociology* in 1936 as "only a half-baked Marxian interpretation of the labor side of Reconstruction and a badly distorted picture of the Negroes' part in Southern life." But she also reminds us that Patricia Hill Collins, the most widely cited critical race theorist in sociology today, has been located in an African American studies department for most of her career. For Glenn, Burawoy's defense of sociology is a defense of privilege, an effort that will reproduce inequalities among disciplines.

Barbara Ehrenreich is also skeptical about the distinctive contributions of sociology. A practicing journalist with a PhD in biology, Ehrenreich writes as a public intellectual, sympathetic to sociology, but without a stake in the discipline. Ehrenreich argues that sociologists must focus on the problems endemic to modern society. To do so requires reaching "out to other disciplines, even at the risk of disrupting boundaries and ceding turf." She makes a case that sociology needs history, psychology, and even biology, asking at least that public sociologists be "willing to go anywhere in pursuit of answers, even to go boldly, when the questions carry them there, where no social scientist has gone before."

THE FUTURE OF PUBLIC SOCIOLOGY?

Visions of the future cannot rely on simple projections of the past. Even in the best of circumstances, as Arthur Stinchcombe has reminded us, we do not know with certainty the future of any social practice. In the case of public sociology, we do not even fully know its past. We do know, to be sure, that some prominent figures of the past (W. E. B. DuBois, Jane Addams), now reclaimed for the discipline, were organic public sociologists in the fullest sense. But we do not know how many sociologists have emulated their efforts in the years since or in what ways they have emulated them. We know, from the pages of *Footnotes* and elsewhere, that many sociologists write for op-ed pages. But we have little idea how frequently they do so or how central they see such writing to their careers. We know that a majority of sociologists teach. But we do not know, if even we could measure it, how many teach reflexively and how many see their teaching focused on instrumental knowledge.

If we do not even know public sociology's past (or its present), we cannot pretend to know its future—whether public sociology will gather strength over the years to come or appear, decades from now, as a curious, nearly forgotten detour on a path leading in some altogether different direction. We can, however, imagine what some of the forces driving public sociology may be.

For several decades, if not longer, sociology has attracted a disproportionate share of scholars critical of American society. These critical impulses within sociology have been expressed in—and reinforced by—demographic changes within the discipline. The feminization of American sociology (well over half of all new PhDs are now women) and its racial diversification (well over one-quarter of all new sociology PhDs are now minorities) have likely increased the numbers of sociologists committed to social justice projects and inclined toward public sociology. Whether this inclination strengthens or weakens over the years to come will depend both on the status of currently disadvantaged groups within American society and on future demographic changes.

We also know that the continued expansion of mass higher education, especially in conjunction with often severe budget constraints, has created a new labor pool of part-time faculty. These part-timers, blocked from more conventional routes, seem likely candidates for developing alternative careers as public sociologists, mixing teaching with advocacy for organizations and publics to which they are variously attached. But we do not know how long or how thoroughly the turn to part-time faculty will continue. And we know even less how well new careers as public sociologists will touch those in more secure positions or what sorts of inroads public sociology might make in the currently most prestigious centers of the discipline. (It is, we might note, entirely to the point that the call for public sociology comes from a president of the American Sociological Association with a long-standing position in one of the country's leading sociology departments—who is himself much better known as a professional and critical sociologist than as a public sociologist.)

We also know, more generally, that the future of public sociology is likely tied intimately to the future of those colleges and universities that employ a large majority of sociologists. In the past, as Piven and Hays both argue in the articles discussed earlier, universities have provided sociologists the freedom to pursue advocacy (as well as freedom from political pressure, as Smith-Lovin and Stinchcombe argue). Increased teaching loads, whether measured in courses taught or by the number of students in courses, would decrease the time available for sociologists to engage with publics beyond the university. An increased emphasis on instrumental knowledge, whether in the name of developing standards of accountability or in a search for increased external funding, would stunt the development of reflexivity. But there are developments moving in other directions as well. By some reports, many colleges and universities, reviving and extending the long mandate of land grant institutions to public service, are trying to encourage service learning, among both their students and their faculty. Whether this encouragement continues (and expands), what forms this encouragement takes, and whether this encouragement is institutionalized in the form of new career paths will all shape the future of public sociology.

We know, finally, that American sociology, in steps however slow and halting, has become less insular in recent years. This is evident in intensified interest in world systems, globalization, and the Global South. But an intensified interest in the world beyond our borders as easily takes the forms of professional sociology, policy sociology, and critical sociology as it does public sociology. Neither does an interest in the world beyond our borders imply that American sociology will, in its organization, become more like Latin American sociology or European sociology, where the widespread practice of public sociology may be an expression of poor prospects for academic employment. And there is nothing inevitable even about the internationalization of American sociology. It is at least imaginable that Americans and American sociologists, tired of international adventurism, will retreat to a political and intellectual isolationism in which models of public sociology from other nations retreat from view.

The future of public sociology will depend, then, on broad structural forces, in the international order, in American society, in the university, even within the discipline itself. But to argue that the future of public sociology will depend only on structural forces is to miss the point of public sociology itself. To take the call to public sociology seriously, whether we are ourselves sympathetic or hostile, is to recognize that reflexive public engagement and advocacy are themselves consequential and that the future is not fixed. Sociologists may not make even their own discipline under conditions of their own choosing, but they do make that discipline. In this sense, the future of public sociology will depend, in some unknown part, on the choices sociologists themselves make, individually and (more importantly) collectively, for themselves and for the discipline as a whole. If this book contributes to making those choices in more informed, more thoughtful ways, it has served its purpose.

NOTE

1. See, particularly, the pieces by William Gamson, Charlotte Ryan, and Charles Derber (2004) in a special section of *Social Problems* devoted to a discussion of public sociology.

REFERENCES

Bellah, Robert, Richard Madsen, William M. Sullivan, Ann Swidler, and Steven Tipton. 1985. *Habits of the Heart: Individualism and Commitment in American Life.* Berkeley: University of California Press.

Coser, Lewis A. 1975. "Presidential Address: Two Methods in Search of a Substance." *American Sociological Review* 40 (6): 691–700 (www.jstor.org.silk .library.umass.edu:2048/browse/00031224/di97430840).

Derber, Charles. 2004. "Public Sociology as a Vocation." Pp. 119–21 in "Public Sociologies: A Symposium from Boston College," M. Burawoy, W. Gamson, C. Ryan, S. Pfohl, D. Vaughan, C. Derber, and J. Schor. *Social Problems* 51 (1): 103–30.

Feagin, Joe R. 2001. "Social Justice and Sociology: Agendas for the Twenty-first Century: Presidential Address." *American Sociological Review* 66 (1): 11–20.

Gamson, William. 2004. "Life on the Interface." Pp. 106–10 in "Public Sociologies: A Symposium from Boston College," M. Burawoy, W. Gamson, C. Ryan, S. Pfohl, D. Vaughan, C. Derber, and J. Schor. *Social Problems* 51 (1): 103–30.

Gans, Herbert J. 1989. "Sociology in America: The Discipline and the Public American Sociological Association, 1988 Presidential Address." *American Sociological Review* 54 (1): 1–16.

Lee, Alfred McClung. 1976. "Sociology for Whom?" *American Sociological Review* 41 (6): 925–36.

Ogburn, William F. 1929. "Presidential Address: The Folkways of a Scientific Sociology." www.asanet.org/galleries/default-file/ogburnpresidentialaddress.pdf.

Riesman, David. 1950. *The Lonely Crowd: A Study of the Changing American Character.* With N. Glazer and R. Denny. New Haven, CT: Yale University Press.

Ryan, Charlotte. 2004. "Can We Be Compañeros?" Pp. 110–13 in "Public Sociologies: A Symposium from Boston College," M. Burawoy, W. Gamson, C. Ryan, S. Pfohl, D. Vaughan, C. Derber, and J. Schor. *Social Problems* 51 (1): 103–30.

MICHAEL BURAWOY

For Public Sociology

> This is how one pictures the angel of history. His face is
> turned towards the past. Where we perceive a chain of
> events, he sees one single catastrophe which keeps piling
> wreckage upon wreckage and hurls it in front of his feet. The
> angel would like to stay, awaken the dead, and make whole
> what has been smashed. But a storm is blowing from Par-
> adise; it has got caught in his wings with such violence that
> the angel can no longer close them. This storm irresistibly
> propels him into the future to which his back is turned, while
> the pile of debris before him grows skyward. This storm is
> what we call progress.
>
> Walter Benjamin, 1940

Walter Benjamin wrote his famous ninth thesis on the philosophy of history as the Nazi army approached his beloved Paris, hallowed sanctu-
ary of civilization's promise. He portrayed this promise in the tragic
figure of the angel of history, battling in vain against civilization's long
march through destruction. To Benjamin, in 1940, the future had never
looked bleaker with capitalism-become-fascism in a joint pact with
socialism-become-Stalinism to overrun the world. Today, at the dawn of
the twenty-first century, although communism has dissolved and fascism is a haunting memory, the debris continues to grow skyward.
Unfettered capitalism fuels market tyrannies and untold inequities on a
global scale, while resurgent democracy too often becomes a thin veil
for powerful interests, disenfranchisement, mendacity, and even violence. Once again the angel of history is swept up in a storm, a terrorist
storm blowing from Paradise.

In its beginning sociology aspired to be such an angel of history,
searching for order in the broken fragments of modernity, seeking to salvage the promise of progress. Thus, Karl Marx recovered socialism from

alienation; Émile Durkheim redeemed organic solidarity from anomie and egoism. Max Weber, despite premonitions of "a polar night of icy darkness," could discover freedom in rationalization and extract meaning from disenchantment. On this side of the Atlantic W. E. B. DuBois pioneered pan-Africanism in reaction to racism and imperialism, while Jane Addams tried to snatch peace and internationalism from the jaws of war. But then the storm of progress got caught in sociology's wings. If our predecessors set out to change the world, we have too often ended up conserving it. Fighting for a place in the academic sun, sociology developed its own specialized knowledge, whether in the form of the brilliant and lucid erudition of Robert Merton (1949), the arcane and grand design of Talcott Parsons (1937, 1951), or the early statistical treatment of mobility and stratification, culminating in the work of Peter Blau and Otis Dudley Duncan (1967). Reviewing the 1950s, Seymour Martin Lipset and Neil Smelser (1961, 1–8) could triumphantly declare sociology's moral prehistory finally over and the path to science fully open. Not for the first time Comtean visions had gripped sociology's professional elite. As before, this burst of "pure science" was short-lived. A few years later, campuses—especially those where sociology was strong—were ignited by political protest for free speech, civil rights, and peace, indicting consensus sociology and its uncritical embrace of science. The angel of history had once again fluttered in the storm.

The dialectic of progress governs our individual careers as well as our collective discipline. The original passion for social justice, economic equality, human rights, sustainable environment, political freedom, or simply a better world that drew so many of us to sociology is channeled into the pursuit of academic credentials. Progress becomes a battery of disciplinary techniques—standardized courses, validated reading lists, bureaucratic rankings, intensive examinations, literature reviews, tailored dissertations, refereed publications, the almighty CV, the job search, the tenure file, and then policing one's colleagues and successors to make sure we all march in step. Still, despite the normalizing pressures of careers, the originating moral impetus is rarely vanquished; the sociological spirit cannot be extinguished so easily.

Constrictions notwithstanding, discipline—in both the individual and collective senses of the word—has borne its fruits. We have spent a century building professional knowledge, translating common sense into science, so that now we are more than ready to embark on a systematic back-translation, taking knowledge back to those from whom it came, making public issues out of private troubles, and thus regenerating sociology's moral fiber. Herein lies the promise and challenge of public sociology, the complement and not the negation of professional sociology.

To understand the production of public sociology, its possibilities and its dangers, its potentialities and its contradictions, its successes and failures, during the last eighteen months I have discussed and debated public sociology in over forty venues, from community colleges to state associations to elite departments across the United States—as well as in England, Canada, Norway, Taiwan, Lebanon, and South Africa. The call for public sociology resonated with audiences wherever I went. Debates resulted in a series of symposia on public sociology, including ones in *Social Problems* (February 2004), *Social Forces* (June 2004), and *Critical Sociology* (Summer 2005). *Footnotes*, the newsletter of the American Sociological Association (ASA), developed a special column on public sociology, the results of which are brought together in *An Invitation to Public Sociology* (American Sociological Association 2004). Departments have organized awards and blogs on public sociology, the ASA has unveiled its own site for public sociology, and introductory textbooks have taken up the theme of public sociology. Sociologists have appeared more regularly in the opinion pages of our national newspapers. The 2004 ASA annual meetings, devoted to the theme of public sociologies, broke all records for attendance and participation and did so by a considerable margin. These dark times have aroused the angel of history from his slumbers.

I offer eleven theses. They begin with the reasons for the appeal of public sociologies today, turning to their multiplicity and their relation to the discipline as a whole—the discipline being understood both as a division of labor and as a field of power. I examine the matrix of professional, policy, public, and critical sociologies as it varies historically and among countries, comparing sociology with other disciplines, before finally turning to what makes sociology so special, not just as a science but as a moral and political force.

THESIS I: THE SCISSORS MOVEMENT

The aspiration for public sociology has become stronger and its realization ever more difficult as sociology has moved left and the world has moved right.

To what shall we attribute the current appeal of public sociology? To be sure, it reminds so many of why they became sociologists, but public sociology has been around for some time, so why might it suddenly take off?

Over the last half century the political center of gravity of sociology has moved in a critical direction while the world it studies has moved in the opposite direction. Thus, in 1968, members of the ASA were asked to vote on a member resolution against the Vietnam War. Of those who voted, two-thirds *opposed* the ASA taking a position, while in a separate opinion question, 54 percent expressed their individual opposition to the war (Rhoades 1981, 60)—roughly the same proportion as in the general population at the time. In 2003, thirty-five years later, a similar member resolution against the war in Iraq was put to the ASA membership and two-thirds *favored* the resolution (*Footnotes*, July-August 2003). Even more significant, in the corresponding opinion poll, 75 percent of those who voted said they were against the war, at a time (late May 2003) when 75 percent of the general population supported the war.[1]

Given the leftward drift of the 1960s, this is an unexpected finding. Despite the turbulence of the 1968 annual meeting in Boston, which included Martin Nicolaus's famous and fearless attack on "fat-cat sociology," and forthright demands from the Caucus of Black Sociologists, the Radical Caucus, and the Caucus of Women Sociologists, oppositional voices were still in a minority. The majority of members had grown up in and imbibed the liberal conservatism of the earlier postwar sociology. Over time, however, the radicalism of the 1960s diffused through the profession, albeit in diluted form. The increasing presence and participation of women and racial minorities and the ascent of the 1960s generation to leadership positions in departments and our association marked a critical drift that is echoed in the content of sociology.[2]

Thus, political sociology turned from the virtues of American electoral democracy to studying the state and its relation to classes, social movements as political process, and the deepening of democratic participation. Sociology of work turned from processes of adaptation to the study of domination and labor movements. Stratification shifted from the study of social mobility within a hierarchy of occupational prestige to the examination of changing structures of social and economic inequality—class, race, and gender. The sociology of development abandoned modernization theory for underdevelopment theory, world systems analyses, and state-orchestrated growth. Race theory moved from theories of assimilation to political economy to the study of racial formations. Social theory introduced more radical interpretations of Weber and Durkheim and incorporated Marx into the canon. If feminism was not quite let into the canon, it certainly had a dramatic impact on most substantive fields of sociology. Globalization is wreaking havoc with sociology's basic unit of analysis—the nation-state—while compelling deparochialization of our discipline. There have, of course, been countermovements—for example, the ascendancy of assimilation studies in immigration or the neoinstitutionalists who document the worldwide diffusion of American institutions—but over the last half century the overwhelming movement has been in a critical direction.

If the succession of political generations and the changing content of sociology constitute one arm of the scissors, the other arm, moving in the opposite direction, is the world we study. Even as the rhetoric of equality and freedom intensifies, so sociologists have documented ever-deepening inequality and domination. Over the last twenty-five years earlier gains in economic security and civil rights have been reversed by market expansion (with their attendant inequalities) and coercive states, violating rights at home and abroad. All too often, market and state have collaborated against humanity in what has commonly come to be known as neoliberalism. To be sure, sociologists have become more sensitive, more focused on the negative, but the evidence they have accumulated does suggest regression in so many arenas. And, of course, as I write, we are governed by a regime that is deeply antisociological in its ethos, hostile to the very idea of "society."

In our own backyard, the university has suffered mounting attacks from the National Association of Scholars for harboring too many liberals. At the same time, facing declining budgets, and under intensified competition, public universities have responded with market solutions—joint ventures with private corporations, advertising campaigns to attract students, fawning over private donors, commodifying education through distance learning, and employing cheap temporary professional labor, not to mention the armies of low-paid service workers (Kirp 2003; Bok 2003). Is the market solution the only solution? Do we have to abandon the very idea of the university as a "public" good? The interest in a public sociology is, in part, a reaction and a response to the privatization of everything. Its vitality depends on the resuscitation of the very idea of "public," another casualty of the storm of progress. Hence the paradox: the widening gap between the sociological ethos and the world we study inspires the demand and, simultaneously, creates the obstacles to public sociology. How should we proceed?

THESIS II: THE MULTIPLICITY OF PUBLIC SOCIOLOGIES

There are multiple public sociologies, reflecting different types of publics and multiple ways of accessing them. Traditional and organic public sociologies are two polar but complementary types. Publics can be destroyed, but they can also be created. Some never disappear—our students are our first and captive public.

What should we mean by public sociology? Public sociology brings sociology into a conversation with publics, understood as people who are themselves involved in conversation. It entails, therefore, a double conversation. Obvious candidates are W. E. B. DuBois, *The Souls of Black Folk* (1903); Gunnar Myrdal, *An American Dilemma* (1994); David Riesman, *The Lonely Crowd* (1950); and Robert Bellah and colleagues, *Habits of the Heart* (1985). What do all these books have in common? They are written by sociologists, they are read beyond the academy, and they become the vehicle of a public discussion about the nature of U.S. society—the nature of its values, the gap between its promise and its reality, its malaise, its tendencies. In the same genre of what I call *traditional public sociology* we can locate sociologists who write in the opinion pages of our national newspapers, where they comment on matters of public importance. Alternatively, journalists may carry academic research into the public realm, as they did with, for example, Chris Uggen and Jeff Manza's (2002) article in the *American Sociological Review* on the political significance of felon disenfranchisement and Devah Pager's (2002) dissertation on the way race swamps the effects of criminal record on the employment prospects of youth. With traditional public sociology the publics being addressed are generally invisible in that they cannot be seen, thin in that they do not generate much internal interaction, and passive in that they do not constitute a movement or organization, and they are usually mainstream. The traditional public sociologist instigates debates within or between publics, although he or she might not actually participate in them.

There is, however, another type of public sociology—*organic public sociology*—in which the sociologist works in close connection with a visible, thick, active, local, and often counterpublic. The bulk of public sociology is indeed of an organic kind—sociologists working with a labor movement, neighborhood associations, communities of faith, immigrant rights groups, human rights organizations. Between the organic public sociologist and a public is a dialogue, a process of mutual education. The recognition of public sociology must extend to the organic kind, which often remains invisible and private and is often considered to be apart from our professional lives. The project of such public sociologies is to make visible the invisible, to make the private public, to validate these organic connections as part of our sociological life.

Traditional and organic public sociologies are not antithetical but complementary. Each informs the other. The broadest debates in society—for example, about family values—can inform and be informed by our work with welfare clients. Debates about NAFTA can shape the sociologist's collaboration with a trade union local; working with prisoners to defend their rights can draw on public debates about the carceral complex. Berkeley graduate students Gretchen Purser, Amy Schalet, and Ofer Sharone (2004) studied the plight of low-paid service workers on campus, bringing them out of the shadows and constituting them as a public to which the university should be accountable. The report drew on wider debates about the working poor, immigrant workers, and the privatization and corporatization of the university, while feeding public discussion about the academy as a principled community. In the best circumstances traditional public sociology frames organic public sociology, while the latter disciplines, grounds, and directs the former.

We can distinguish between different types of public sociologist and speak of different publics, but how are the two sides—the academic and the extra-academic—brought into dialogue? Why should anyone listen to us rather than the other messages streaming through the media? Are we too critical to capture the attention of our publics? Alan Wolfe (1989), Robert Putnam (2001), and Theda Skocpol (2003) go further and warn that publics are disappearing—destroyed by the market, colonized by the media, or stymied by bureaucracy. The very existence of a vast swath of public sociology, however, does suggest there is no shortage of publics if we but care to seek them out. But we do have a lot to learn about engaging them. We are still at a primitive stage in our project. We should not think of publics as fixed but in flux, and we can participate in their creation as well as their transformation. Indeed, part of our business as sociologists is to define human categories—people with AIDS, women with breast cancer, women, gays—and if we do so with their collaboration, we create publics. The category "women" became the basis of a public—an active, thick, visible, national, nay, international counterpublic—because intellectuals, sociologists among them, defined women as marginalized, left out, oppressed, and silenced, that is, defined them in ways they recognized. From this brief excursion through the variety of publics, it is clear that public sociology needs to develop a *sociology of publics*—working through and beyond a lineage that would include Robert Park ([1904] 1972), Walter Lippmann (1922), John Dewey (1927), Hannah Arendt (1958), Jürgen Habermas ([1962] 1991), Richard Sennett (1977), Nancy Fraser (1997), and Michael Warner (2002)—to better appreciate the possibilities and pitfalls of public sociology.

Beyond creating other publics, we can constitute ourselves as a public that acts in the political arena. As Durkheim famously insisted, professional associations should be an integral element of national political life—and not just to defend their own narrow professional interests. So the American Sociological Association has much to contribute to public debate, as indeed it has done, when it submitted an amicus curiae brief to the Supreme Court in the Michigan affirmative action case, when it declared that sociological research demonstrated the existence of racism and that racism has both social causes and consequences, when its members adopted resolutions against the war in Iraq and against a constitutional amendment that would outlaw same-sex marriage, and when the ASA Council protested the imprisonment of Egyptian sociologist Saad Ibrahim. Speaking on behalf of all sociologists is difficult and dangerous. We should be sure to arrive at public positions through open dialogue, through free and equal participation of our membership, through deepening our internal democracy. The multiplicity of public sociologies reflects not only different publics but different value commitments on the part of sociologists. Public sociology has no intrinsic normative valence, other than the commitment to dialogue around issues raised in and by sociology. It can as well support Christian fundamentalism as it can liberation sociology or communitarianism. If sociology actually supports more liberal or critical public sociologies, that is a consequence of the evolving ethos of the sociological community.

There is one public that will not disappear before we do—our students. Every year we create approximately twenty-five thousand new BAs who have majored in sociology. What does it mean to think of them as a potential public? It surely does not mean we should treat them as empty vessels into which we pour our mature wine, nor blank slates upon which we inscribe our profound knowledge. Rather we must think of them as carriers of a rich lived experience that we elaborate into a deeper self-understanding of the historical and social contexts that have made them who they are. With the aid of our grand traditions of sociology, we turn their private troubles into public issues.

We do this by engaging their lives, not suspending them; starting from where they are, not from where we are. Education becomes a series of dialogues on the terrain of sociology that we foster—a dialogue between ourselves and students, between students and their own experiences, among students themselves, and finally a dialogue of students with publics beyond the university. Service learning is the prototype: as they learn, students become ambassadors of sociology to the wider world, just as they bring back to the classroom their engagement with diverse publics.[3] As teachers, we are all potentially public sociologists.

It is one thing to validate and legitimate public sociology by recognizing its existence, bringing it out from the private sphere into the open, where it can be examined and dissected; it is another thing to make it an integral part of our discipline, which brings me to Thesis III.

THESIS III: THE DIVISION OF SOCIOLOGICAL LABOR

Public sociology is part of a broader division of sociological labor that also includes policy sociology, professional sociology, and critical sociology.

Champion of traditional public sociology C. Wright Mills (1959), and many others since him, would turn all sociology into public sociology. Mills harked back to the late nineteenth-century forefathers, for whom scholarly and moral enterprises were indistinguishable. There is no turning back, however, to that earlier period before the academic revolution. Instead we have to move forward and work from where we really are, from the division of sociological labor.

The first step is to distinguish public sociology from *policy sociology*. Policy sociology is sociology in the service of a goal defined by a client. Policy sociology's raison d'être is to provide solutions to problems that are presented to us, or to legitimate solutions that have already been reached. Some clients specify the task of the sociologist with a narrow contract, whereas other clients are more like patrons defining broad policy agendas. Being an expert witness, for example, an important service to the community, is a relatively well-defined relation with a client, whereas funding from the State Department to investigate the causes of terrorism or poverty might offer a much more open research agenda.

Public sociology, by contrast, strikes up a dialogic relation between sociologist and public in which the agenda of each is brought to the table, in which each adjusts to the other. In public sociology, discussion often involves values or goals that are not automatically shared by both sides, so that reciprocity or, as Habermas (1984) calls it, "communicative action" is often hard to sustain. Still, it is the goal of public sociology to develop such a conversation.

Barbara Ehrenreich's bestselling *Nickel and Dimed* (2002)—an ethnography of low-wage work that indicted, among others, Wal-Mart's employment practices, is an example of public sociology, whereas William Bielby's (2003) expert testimony in the sexual discrimination suit against the same company would be a case of policy sociology. The approaches of public and policy sociology are neither mutually exclusive nor even antagonistic. As in this case, they are often complementary. Policy sociology can turn into public sociology, especially when the policy fails as in the case of James Coleman's (1966, 1975) busing proposals or when the government refuses to support policy proposals such as William Julius Wilson's (1996) recommendation to create jobs in order to alleviate racialized poverty, or Paul Starr's involvement in the abortive health care reforms of the Clinton administration. Equally, public sociology can often turn into policy sociology. Diane Vaughan's (2004) widely reported engagement with the media over the *Columbia* shuttle disaster, based on her earlier research into the *Challenger* disaster, paved the way for her ideas to be taken up in the report of the *Columbia* Accident Investigation Board (2003) and, in particular, its indictment of the organizational culture of the National Aeronautical and Space Administration (NASA).

There can be neither policy nor public sociology without a *professional sociology* that supplies true and tested methods, accumulated bodies of knowledge, orienting questions, and conceptual frameworks. Professional sociology is not the enemy of policy and public sociology but the sine qua non of their existence—providing both legitimacy and expertise for policy and public sociology. Professional sociology consists first and foremost of multiple intersecting research programs, each with their assumptions, exemplars, defining questions, conceptual apparatuses, and evolving theories.[4] Most subfields contain well-established research programs, such as organization theory, stratification, political sociology, sociology of culture, sociology of the family, race, economic sociology, and so forth. There are often research programs within subfields, such as organizational ecology within organization theory. Research programs advance by tackling their defining puzzles, which come either from external anomalies (inconsistencies between predictions and empirical findings) or from internal contradictions. Thus, the research program on social movements was established by displacing the "irrationalist" and psychological theories of collective behavior and building a new framework around the idea of resource mobilization, which in turn led to the formulation of a political process model, framing, and, most recently, the attempt to incorporate emotions. Within each research program, exemplary studies solve one set of puzzles and at the same time create new ones, turning the research program in new directions. Research programs degenerate as they become swamped by anomalies and contradictions or when attempts to absorb puzzles become more a face-saving device than a genuine theoretical innovation. Jeff Goodwin and Jim Jasper (2004, chap. 1) argue that such has been the fate of the social movement theory as it has become overly general and ingrown.

It is the role of *critical sociology,* my fourth type of sociology, to examine the foundations—both the explicit and the implicit, both normative and descriptive—of the research programs of professional sociology. We think here of the work of Robert Lynd (1939), who complained that social science was abdicating its responsibility to confront the pressing cultural and institutional problems of the time by obsessing about technique and specialization. C. Wright Mills (1959) indicted the professional sociology of the 1950s for its irrelevance, veering toward abstruse "grand theory" or meaningless "abstracted empiricism" that divorced data from context. Alvin Gouldner (1970) took structural functionalism to task for its domain assumptions about a consensus society that were out of tune with the escalating conflicts of the 1960s. Feminism, queer theory, and critical race theory have hauled professional sociology over the coals for overlooking the ubiquity and profundity of gender, sexual, and racial oppressions. In each case critical sociology attempts to make professional sociology aware of its biases and silences, promoting new research programs built on alternative foundations. Critical sociology is the conscience of professional sociology, just as public sociology is the conscience of policy sociology.

Critical sociology also gives us the two questions that place our four sociologies in relation to each other. The first question is one posed by Alfred McClung Lee in his presidential address, "Sociology for Whom?" (1976). Are we just talking to ourselves (an academic audience), or are we also addressing others (an extra-academic audience)? To pose this question is to answer it, since few would argue for a hermetically sealed discipline or defend pursuing knowledge simply for knowledge's sake. To defend engaging extra-academic audiences, whether serving clients or talking to publics, is not to deny the dangers and risks that go with it, but to say that it is necessary despite or even because of those dangers and risks.

TABLE I. DIVISION OF SOCIOLOGICAL LABOR

	Academic Audience	Extra-Academic Audience
Instrumental Knowledge	Professional	Policy
Reflexive Knowledge	Critical	Public

The second question is Lynd's question: "Sociology for what?"Should we be concerned with the ends of society or only with the means to reach those ends? This is the distinction underlying Max Weber's discussion of technical and value rationality. Weber and, following him, the Frankfurt School were concerned that technical rationality was supplanting value discussion, what Max Horkheimer ([1947] 1974) referred to as the eclipse of reason or what he and his collaborator Theodor Adorno ([1944] 1969) called the dialectic of enlightenment. I call the one type of knowledge *instrumental knowledge,* whether it be the puzzle solving of professional sociology or the problem solving of policy sociology. I call the other *reflexive knowledge* because it is concerned with a dialogue about ends, whether the dialogue takes place within the academic community about the foundations of its research programs or between academics and various publics about the direction of society. Reflexive knowledge interrogates the value premises of society as well as our profession. The overall scheme is summarized in Table 1.[5]

In practice, any given piece of sociology can straddle these ideal types or move across them over time. For example, already I have noted that the distinction between public and policy sociology can often blur— sociology can simultaneously serve a client and generate public debate.

Categories are social products. This categorization of sociological labor redefines the way we regard ourselves. I'm engaging in what Pierre Bourdieu ([1979] 1986, [1984] 1988) would call a classification struggle, displacing debates about quantitative and qualitative techniques, positivist and interpretive methodologies, micro- and macrosociology by centering two questions: for whom and for what do we pursue sociology? The remaining theses attempt to justify and expand this classification system.

THESIS IV: THE ELABORATION OF INTERNAL COMPLEXITY

The questions "Knowledge for whom?" and "Knowledge for what?" define the fundamental character of our discipline. They not only divide sociology into four different types but allow us to understand how each type is internally constructed.

Our four types of knowledge represent not only a functional differentiation of sociology but also four distinct perspectives on sociology. The division of sociological labor looks very different from the standpoint of critical sociology as compared, for example, with the view from policy sociology! Indeed, critical sociology largely defines itself by its opposition to professional ("mainstream") sociology, itself viewed as inseparable from renegade policy sociology. Policy sociology pays back in kind, attacking critical sociology for politicizing and thereby discrediting the discipline. Thus, from within each category we tend to essentialize, homogenize, and stereotype the others. We must endeavor, therefore, to recognize the complexity of all four types of sociology. We can best do this by once again posing our two basic questions: knowledge for whom and knowledge for what? This results in an internal differentiation of each type of sociology and, therefore, a more nuanced picture. We also learn about the tensions within each type driving it in this direction or that.

Let us begin with professional sociology. At its core is the creation, elaboration, and degeneration of multiple research programs. But there is also a policy dimension of professional sociology that defends sociological research in the wider world—defense of funds for politically contested research, such as the study of sexual behavior; the determination of human subjects protocols; the pursuit of government support, say, for minority fellowship programs, and so forth. This policy dimension of professional sociology is concentrated in the office of the American Sociological Association and is represented in the pages of its newsletter, *Footnotes*. Then there is the public face of professional sociology, presenting research findings in an accessible manner for a lay audience. This was the avowed purpose of the new magazine *Contexts*, but a similar function is performed by the regular congressional briefings organized by the ASA office. Here, also, we find the plethora of teachers who disseminate the findings of sociological research and, of course, the writing of textbooks. It is a delicate line that separates this public face of professional sociology from public sociology itself, but the former is more intimately concerned with securing the conditions for our core professional activities.

Finally, there is the critical face of professional sociology—debates within and between research programs such as those over the relative importance of class and race, over the effects of globalization, over patterns of overwork, over the class bases of electoral politics, over the

TABLE 2. DISSECTING PROFESSIONAL SOCIOLOGY

Professional	*Policy*
Research conducted within research programs that define assumptions, theories, concepts, questions, and puzzles	Defense of sociological research, human subjects, funding, congressional briefings
Critical	*Public*
Critical debates of the discipline within and between research programs	Concern for the public image of sociology, presenting findings in an accessible manner, teaching basics of sociology, and writing textbooks

sources of underdevelopment, and so forth. Such critical debates are the subject of the articles in the *Annual Review of Sociology*, and they inject the necessary dynamism into our research programs. The four divisions of professional sociology are represented in Table 2.

Because of its size, we can discern a functional differentiation, or as Andrew Abbott (2001) might call it, "fractalization," of professional sociology, but the other types of sociology are less internally developed so that it is better to talk of their different aspects or dimensions. Thus, the core activity of public sociology—the dialogue between sociologists and their publics—is supported (or not) by professional, critical, and policy moments. Take, for example, Boston College's Media Research and Action Project, which brings sociologists together with community organizers to discover how best to present social issues to the media. There is a professional moment to this project based on William Gamson's idea of framing, a critical moment based on the limited ways in which the media operate, and a policy moment that grapples with the concrete aims of community organizers. Charlotte Ryan (2004) describes the tensions within the project that stem from the contradictory demands between the immediacy of public sociology and the career rhythms of professional sociology, while Gamson (2004) underlines the university's limited economic commitment to a project to empower local communities.

Policy sociology also has its professional, critical, and public moments. Here an interesting case is Judy Stacey's (2004) experience as an expert witness defending same-sex marriage in Ontario, Canada. The legal opponents of same-sex marriage drew on her widely read article published in the *American Sociological Review* (Stacey and Biblarz 2001). The authors argued that while studies show some slight differences in the effects of gay parenting on children—that they were more open to sexual diversity—there was no evidence that the effects were in any way "harmful." Opponents of same-sex marriage argued that Stacey and Biblarz had drawn on studies so scientifically weak that no such conclusions could be drawn. Judy Stacey, therefore, found herself in the unaccustomed position of defending the scientific rigor of her conclusions. Moreover, her defense of gay civil liberties entailed the defense of marriage—an institution she had subjected to intense criticism in her scholarly writings. In this case, we see how constraining policy sociology can be and how its dependence upon professional sociology can pit it against critical and public sociologies. The four faces of any given type of sociology may not be in harmony with each other.

We can see this again in critical sociology. In her classic article "A Sociology for Women," Dorothy Smith (1987, chap. 2) took sociology to task for its universalization of the male standpoint, especially the standpoint of ruling men who command the macrostructures of society. Drawing on the canonical writings of Alfred Schutz, she elaborates the standpoint of women as rooted in the microstructures of everyday life—the invisible labor that supports the macrostructures. Patricia Hill Collins (1991) further developed standpoint analysis by insisting that insight into society comes from those who are multiply oppressed—poor black women—but she too drew on conventional social theory, in her case not Schutz but Georg Simmel and Robert Merton, to elaborate the critique of professional sociology. Moreover, for her there was a public moment too—the connection of black female intellectuals to the culture of poor black women was necessary to bring greater universality to professional sociology. Thus, we see the professional and public moments of critical sociology, but what of its policy moment? Could one argue that here lies the realpolitik of defending spaces for critical thought within the university, spaces that would include interdisciplinary programs, institutes, and the struggle for representation?

These are just a few examples to illustrate the complexity of each type of sociology, recognizing their academic and extra-academic as well as their instrumental and reflexive dimensions. We should not forget this complex internal composition as we refocus on the relations among the four major types.

THESIS V: LOCATING THE SOCIOLOGIST

A distinction must be made between sociology and its internal divisions on the one side and sociologists and their trajectories on the other. The life of the sociologist is propelled by the mismatch of her or his sociological habitus and the structure of the disciplinary field as a whole.

We should distinguish between the division of sociological labor and the sociologists who inhabit one or more places within it. About 30 percent of PhDs are employed outside the university, primarily in the world of policy research, from where they may venture into the public realm (Kang 2003). The 70 percent of PhDs who teach in universities occupy the professional quadrant, conducting research or disseminating its results, but they may hold positions in other quadrants too, at least if they have tenure-track positions. By contrast, the army of contingent workers—adjuncts, temporary lecturers, part-time instructors—are stuck in a single place, paid a pittance (two thousand dollars to four thousand dollars a course) for their often dedicated teaching, with insecure employment and usually without benefits (Spalter-Roth and Erskine 2004). They are more prevalent in the high-prestige universities, where they can amount to 40 percent of employees teaching up to 40 percent of courses. These are the underlaborers who subsidize the research and the salaries of the permanent faculty, releasing them for other activities.

Thus, many of our most distinguished sociologists have occupied multiple locations. James Coleman, for example, simultaneously worked in both professional and policy worlds while being hostile to critical and public sociologies. Christopher Jencks, who has worked in similar policy fields, is unusual in combining critical and public moments with professional and policy commitments. Arlie Hochschild's sociology of emotions is strung out between professional and critical sociology, whereas her research on work and family combines public and policy sociology. Of course, these sociologists have or had comfortable positions in top-ranked sociology departments, where conditions of work permit multiple locations. Most of us occupy only one quadrant at a time. So we should also focus on careers.

Sociologists not only are simultaneously located in different positions, but assume trajectories through time among our four types of sociology. Before the consolidation of professional careers, movement among the quadrants was more erratic. Increasingly disaffected with the academy and marginalized within it by his race, after completing *The Philadelphia Negro* in 1899, and after setting up and running the Atlanta Sociological Laboratory at the University of Atlanta between 1897 and 1910, W. E. B. DuBois left academia to found the National Association for the

Advancement of Colored People (NAACP) and became editor of its magazine, *Crisis*. In this public role he wrote all sorts of popular essays, inevitably influenced by his sociology. In 1934 he returned to the academy to chair the sociology department at Atlanta, where he finished another classic monograph, *Black Reconstruction*, only to depart once again, after World War II, for national and international public venues. His relentless campaigns for racial justice were the acme of public sociology, although, of course, his ultimate aim was always to change policy. Public sociology is often an avenue for the marginalized, locked out of the policy arena and ostracized in the academy.

While W. E. B. DuBois was taking the route out of the academy, his nemesis, another major figure in the sociology of race, Robert Park, was traveling in the opposite direction.[6] After years as a journalist, which included radical exposés of Belgium's atrocities in the Congo, he became Booker T. Washington's private secretary and research analyst before entering, and then shaping and professionalizing, the department of sociology at the University of Chicago (Lyman 1992).

C. Wright Mills was of a later generation, but like DuBois he became increasingly disaffected with the academy. After completing his undergraduate degree in philosophy at the University of Texas, he went to Wisconsin to work with German émigré Hans Gerth. There he wrote his dissertation on pragmatism. Robert Merton and Paul Lazarsfeld recruited him to Columbia University because he showed such promise as a professional sociologist. Unable to tolerate the "illiberal practicality" of Lazarsfeld's Bureau of Applied Research, he turned from instrumental sociology to a public sociology—*The New Men of Power, White Collar,* and *The Power Elite*. At the end of his short life he would return to the promise and betrayal of sociology in his inspirational *The Sociological Imagination*. This turn to critical sociology coincided with a move beyond sociology into the realm of the public intellectual with *Listen, Yankee!* and *The Causes of World War Three*—books that were only distantly connected to sociology.[7]

Today careers in sociology are more heavily regimented than they were in Mills's time. A typical graduate student—perhaps inspired by an undergraduate teacher or burned out from a draining social movement—enters graduate school with a critical disposition, wanting to learn more about the possibilities of social change, whether this be limiting the spread of AIDS in Africa, the deflection of youth violence, the conditions of success of feminist movements in Turkey and Iran, family as a source of morality, variation in support for capital punishment, public misconstrual of Islam, and so forth. There she confronts a succession of required courses, each with its own abstruse texts to be mastered or abstract techniques to be acquired. After three or four years she is ready to take the qualifying or preliminary examinations in three or four areas, whereupon she embarks on her dissertation. The whole process can take anything from five years up. It is as if graduate school is organized to winnow away at the moral commitments that inspired the interest in sociology in the first place.

Just as Durkheim stressed the noncontractual elements of contract—the underlying consensus and trust without which contracts would be impossible—so equally we must appreciate the importance of the non-careerist underpinnings of careers. Many of the 50 percent to 70 percent of graduate students who survive to receive their PhD sustain their original commitment by doing public sociology on the side—often hidden from their supervisor. How often have I heard faculty advise their students to leave public sociology until after tenure—not realizing (or realizing all too well?) that public sociology is what keeps sociological passion alive. If they follow their advisor's advice, they may end up a contingent worker, in which case there will be even less time for public sociology, or they may be lucky enough to find a tenure-track job, in which case they have to worry about publishing articles in accredited journals or publishing books with recognized university presses. Once they have tenure, they are free to indulge their youthful passions, but by then they are no longer youthful. They may have lost all interest in public sociology, preferring the more lucrative policy world of consultants or a niche in professional sociology. Better to indulge the commitment to public sociology from the beginning, and that way ignite the torch of professional sociology.

The differentiation of sociological labor with its attendant specialization can create anxiety for the sociological habitus that hankers after a unity of reflexive and instrumental knowledge, or a habitus that desires both academic and extra-academic audiences. The tension between institution and habitus drives sociologists restlessly from quadrant to quadrant, where they may settle for ritualistic accommodation before moving on, or abandon the discipline altogether. Still, there are always those whose habitus adapts well to specialization and whose energy and passion are infectious, spilling over into the other quadrants. As I shall now argue, specialization is not inimical to public sociology.

THESIS VI: THE NORMATIVE MODEL AND ITS PATHOLOGIES

The flourishing of our discipline depends upon a shared ethos, under-pinning the reciprocal interdependence of professional, policy, public, and critical sociologies. In being overresponsive to their different audiences, however, each type of sociology can assume pathological forms, threatening the vitality of the whole.

Those who have endorsed public sociology have often been openly contemptuous of professional sociology. Russell Jacoby's *The Last Intellectuals* (1987) began a series of commentaries that lament the retreat of the public intellectual into a cocoon of professionalization. Thus, Orlando Patterson (2002) celebrates David Riesman as "the last sociologist" because Riesman, and others of his generation, tackled issues of great public significance, whereas the professional sociology of today tests narrow hypotheses, mimicking the natural sciences. In asking "Whatever happened to sociology?" Peter Berger (2002) answers that the field has fallen victim to methodological fetishism and an obsession with trivial topics. But he also complains that the 1960s generation has turned sociology from a science into an ideology. He captures the cool reception of public sociology among many professional sociologists who fear public involvement will corrupt science and threaten the legitimacy of the discipline as well as the material resources it will have at its disposal.

I take the opposite view—that between professional and public sociology there should be, and there often is, respect and synergy. Far from being incompatible, the two are like Siamese twins. Indeed, my normative vision of the discipline of sociology is of reciprocal interdependence among our four types—an organic solidarity in which each type of sociology derives energy, meaning, and imagination from its connection to the others.

As I have already insisted, at the heart of our discipline is its professional component. Without a professional sociology, there can be no policy or public sociology, nor can there be a critical sociology—for there would be nothing to criticize. Equally, professional sociology depends for its vitality upon the continual challenge of public issues through the vehicle of public sociology. It was the civil rights movement that transformed sociologists' understanding of politics; it was the feminist movement that gave new direction to so many spheres of sociology. In both cases it was sociologists, engaged with and participating in the movements, who infused new ideas into sociology. Similarly, Linda Waite and Maggie Gallagher's (2000) public defense of marriage generated lively debate within our profession. Critical sociology may be a thorn in the side of professional sociology, but it is crucial in forcing awareness of the assumptions we make so that from time to time we may change those assumptions. How bold and invigorating were Alvin Gouldner's (1970) challenges to structural functionalism, but also to the way policy sociology could become the unwitting agent of oppressive social control. Today we might include within the rubric of critical sociology the movement for "pure sociology," a scientific sociology purged of public engagement. What was professional sociology yesterday can be critical today. Policy sociology, for its part, has reenergized the sociology of inequality with its research into poverty and education. More recently, medical research has married all four sociologies through collaboration with citizen groups around such illnesses as breast cancer, building new participatory models of science (Brown et al. 2004; McCormick et al. 2004).

Such examples of synergy are plentiful, but we should be wary of thinking that the integration of our discipline is easy. Connections across the four sociologies are often difficult to accomplish because they call for profoundly different cognitive practices, different along many dimensions—form of knowledge, truth, legitimacy, accountability, and politics, culminating in their own distinctive pathology. Table 3 highlights these differences.

The knowledge we associate with professional sociology is based on the development of research programs, different from the concrete knowledge required by policy clients, different from the communicative knowledge exchanged between sociologists and their publics, which in turn is different from the foundational knowledge of critical sociology. From this follows the notion of truth to which each adheres. In the case of professional sociology, the focus is on producing theories that correspond to the empirical world; in the case of policy sociology, knowledge has to be "practical" or "useful"; with public sociology, knowledge is based on consensus between sociologists and their publics; and for critical sociology, truth is nothing without a normative foundation to guide it. Each type of sociology has its own legitimation: professional sociology justifies itself on the basis of scientific norms, policy sociology on the basis of its effectiveness, public sociology on the basis of its relevance, and critical sociology has to supply moral visions. Each type of sociology also has its own accountability. Professional sociology is accountable to peer review, policy sociology to its clients, and public sociology to a designated public, whereas critical sociology is account-

TABLE 3. ELABORATING THE TYPES
OF SOCIOLOGICAL KNOWLEDGE

	Academic	Extra-Academic
Instrumental	*Professional Sociology*	*Policy Sociology*
Knowledge	Theoretical/empirical	Concrete
Truth	Correspondence	Pragmatic
Legitimacy	Scientific norms	Effectiveness
Accountability	Peers	Clients
Politics	Professional self-interest	Policy intervention
Pathology	Self-referentiality	Servility
Reflexive	*Critical Sociology*	*Public Sociology*
Knowledge	Foundational	Communicative
Truth	Normative	Consensus
Legitimacy	Moral vision	Relevance
Accountability	Critical intellectuals	Designated publics
Politics	Internal debate	Public dialogue
Pathology	Dogmatism	Faddishness

able to a community of critical intellectuals who may transcend disciplinary boundaries. Furthermore, each type of sociology has its own politics. Professional sociology defends the conditions of science, policy sociology proposes policy interventions, and public sociology understands politics as democratic dialogue, whereas critical sociology is committed to opening up debate within our discipline.

Finally, and most significantly, each type of sociology suffers from its own pathology, arising from its cognitive practice and its embeddedness in divergent institutions. Those who speak only to a narrow circle of fellow academics easily regress toward insularity. In the pursuit of puzzle solving, defined by our research programs, professional sociology can easily become focused on the seemingly irrelevant.[8] In our attempt to defend our place in the world of science, we do have an interest in monopolizing inaccessible knowledge, which can lead to incomprehensible grandiosity or narrow "methodism." No less than professional sociology, critical sociology has its own pathological tendencies toward ingrown sectarianism—communities of dogma that no longer offer any serious engagement with professional sociology or the infusion of values into public sociology. On the other side, policy sociology is all too easily captured by clients who impose strict contractual obligations on their funding, distortions that can reverberate back into professional sociology. If market research had dominated the funding of policy sociology, as Mills feared it would, then we could all be held for ransom.

The migration of sociologists into business, education, and policy schools may have tempered this pathology but certainly has not insulated the discipline from such pressures. Public sociology, no less than policy sociology, can be held hostage to outside forces. In pursuit of popularity, public sociology is tempted to pander to and flatter its publics, thereby compromising professional and critical commitments. There is, of course, the other danger, that public sociology may speak down to its publics, a sort of intellectual vanguardism. Indeed, one might detect such a pathology in C. Wright Mills's contempt for mass society.

These pathologies are real tendencies so that the critical views of Jacoby, Patterson, Berger, and others with regard to professional sociology are not without foundation. These critics err, however, in reducing the pathological to the normal. They conveniently miss the important, relevant research of professional sociology, showcased, for example, in the pages of *Contexts,* just as they overlook the pathologies of their own types of sociology. The professionals are no less guilty of pathologizing public sociology as "pop sociology" while overlooking the ubiquitous and robust but, often, less accessible public sociology. As a community we have too easily gone to war with each "other," blind to the necessary interdependence of our divergent knowledges. We need to bind ourselves to the mast, making our professional, policy, public, and critical sociologies mutually accountable. In that way we would also contain the development of pathologies. Institutionalizing reciprocal interchange would also require us to develop a common ethos that recognizes the validity of all four types of sociology—a commitment based on the urgency of the problems we study. In this best of all worlds, in this normative vision, one would not have to be a public sociologist to contribute to public sociology; one could do so by being a good professional, critical, or policy sociologist. The flourishing of each sociology would enhance the flourishing of all.

THESIS VII: THE DISCIPLINE AS A FIELD OF POWER

In reality, disciplines are fields of power in which reciprocal interdependence becomes asymmetrical and antagonistic. The result, at least in the United States, is a form of domination in which instrumental knowledge prevails over reflexive knowledge.

Our angel of history, having aroused himself in the 1970s, was swept back in another storm during the 1980s. Sociology was in crisis—undergraduate enrollments plummeted, the job situation for qualified sociologists worsened, there were rumors of department closures, and intellectually the discipline seemed to lose direction. From the pen of Irving Louis Horowitz came *The Decomposition of Sociology* (1993), complaining of the politicization of sociology. James Coleman (1991, 1992) devoted articles to the dangers of political correctness and the invasion of the academy by the social norm. Stephen Cole's edited collection *What's Wrong with Sociology?* (2001) brought together such distinguished sociologists as Peter Berger, Joan Huber, Randall Collins, Seymour Martin Lipset, James Davis, Mayer Zald, Arthur Stinchcombe, and Howard Becker. They mourned sociology's fragmentation, incoherence, and noncumulativeness as though a true science—using their image of natural science or economics—is always integrated, coherent, and cumulative! Their 1950s optimism had turned sour in the face of the barrage of critical challenges to consensus sociology during the 1960s and 1970s. Now the chickens were coming home to roost, and sociology, or their vision of it, was in jeopardy.

Perhaps the most interesting and thoroughgoing of this genre of writing was Stephen Turner and Jonathan Turner's *The Impossible Science* (1990), which reconstructed the history of sociology from this bleak standpoint. From the beginning, they aver, sociology had neither a sustainable audience nor reliable clients and patrons. It was continually overrun by political forces, interrupted by a transitory scientific ascendancy in the period after World War II. If there is a common thread running through all these narratives of decline, it is one that attributes sociology's malaise to the subversive power of its reflexive knowledge, whether this be in the form of critical or public sociology.

In one respect I concur with the "declinists": our discipline is not only a potentially integrated division of labor but also a *field of power,* a more or less stable hierarchy of antagonistic knowledges. My disagreement, however, lies with their evaluation of the state of sociology and the balance of power within our discipline. Sociology's decline in the 1980s was short-lived. Far from being in the doldrums, today sociology has never been in better shape. The number of BAs in sociology has been increasing steadily since 1985, overtaking economics and history and nearly catching up with political science. The production of PhDs still lags behind these neighboring disciplines, but our numbers have been growing steadily since 1989. They will, presumably, continue to grow to meet the demand for undergraduate teaching, although the trend toward adjunct and contingent labor shows no sign of abating. Membership of the American Sociological Association has been mounting rapidly for the last four years, restoring the all-time highs of the 1970s. Given a political climate hostile to sociology, this is perhaps strange, yet it could be that this very climate is drawing people to the critical and public moments of sociology.

My second point of disagreement with the "declinists" concerns the threat to sociology. I believe it is the reflexive dimension of sociology that is in danger, not the instrumental dimension. At least in the United States professional and policy sociologies—the one supplying careers and the other supplying funds—dictate the direction of the discipline. Critical sociology's supply of values and public sociology's supply of influence do not match the power of careers and money. There may be dialogue along the vertical dimension of Table 1, but the real bonds of symbiosis lie in the horizontal direction, creating a ruling coalition of professional and policy sociology and a subaltern mutuality of critical and public sociology. This pattern of domination derives from the embeddedness of the discipline in a wider constellation of power and interests. In our society money and power speak louder than values and influence. In the United States capitalism is especially raw with a public sphere that is not only weak but overrun by armies of experts and a plethora of media. The sociological voice is easily drowned out. Just as public sociology has to face a competitive public sphere, so critical sociology encounters the balkanization of disciplines, and as a result critical discussion is deprived of access to its most powerful engine—parallel dispositions in other disciplines.

The balance of power may be weighted in favor of instrumental knowledge, but we can still make our discipline ourselves, creating the spaces to manufacture a bolder and more vital vision. To be sure, there is a contradiction between professional sociology's accountability to peers and public sociology's accountability to publics, but must this lead to warring camps—each pathologizing the other? To be sure, critical and policy sociologies are at odds—the one clinging to its autonomy and the other to its clients—but if each would recognize parts of the other in itself, mutuality could displace antagonism. Instead of driving the discipline into separate spheres, we might develop a variety of synergies and fruitful engagements.

Here there is no space to explore any further the potential antagonisms and alliances within this field of power. Suffice it to say, if our discipline can be held together only under a system of domination, let that system be one of hegemony rather than despotism. That is to say, the subaltern knowledges (critical and public) should be allowed breathing space to develop their own capacities and to inject dynamism back into the dominant knowledges. Professional and policy sociology should recognize their enlightened interest in flourishing critical and public sociologies. However disruptive in the short term, in the long term instrumental knowledge cannot thrive without challenges from reflexive knowledges, that is, from the renewal and redirection of the values that underpin their research, values that are drawn from and recharged by the wider society.

We have sketched out the field of power that comprises the relations among the four sociologies in a relatively abstract manner. Their concrete combination will vary among departments, over time within a single country, and among countries, and even assume a changing global configuration. Accordingly, the next three theses explore the specificity of the contemporary configuration of United States sociology by pursuing a series of comparisons, and in this way we will deepen our encounter with the national and global forces shaping disciplinary fields.

THESIS VIII: HISTORY AND HIERARCHY

In the United States the domination of professional sociology emerged through successive dialogues with public, policy, and critical sociologies. But even here the strength of professional sociology is concentrated in the research departments at the top of a highly stratified system of university education, while at the subaltern levels public sociology is often more important, if less visible.

Today we accept the domination of professional sociology as a normal feature of United States sociology, but it is actually a quite recent phenomenon. We can plot the history of United States sociology as the deepening of professional sociology in three successive periods.

Professional sociology began in the middle of the nineteenth century as a dialogue between ameliorative, philanthropic, and reform groups on the one side, and the early sociologists on the other side. The latter often came from a religious background, but they transferred their moral zeal to the fledgling secular science of sociology. After the Civil War the exploration of social problems developed through the collection and analysis of labor statistics as well as social surveys of the poor. Collecting data to demonstrate the plight of the lower classes became a movement unto itself that laid the foundations of professional sociology. Sociologists would remain in close contact with all manner of groups in a burgeoning civil society even after the formation of the

American Sociological Society, as it was called then, in 1905. In its origins, therefore, sociology was inherently public.

The second phase of sociology saw the shift of engagement from publics to foundations and government. Beginning in the 1920s, with the Rockefeller Foundation's support for the Institute for Social and Religious Research (which would sponsor the famous Middletown studies), and then its support for community research at the University of Chicago and at the University of North Carolina, foundations became increasingly active in promoting sociology. At the same time rural sociology managed to create a research base within the state itself (Larson and Zimmerman 2003). As director of the President's Research Committee on Social Trends, William Ogburn pulled together a massive volume titled *Recent Social Trends in the United States* (1933). During World War II, state-sponsored sociology continued, the most famous being Samuel Stouffer's (1949) multivolume study of morale within the United States Army. After the war a new source of funding appeared, namely, the corporate financing of survey research, epitomized by Lazarsfeld's work at the Bureau of Applied Social Research at Columbia University. The more sociology depended upon commercial and government funding, the more it developed rigorous statistical methods for the analysis of empirical data, which invited criticisms from many quarters.

The third phase of American sociology, therefore, was marked by critical sociology's engagement with professional sociology. Its inspiration was Robert Lynd (1939), who criticized sociology's narrowing of scope and its claims of value neutrality. It was perhaps most famously continued by C. Wright Mills (1959), who referred to sociology's originating engagement with publics as "liberal practicality" and to the second period of corporate and state funding as "illiberal practicality." He did not realize, however, that he was inaugurating a third phase of "critical sociology," which would redirect both theoretical and methodological trends within the discipline. Alvin Gouldner (1970) produced a milestone in this third phase, attacking the foundations of structural functionalism and allied sociologies and creating space for new theoretical tendencies influenced by feminism and Marxism. This critical sociology provided the energy and imagination behind the reconstruction of professional sociology in the 1980s and 1990s.

From where will the next impetus for sociology come? Thesis I claimed that the gap between the sociological ethos and the world is propelling sociology into the public arena. Moreover, professional sociology has now reached a level of maturity and self-confidence such that it can return to its civic roots and promote public sociology from a position of strength—an engagement with the profound and disturbing global trends of our time. If the original public sociology of the nineteenth century was inevitably provincial, it nonetheless laid the foundation for the ambitious professional sociology of the twentieth century, which, in turn, has created the basis for its own transcendence—a twenty-first-century public sociology of global dimensions.

This is not to discount the importance of local public sociology, the organic connections between sociologists and immediate communities—far from it. After all, the global only manifests itself through and is constituted out of local processes. We must recognize that so much local public sociology is already taking place in our state systems of education where faculty bear the burden of huge teaching loads. If they can squeeze some time beyond teaching, they take their public sociology out of the classroom and into the community. We do not know about these extracurricular public sociologies because their practitioners rarely have the time to write them up. Fortunately, Kerry Strand and colleagues (2003) have cast a beam onto this hidden terrain by putting together a handbook on organic public sociologies, or what they call community-based research. The volume lays out a set of principles and practices as well as numerous examples, many of which combine research, teaching, and service.

The broader point is that the U.S. system of higher education is a large sprawling set of institutions, steeply hierarchical and enormously diverse. Therefore, the configuration of our four sociologies looks very different at different levels and in different places. The concentration of research and professionalism in the upper reaches of our university system is made possible, at least in part, by the overburdening of our teaching institutions, the four-year and two-year colleges. The configuration of sociologies in these institutions is analogous to that in poorly resourced parts of the world. As the next thesis intimates, diversity within the United States mirrors diversity at the global level.

THESIS IX: PROVINCIALIZING AMERICAN SOCIOLOGY

United States sociology presents itself as universal, but it is particular— not just in its content but also in its form, that is, in its configuration of our four types of sociology. At the same time it exercises enormous influence over other national sociologies, and not always to their advantage. Thus, we need to remold not only the national but also the global division of sociological labor.

The term *public sociology* is an American invention. If, in other countries, it is the essence of sociology, for us it is but a part of our discipline, and a small one at that. Indeed, for some U.S. sociologists it does not belong in our discipline at all. When I travel to South Africa, however, to talk about public sociology—and this would be true of many countries in the world—my audiences look at me nonplussed. What else could sociology be, if not an engagement with diverse publics about public issues? That the American Sociological Association would devote our annual meetings to public sociologies speaks volumes about the strength of professional sociology in the United States. Moreover, in a world where national professional sociologies are often weaker than public sociologies, focusing on the latter signifies a challenge to the international hegemony of United States sociology and points toward sociology's reconstruction nationally and globally.

The configuration of our four types of sociology varies from country to country. In the Global South, as I have intimated, sociology has often a strong public presence. Visiting South Africa in 1990, I was surprised to discover the close connection between sociology and the anti-apartheid struggles, especially the labor movement but also diverse civic organizations. While in the United States we were theorizing social movements, in South Africa sociologists were making social movements! This project drove their sociology, stimulating a whole new field of research—social movement unionism—which U.S. sociologists rediscovered, as though it were a brand-new idea, twenty years later! But South African sociology focused not only on social mobilization but on the targets of such mobilization. Sociologists analyzed the character and tendencies of the apartheid state and debated the strategy of the anti-apartheid movement. They asked whether they should be servants or critics of the movement. Today, however, ten years after apartheid, South Africa presents a less favorable context for public sociology, as sociologists are drawn off into NGOs, corporations, or state apparatuses; as the new government calls on sociologists to withdraw from the trenches of civil society and focus on teaching; and as social research is channeled into immediate policy issues or "benchmarked" to "international," that is, American, professional standards. The demobilization of civil society has gone hand in hand with a shift from reflexive to instrumental sociology (Sitas 1997; Webster 2004).

Similar tendencies can be found elsewhere, but each with their national specificity. Take the Soviet Union. Sociology disappeared underground in the Stalin era, only to resurface as a weapon of official and unofficial critique under the post-Stalin regimes. Opinion research became a form of public sociology during the thaw of the 1960s, before it was monopolized by the party apparatus. Under the stalwart leadership of Tatyana Zaslavskaya, Perestroika brought sociologists out in force. Sociology became intimately connected to the eruption of civil society. With the evisceration of civil society in the post-Soviet period, however, the fledgling sociology proved defenseless against the invasion of market forces. With but a few exceptions, sociology was banished to business schools and to centers of opinion and market research. Where it exists as a serious intellectual enterprise, it is often funded by Western foundations, employing sociologists trained in England or the United States.

The situation is very different in Scandinavian countries with their strong social democratic traditions. Here sociology grew up with the welfare state, which conferred a strong policy orientation but an equally strong public moment. Norwegian sociology, very much influenced by American sociology, was nonetheless also geared to the policy world, and here the feminist input was very important. With a population of only 5 million and less than two hundred registered sociologists, the professional community is small, so that the more ambitious seek a place in the wider society, whether in government or as public intellectuals. They are regular contributors to newspapers, radio, and television. Norwegians have energetically taken their public sociologies abroad, becoming an international hub with links not just to the United States but to Europe and countries of the Global South.

The rest of Europe is quite variable. France has one of the longest traditions of professional sociology and at the same time cultivated a traditional public sociology, with such leading lights as Raymond Aron, Pierre Bourdieu, and Alain Touraine. In England professional sociology is of a more recent, post–World War II vintage, easily vulnerable to the Thatcher regime that sought to muzzle public and policy initiatives while strengthening a parochial inward-looking profession. The return of a Labour government gave sociology a new lease on life, expanding the sphere of policy research and propelling its most illustrious and prolific public sociologist, Anthony Giddens, into the House of Lords.

In mapping the fields of national sociologies, one learns not only how particular is the sociology of the United States but also how powerful and influential it is. Turning out six hundred doctorates a year, it strides like a giant over world sociology. Many of the leading sociologists, teaching in other parts of the world, were trained in the United States. The American Sociological Association has almost fourteen thousand members with twenty-four full-time staff. But it is not simply the domination of numbers and resources—increasingly, governments around the world are holding their own academics, sociologists included, accountable to "international" standards, which means publishing in "Western" journals and, in particular, American journals. It's happening in South Africa and Taiwan but also in countries with considerable resources, such as Norway. Driven by connections to the West and publishing in English, national sociologies lose their engagement with national problems and local issues. Within each country, states nurture global pressures, which fracture the national division of sociological labor, driving wedges among the four sociologies.

Without conspiracy or deliberation on the part of its practitioners, United States sociology becomes world hegemonic. We, therefore, have a special responsibility to provincialize our own sociology, to bring it down from the pedestal of universality and recognize its distinctive character and national power. We have to develop a dialogue, once again, with other national sociologies, recognizing their local traditions or their aspirations to indigenize sociology. We have to think in global terms, to recognize the emergent global division of sociological labor. If the United States rules the roost with its professional sociology, then we have to foster public sociologies of the Global South and the policy sociologies of Europe. We have to encourage networks of critical sociologies that transcend not just disciplines but also national boundaries. We should apply our sociology to ourselves and become more conscious of the global forces that are driving our discipline, so that we may channel them rather than be channeled by them.

THESIS X: DIVIDING THE DISCIPLINES

The social sciences distinguish themselves from the humanities and the natural sciences by their combination of both instrumental and reflexive knowledge—a combination that is itself variable, and thereby giving different opportunities for public and policy interventions. Interdisciplinary knowledge takes different forms in each quadrant of the sociological field.

It is said that the division of the disciplines is an arbitrary product of nineteenth-century European history, that the present disciplinary specialization is anachronistic, and that we should move ahead toward a unified social science. This positivist fantasy was recently resurrected by Immanuel Wallerstein and colleagues (1996) in the report of the Gulbenkian Commission on the Restructuring of the Social Sciences. The project looks harmless enough, but in failing to pose the questions "Knowledge for whom?" and "Knowledge for what?" the new unified social science all too easily dissolves reflexivity, that is, the critical and public moments of social science. In a world of domination, unity too easily becomes the unity of the powerful. To declare the division of the disciplines as arbitrary, just because they were created at a particular moment of history, is to miss their ongoing and changing meaning and the interests they represent. It is to commit the genetic fallacy. In order to underline the grounds for the division of the disciplines, and in the interests of brevity, I fall back on schematic portraits of academic fields, inevitably sacrificing attention to both internal differentiation and variation over time and place.

The natural sciences are largely based on instrumental knowledge, rooted in research programs whose development is governed by scientific communities. The extra-academic audience is from the policy world—industry or government—ready to exploit scientific discoveries. Increasingly, this extra-academic audience enters the academy to direct or oversee its research, prompting opposition to collusive relations, whether these be in the area of medical research, nuclear physics, or bioengineering (Epstein 1996; Moore 1996; Schurman and Munro 2004). Such critical reflexivity, often extending into public debate, is not the essence of natural science as it is of the humanities. Thus, works of art or literature are ultimately validated on the basis of a dialogue among narrower groups of cognoscenti or within broader publics. Their truth is established through their aesthetic value based on discursive evaluation, that is, as critical and public knowledges, although, of course, they may be elaborated into schools of instrumental knowledge and even enter the policy world.

The social sciences are at the crossroads of the humanities and the natural sciences, since in their very definition they partake in both instrumental and reflexive knowledge. The balance between these two types of knowledge, however, varies among the social sciences. Economics, for example, is as close as the social sciences get to what we might call a paradigmatic science, dominated by a single research program (neoclassical economics). The organization of the discipline reflects this with its paucity of prizes (Clark Medal and Nobel Prize), elite control of the major journals, clear rankings not just of departments but of individual economists, and the absence of autonomously organized subfields. Dissident economists survive only if they can first establish themselves in professional terms. Indeed, one might liken professional economics to the discipline of the Communist Party with its dissidents and its coherent doctrine that it seeks to spread the world over, all in the name of freedom.[9] The internal coherence of economics gives it greater prestige within the academic world and greater effectiveness in the policy world.

If economics is like the Communist Party, American sociology is more like Anarcho-Syndicalism, a decentralized participatory democracy. It is based on multiple and overlapping research traditions, reflected in its very active forty-three sections and their ever-proliferating awards (Ennis 1992) and in the over two hundred sociology journals (Turner and Turner 1990, 159). Our institutional mode of operation reflects our multiple perspectives—although not always adequately. The discipline, a hierarchical and elitist caste system though it is (Burris 2004), nonetheless is more open than economics as measured by faculty mobility between departments and the patterns of recruitment of graduate students (Han 2003). The discipline is more democratic in its elections of officers. Member resolutions are not restricted to professional concerns, and they require the support of only 3 percent of the membership to be put to a vote. Thus, if economics is more effective in the policy world, the structure of the discipline of sociology is organized to be responsive to diverse publics. To the extent that our comparative advantage lies in the public sphere, we are more likely to influence policy indirectly via our public engagements.

Looking at the other social sciences, political science is a balkanized field, but one more inclined toward policy than publics, toward instrumental rather than reflexive knowledge. Today tendencies toward rational choice modeling have led to a reaction in a reflexive direction. The Perestroika movement within political science upholds a more institutional approach to politics and buttresses political theory as critical theory. Anthropology and geography are also balkanized across the instrumental-reflexive divide, so that cultural anthropology and human geography often react against the scientific models of their colleagues, while serving as bridges to the humanities. Philosophy, another crossover between social sciences and humanities, finds its distinctive niche in critical knowledge.

Disciplinary divides are far stronger in the United States than elsewhere, so that "interdisciplinary" knowledge leads a precarious existence at the boundaries of our disciplines. Each of the four types of sociology develops a distinctive exchange and collaboration with neighboring disciplines. At the interface of professional knowledge there is a *cross-disciplinary borrowing*. When economic sociology and political sociology borrow from the neighboring disciplines, the result is still distinctively part of sociology—the social bases of markets and politics. At the interface of critical knowledge, there is a *trans-disciplinary infusion*. Feminism, poststructuralism, and critical race theory have all left their mark on critical sociology's engagement with professional sociology. But the infusion has always been limited. The development of public knowledge often comes about through *multidisciplinary collaboration* as, for example, in "participatory action research" that brings communities together with academics from complementary disciplines. A community defines an issue—public housing, environmental pollution, disease, living wage, schooling, and the like—and then works together with a multidisciplinary team to frame and formulate approaches. Finally, in the policy world there is *joint-disciplinary coordination*, which often reflects a hierarchy of disciplines. Thus, state-funded area studies often work with well-defined policy goals that give precedence to political science and economics.

Having recognized the power of the disciplinary divide, captured in varying combinations of instrumental and reflexive knowledge, we must now ask what this variation signifies. Specifically, is there anything distinctive about sociological knowledge and the interests it represents? Might we as well be economists or political scientists and by happenstance end up as sociologists—a matter of little consequence, a biographical accident? Do we have an identity of our own among the social sciences? This brings me to my final thesis.

THESIS XI: SOCIOLOGIST AS PARTISAN[10]

If the standpoint of economics is the market and its expansion, and the standpoint of political science is the state and the guarantee of political stability, then the standpoint of sociology is civil society and the defense of the social. In times of market tyranny and state despotism, sociology—and in particular its public face—defends the interests of humanity.

The social sciences are not a melting pot of disciplines, because the disciplines represent different and opposed interests—first and foremost interests in the preservation of the grounds upon which their knowledge stands. Economics, as we know it today, depends on the existence of markets with an interest in their expansion, and political science depends on the state with an interest in political stability, while sociology depends on civil society with an interest in the expansion of the social.

But what is civil society? For the purposes of my argument here, we can define it as a product of late nineteenth-century Western capitalism that produced associations, movements, and publics that were outside both state and economy—political parties, trade unions, schooling, communities of faith, print media, and a variety of voluntary organizations. This congeries of associational life is the unique standpoint of sociology, so that when it disappears—Stalin's Soviet Union, Hitler's Germany, Pinochet's Chile—sociology disappears too. When civil society flourishes—Perestroika Russia or late apartheid South Africa—so does sociology.

Sociology may be connected to society by an umbilical cord, but of course, this is not to say sociology only studies civil society—far from it. But it studies the state or the economy from the *standpoint of civil society*. Political sociology, for example, is not the same as political science. It examines the social preconditions of politics and the politicization of the social, just as economic sociology is very different from economics; indeed it looks at what economists overlook, the social foundations of the market.

This tripartite division of the social sciences—I have no space here to include such neighbors as geography, history, and anthropology—was true of their birth in the nineteenth century, but it became blurred in the twentieth century (with the fusing and overlapping boundaries of state, economy, and society). For the last thirty years, however, this three-way separation has been undergoing renaissance, spearheaded by state unilateralism on the one side and market fundamentalism on the other. Through this period civil society has been colonized and co-opted by markets and states. Still, opposition to these twin forces comes, if it comes at all, from civil society, understood in its local, national, and transnational expressions. In this sense sociology's affiliation with civil society, that is public sociology, represents the interests of humanity—interests in keeping at bay both state despotism and market tyranny.

Let me immediately qualify what I've said. First, I do believe that economics and political science, between them, have manufactured the ideological time bombs that have justified the excesses of markets and states, excesses that are destroying the foundations of the public university, that is, their own academic conditions of existence, as well as so much else. Still, while acknowledging this, I would not want to write off all political scientists and economists. Disciplines, after all, are fields of power, each with its dominant and oppositional forces. Think of the Perestroika movement in political science or the network of Post-Autistic Economics—an economics that recognizes individuals as mature and multifaceted human beings. As sociologists we can find and, indeed, have found allies in and collaborated with these oppositional formations.

The field of sociology is also divided. Civil society, after all, is not some harmonious communalism, but it is riven by segregations, dominations, and exploitations.[11] Historically, civil society has been male and white. As it has become more inclusive, it has also been invaded by state and market, reflected in sociology by the uncritical use of such concepts as social capital. Civil society is very much a contested terrain but still, I would argue, in the present conjuncture the best possible terrain for the defense of humanity—a defense that would be aided by the cultivation of a critically disposed public sociology.

How can we accomplish this goal? As I have already suggested in Thesis VII, the institutional division of sociological labor and the corresponding field of power have hitherto restricted the expansion of public sociologies. We would not have to defend public sociology if there were not obstacles to its realization. To surmount them requires commitment and sacrifice that many have already made and continue to make. That was why they became sociologists—not to make money but a better world. So, there already exist a plethora of public sociologies. But there are also new developments. Thus, the magazine *Contexts* has taken a major step in the direction of public sociology. The ASA head office has made vigorous efforts in outreach and lobbying, with its congressional briefings and its regular press releases, but also in the columns of our newsletter, *Footnotes*. This year the ASA has introduced a new award that will recognize excellence in the reporting of sociology in the media. We need to cultivate a collaborative relation between sociology and journalism, for journalists are a public unto themselves as well as standing between us and a multitude of other publics.

The ASA has also established a task force for the institutionalization of public sociologies, which will consider three key issues. First, it will consider how to recognize and validate the public sociology that already exists, making the invisible visible, making the private public. Second, the task force will consider how to introduce incentives for public sociology, to reward the pursuit of public sociology that is so often slighted in merits and promotions. Already departments have created awards and blogs and have begun designing course syllabi for public sociology. Third, if we are going to acknowledge and reward public sociology, then we must develop criteria to distinguish good from bad public sociology. And we must ask who should evaluate public sociology. We must encourage the very best of public sociology whatever that may mean. Public sociology cannot be second-rate sociology.

Important though these institutional changes are, the success of public sociology will not come from above but from below. It will come when public sociology captures the imagination of sociologists, when sociologists recognize public sociology as important in its own right with its own rewards, and when sociologists then carry it forward as a social movement beyond the academy. I envision myriads of nodes, each forging collaborations of sociologists with their publics, flowing together into a single current. They will draw on a century of extensive research, elaborate theories, practical interventions, and critical thinking, reaching common understandings across multiple boundaries, not least but not only across national boundaries, and in so doing shedding insularities of old. Our angel of history will then spread her wings and soar above the storm.

NOTES

Reprinted and adapted with permission of the American Sociological Association. Originally published in the *American Sociological Review*, volume 70, no. 1, February 2005. Innumerable people, impossible to acknowledge by name, have contributed to this project. However, the author would like to thank Sally Hillsman, Bobbie Spalter-Roth, and Carla Howery in the American Sociological Association office, all of whom helped in many ways, not least in providing facts and figures and organizing speaking engagements. For their comments on a draft of this paper, thanks to Barbara Risman, Don Tomaskovic-Devey, and their students, as well as to Chas Camic and Jerry Jacobs. The live version of this address can be obtained on DVD from the American Sociological Association.

1. Data for public support of the Vietnam War come from Mueller (1973, table 3.3), while data for public support of the war in Iraq come from Gallup polls.

2. In 1968, the nineteen elected members of the ASA Council were white and male, except for one woman, Mirra Komarovsky. In 2004, the twenty-member council was exactly 50 percent female and 50 percent minority. As to the broad profession, between 1966 and 1969, 18.6 percent of sociology PhDs were earned by women, whereas the figure was 58.4 percent in 2001. Figures for racial breakdown begin later. In 1980, 14.4 percent of sociology PhDs were earned by minorities, whereas in 2001 the figure was 25.6 percent.

3. There is a vast literature on service learning. Two volumes of special relevance to sociology are Ostrow, Hesser, and Enos (1999) and Marullo and Edwards (2000).

4. In the formulation of the idea of research programs, I have been very influenced by Imre Lakatos (1978) and his debates with Thomas Kuhn, Karl Popper, and others.

5. This scheme bears an uncanny resemblance to Talcott Parsons's (1961) famous four functions—adaptation, goal attainment, integration, and latency (pattern maintenance) (AGIL)—that any system has to fulfill to survive. If critical sociology corresponds to latency function based on value commitments, and public sociology corresponds to integration, where influence is the medium of exchange, then policy sociology corresponds to goal attainment, and professional sociology with its economy of credentials corresponds to adaptation. Habermas (1984, chap. 7) gives Parsons a critical twist by referring to the colonization of the life-world (latency and integration) by the system (adaptation and goal attainment). As we shall see, Thesis VII combines Habermas's colonization thesis with Bourdieu's (1988 [1984]) field analysis of the academic world.

6. Thanks to Stephen Steinberg for pointing out this coincidence. Although he played a major role in professionalizing sociology, Park did not give up social reform, and this despite his endorsement of detached social science and his proclaimed opposition to the action sociology of the women of Hull House.

7. The distinction between "public sociologist" and "public intellectual" is important—the former is a specialist variety of the latter, limiting public commentary to areas of established expertise rather than expounding on topics of broad interest (Gans 2002).

8. I say "seemingly" irrelevant because first and foremost one's research program defines what is anomalous or contradictory. If the results seem trivial, then the research program itself must bear the burden of relevance and insight.

9. Marion Fourcade-Gourinchas (2004) documents the enormous international influence of American economics. Working off the ideas of Amartya Sen (1999), Peter Evans (2004) has striven valiantly to push economics toward an organic public engagement, an economics sensitive to local issues and deliberative democracy.

10. Taken from Alvin Gouldner's (1968) essay of the same title. Equally pertinent to Thesis XI are the challenging words of Pierre Bourdieu: "The ethnosociologist is a sort of organic intellectual of humankind who, as a collective agent, can contribute to denaturalizing and defatalizing existence by putting her competency at the service of a universalism rooted in the understanding of particularisms" (cited in Wacquant 2004).

11. It is here that I part company with the Durkheimian perspective of communitarians such as Amitai Etzioni (1993) and Philip Selznick (2002), who focus on the moral relation of the individual to society and who regard hierarchies, dominations, exclusions, and so forth as unfortunate interferences. Just as they do not center the divisions of society, they also sidestep divisions within sociology and within the academy more generally.

REFERENCES

Abbott, Andrew. 2001. *Chaos of Disciplines*. Chicago: University of Chicago Press.

American Sociological Association. 2004. *An Invitation to Public Sociology*. Washington, DC: American Sociological Association.

Arendt, Hannah. 1958. *The Human Condition.* Chicago: University of Chicago Press.

Bellah, Robert, Richard Madsen, William M. Sullivan, Ann Swidler, and Steven Tipton. 1985. *Habits of the Heart: Individualism and Commitment in American Life.* Berkeley: University of California Press.

Benjamin, Walter. 1968. *Illuminations.* Edited and with an introduction by Hannah Arendt. New York: Harcourt Brace Jovanovich.

Berger, Peter. 2002. "Whatever Happened to Sociology?" *First Things* 126: 27–29.

Bielby, William. 2003. *Betty Dukes et al. v. Wal-Mart Stores, Inc.*

Blau, Peter, and Otis Dudley Duncan. 1967. *The American Occupational Structure.* New York: John Wiley.

Bok, Derek. 2003. *Universities in the Marketplace: The Commercialization of Higher Education.* Princeton, NJ: Princeton University Press.

Bourdieu, Pierre. (1979) 1986. *Distinction: A Social Critique of the Judgment of Taste.* New York: Routledge and Kegan Paul.

———. (1984) 1988. *Homo Academicus.* Stanford, CA: Stanford University Press

Brown, Phil, Stephen Zavestoski, Sabrina McCormick, Brian Mayer, Rachel Morello-Frosch, and Rebecca Gasio Altman. 2004. "Embodied Health Movements: New Approaches to Social Movements in Health." *Sociology of Health and Illness* 26: 50–80.

Burris, Val. 2004. "The Academic Caste System: Prestige Hierarchies in PhD Exchange Networks." *American Sociological Review* 69: 239–64.

Cole, Stephen, ed. 2001. *What's Wrong with Sociology?* New Brunswick, NJ: Transaction Publishers.

Coleman, James. 1966. *Equality of Educational Opportunity.* Washington, DC: United States Department of Health, Education, and Welfare.

———. 1975. *Trends in School Segregation, 1968–1973.* Washington, DC: Urban Institute.

———. 1991. "A Quiet Threat to Academic Freedom." *National Review* 43: 28–34.

———. 1992. "The Power of Social Norms." *Duke Dialogue* 3.

Collins, Patricia Hill. 1991. *Black Feminist Thought: Knowledge, Consciousness, and the Politics of Empowerment.* New York: Routledge.

Columbia Accident Investigation Board. 2003. *Report.* Vol. I. Washington, DC: Government Printing Office.

Dewey, John. 1927. *The Public and Its Problems.* New York: Henry Holt.

DuBois, W. E. B. 1903. *The Souls of Black Folk.* New York: A. C. McClurg.

Ehrenreich, Barbara. 2002. *Nickel and Dimed: On (Not) Getting By in America.* New York: Henry Holt.

Ennis, James. 1992. "The Social Organization of Sociological Knowledge: Modeling the Intersection of Specialties." *American Sociological Review* 57: 259–65.

Epstein, Steven. 1996. *Impure Science: AIDS, Activism, and the Politics of Knowledge.* Berkeley: University of California Press.

Etzioni, Amitai. 1993. *The Spirit of Community: Rights, Responsibilities, and the Communitarian Agenda.* New York: Simon & Schuster.

Evans, Peter. 2004. "Development as Institutional Change: The Pitfalls of Monocropping and the Potentials of Deliberation." *Studies in Comparative International Development* 38: 30–53.

Fourcade-Gourinchas, Marion. 2004. "The Construction of a Global Profession: The Case of Economics." Unpublished manuscript. Department of Sociology, University of California, Berkeley.

Fraser, Nancy. 1997. *Justice Interruptus: Critical Reflections on the "Postsocialist" Condition*. New York: Routledge.

Gamson, William. 2004. "Life on the Interface." *Social Problems* 51: 106–10.

Gans, Herbert. 2002. "More of Us Should Become Public Sociologists." *Footnotes* 30 (July/August): 10.

Goodwin, Jeff, and Jim Jasper, eds. 2004. *Rethinking Social Movements: Structure, Meaning, and Emotion*. Lanham, MD: Rowman & Littlefield.

Gouldner, Alvin. 1968. "The Sociologist as Partisan: Sociology and the Welfare State." *American Sociologist* 3: 103–16.

———. 1970. *The Coming Crisis of Western Sociology*. New York: Basic Books.

Habermas, Jürgen. 1984. *The Theory of Communicative Action*. 2 vols. Boston: Beacon.

———. (1962) 1991. *The Structural Transformation of the Public Sphere: An Inquiry into a Category of Bourgeois Society*. Cambridge, MA: MIT Press.

Han, Shin-Kap. 2003. "Tribal Regimes in Academia: A Comparative Analysis of Market Structure across Disciplines." *Social Networks* 25: 251–80.

Horkheimer, Max. (1947) 1974. *Eclipse of Reason*. New York: Seabury Press.

Horkheimer, Max, and Theodor Adorno. (1944) 1969. *Dialectic of Enlightenment*. New York: Seabury Press.

Horowitz, Irving Louis. 1993. *The Decomposition of Sociology*. New York: Oxford University Press.

Jacoby, Russell. 1987. *The Last Intellectuals: American Culture in the Age of Academe*. New York: Noonday Press.

Kang, Kelly. 2003. *Characteristics of Doctoral Scientists and Engineers in the United States: 2001*. Arlington, VA: National Science Foundation, Division of Science Resources Statistics.

Kirp, David. 2003. *Shakespeare, Einstein, and the Bottom Line: The Marketing of Higher Education*. Cambridge, MA: Harvard University Press.

Lakatos, Imre. 1978. *The Methodology of Scientific Research Programmes*. Cambridge: Cambridge University Press.

Larson, Olaf, and Julie Zimmerman. 2003. *Sociology in Government: The Galpin-Taylor Years in the U.S. Department of Agriculture, 1919–1953*. University Park: University of Pennsylvania Press.

Lee, Alfred McClung. 1976. "Sociology for Whom?" *American Sociological Review* 41: 925–36.

Lippmann, Walter. 1922. *Public Opinion*. New York: Harcourt, Brace.

Lipset, Seymour Martin, and Neil J. Smelser. 1961. *Sociology: The Progress of a Decade*. Englewood Cliffs, NJ: Prentice-Hall.

Lyman, Stanford. 1992. *Militarism, Imperialism, and Racial Accommodation: An Analysis and Interpretation of the Early Writings of Robert E. Park*. Fayetteville: University of Arkansas Press.

Lynd, Robert. 1939. *Knowledge for What? The Place of Social Sciences in American Culture.* Princeton, NJ: Princeton University Press.

Marullo, Sam, and Bob Edwards, eds. 2000. "Service-Learning Pedagogy as Universities' Response to Troubled Times." Special issue of *American Behavioral Scientist* 43: 741–912.

McCormick, Sabrina, Julia Brody, Phil Brown, and Ruth Polk. 2004. "Public Involvement in Breast Cancer Research: An Analysis and Model for Future Research." *International Journal of Health Services* 34 (4): 625–46.

Merton, Robert. 1949. *Social Theory and Social Structure.* Glencoe, IL: The Free Press.

Mills, C. Wright. 1959. *The Sociological Imagination.* New York: Oxford University Press.

Moore, Kelly. 1996. "Organizing Integrity: American Science and the Creation of Public Interest Organizations, 1955–1975." *American Journal of Sociology* 101: 1592–1627.

Mueller, John. 1973. *War, Presidents, and Public Opinion.* New York: John Wiley.

Myrdal, Gunnar. 1944. *An American Dilemma: The Negro Problem and Modern Democracy.* New York: Harper & Row.

Ogburn, William. *See* President's Research Committee on Social Trends.

Ostrow, James, Garry Hesser, and Sandra Enos, eds. 1999. *Cultivating the Sociological Imagination: Concepts and Models for Service-Learning in Sociology.* Washington, DC: American Association for Higher Education.

Pager, Devah. 2002. "The Mark of a Criminal Record." PhD diss., Department of Sociology, University of Wisconsin, Madison.

Park, Robert. (1904) 1972. *The Crowd and the Public.* Chicago: University of Chicago Press.

Parsons, Talcott. 1937. *The Structure of Social Action: A Study in Social Theory with Special Reference to a Group of Recent European Writers.* New York: McGraw Hill.

———. 1951. *The Social System.* New York: The Free Press.

———. 1961. "An Outline of the Social System." In *Theories of Society: Foundations of Modern Sociological Theory,* ed. T. Parsons, E. Shils, K. Naegele, and J. Pitts, 30–79. New York: The Free Press.

Patterson, Orlando. 2002. "The Last Sociologist." *New York Times.* 19 May.

President's Research Committee on Social Trends. 1933. *Recent Social Trends in the United States.* New York: McGraw-Hill.

Purser, Gretchen, Amy Schalet, and Ofer Sharone. 2004. "Berkeley's Betrayal: Wages and Working Conditions at Cal." Presented at the annual meeting of the American Sociological Association, San Francisco, CA. 16 August.

Putnam, Robert. 2001. *Bowling Alone: The Collapse and Revival of American Community.* New York: Simon & Schuster.

Rhoades, Lawrence. 1981. *A History of the American Sociological Association, 1905–1980.* Washington, DC: American Sociological Association.

Riesman, David. 1950. *The Lonely Crowd: A Study of the Changing American Character.* With N. Glazer and R. Denny. New Haven, CT: Yale University Press.

Ryan, Charlotte. 2004. "Can We Be Compañeros?" *Social Problems* 51: 110–13.

Schurman, Rachel, and William Munro. 2004. "Intellectuals, Ideology, and Social Networks: The Process of Grievance Construction in the Anti-Genetic Engineering Movement." Unpublished manuscript. Department of Sociology, University of Illinois, Urbana-Champaign.

Selznick, Philip. 2002. *The Communitarian Persuasion.* Baltimore: Johns Hopkins University Press.

Sen, Amartya. 1999. *Development as Freedom.* New York: Random House.

Sennett, Richard. 1977. *The Fall of Public Man.* New York: W. W. Norton.

Sitas, Ari. 1997. "The Waning of Sociology in South Africa." *Society in Transition* 28: 12–19.

Skocpol, Theda. 2003. *Diminished Democracy: From Membership to Management in American Civic Life.* Norman: University of Oklahoma Press.

Smith, Dorothy. 1987. *The Everyday World as Problematic: A Feminist Sociology.* Boston: Northeastern University Press.

Spalter-Roth, Roberta, and William Erskine. 2004. *Academic Relations: The Use of Supplementary Faculty.* Washington, DC: American Sociological Association.

Stacey, Judith. 2004. "Marital Suitors Court Social Science Spin-Sters: The Unwittingly Conservative Effects of Public Sociology." *Social Problems* 51: 131–45.

Stacey, Judith, and Timothy Biblarz. 2001. "(How) Does the Sexual Orientation of Parents Matter?" *American Sociological Review* 66: 159–83.

Stouffer, Samuel A., Edward A. Suchman, Leland C. DeVinney, Shirley A. Star, and Robin M. Williams Jr. 1949. *The American Soldier.* 2 vols. Princeton, NJ: Princeton University Press.

Strand, Kerry, Sam Marullo, Nick Cutforth, Randy Stoecker, and Patrick Donohue. 2003. *Community-Based Research and Higher Education.* San Francisco: Jossey-Bass.

Turner, Stephen, and Jonathan Turner. 1990. *The Impossible Science: An Institutional Analysis of American Sociology.* London and Newbury Park, CA: Sage Publications.

Uggen, Christopher, and Jeffrey Manza. 2002. "Democratic Contraction? Political Consequences of Felon Disenfranchisement in the United States." *American Sociological Review* 67: 777–803.

Vaughan, Diane. 2004. "Public Sociologist by Accident." *Social Problems* 51: 115–18.

Wacquant, Loïc. 2004. "Following Bourdieu into the Field." *Ethnography* 5 (4).

Waite, Linda, and Maggie Gallagher. 2000. *The Case for Marriage: Why Married People Are Happier, Healthier, and Better Off Financially.* New York: Doubleday.

Wallerstein, Immanuel, Calestous Juma, Evelyn Fox Keller, Jurgen Kocka, Domenique Lecourt, V. Y. Mudkimbe, Kinhide Miushakoji, Ilya Prigogine, Peter J. Taylor, and Michel-Rolph Trouillot. 1996. *Open the Social Sciences: Report of the Gulbenkian Commission on the Restructuring of the Social Sciences.* Stanford, CA: Stanford University Press.

Warner, Michael. 2002. *Publics and Counterpublics.* New York: Zone Books.

Webster, Edward. 2004. "Sociology in South Africa: Its Past, Present, and Future." *Society in Transition* 35: 27–41.

Wilson, William Julius. 1996. *When Work Disappears: The World of the New Urban Poor.* New York: Knopf.

Wolfe, Alan. 1989. *Whose Keeper? Social Science and Moral Obligation.* Berkeley: University of California Press.

INSTITUTIONALIZING
PUBLIC SOCIOLOGY

ALAIN TOURAINE

Public Sociology and the End of Society

Burawoy's discourse starts with the sudden feeling of our double failure: the time has come to overcome the meaningless contradiction between professional sociology and critical sociology, both of which are equally irrelevant to fulfilling our expectations. The first, which reached its most elaborate form in Talcott Parsons's system building, declined rapidly during the 1970s, when the Vietnam War and the campaigns for the civil rights of black Americans (renamed African Americans) led to a sharp rejection of the idea of social system, an idea that appeared to conceal processes of domination, conquest, or repression that were penetrating more and more rapidly into all sectors of social life. Today it is impossible to imagine a movement back to Parsons's concepts, unless one stays inside academic institutions, which protect some professors from the turmoil coming from the rest of the world.

The second, critical sociology, even more rapidly lost its strength, not only because it could no longer make an alliance with "the socialist camp"—Russian, Cuban, or Chinese—but because it was ruined by its own social determinism, a determinism that rejects any possibility of social or political movements breaking a system of domination that determines the categories for representations of all actors. The best example of this self-destruction of critical sociology is the wide success in Latin America of the most radical form of the theory of dependency. If "nothing can be done," we can just denounce a foreign domination or sacrifice our lives, as Che Guevara did.

Some slothful thinkers and writers believe that these difficulties can be overcome by lowering the level of analysis. They point out that daily life and ordinary speech provide concrete examples of instances where professional sociology and critical thoughts are combined, in the same way that our judgments are often both positive and normative. But one cannot solve the problem by dissolving it into smoothing statements.

Burawoy's proposal can be reformulated as an invitation to find an entirely different solution. He suggests that we add to these two opposite orientations of sociology others that are different from them but have some common components. Policy-oriented sociology studies decision-making processes and detects involuntary action and offers a critique of the illusory idea that we are determined by our position in a hierarchical system. Public sociology is the penetration of professional sociology into a public space so that its insights can be used to support interests and values.

Without a doubt, many commentators will study the relationship among these four sectors of sociological thought. But I prefer to use my situation as an outsider, as a foreigner who elaborates his ideas by using elements coming from European, North American, and Latin American intellectual life. From this vantage point I read these very insightful proposals from a somewhat different point of view, but I accept, from the beginning, the main orientations of Burawoy's analysis. Instead of considering the opposition or complementarity between professional and public sociology as different forms of knowledge, I will concentrate on theoretical differences between the main orientations of sociological research but acknowledge that our ideas are affected by differences between our historical and social situations.

My starting point is that the subject matter of sociology no longer corresponds to its "classical" definition. From Durkheim to Parsons and their followers, what we call classical sociology has defined itself as the study of the processes through which a society is integrated, rejects what it considers as its enemies, and controls its internal conflicts and processes of change. It is easy to understand that "strong" and stable societies are more likely to analyze themselves along this line, while such an analysis is more difficult for dual societies, those that are dependent or colonized, in deep crisis or invaded, fragmented or divided by cultural and social conflicts. These societies are more sensitive to an opposition: on the one hand, their situation and key social processes are seen as mainly controlled from the outside—the famous globalization. On the other hand, their people are defined mainly in cultural, ethnic, or religious terms. This produces an absence of correspondence between these two forms of analysis, so that we end up with nonsocially defined situations and nonsocially defined people.

Such a situation, which corresponds to the experience of most of us, makes it necessary to define sociology as the search for processes of action, social or political, that try to fill the gap between situations and representations. Sociology, then, is no longer defined as the study of society or social systems in general but as the study of processes through which economic or political determinants, on the one side, and cultural and socially defined individuals and groups, on the other, can be connected, giving birth to collective action, political processes, and personal and collective attitudes.

"Classical" sociology has in any case been destroyed by attacks coming from many different sides. During the last half century two types of attacks have been particularly dangerous. The first comes from a triumphant capitalism, that is, from the destruction of social and political controls that regulate economic life. This is the real meaning of globalization: a world economy cannot be controlled by a national or regional political authority or social protests. The second comes from within sociology itself. Social organization is analyzed no longer in terms of functionality or disfunctionality but as a set of processes through which a system of domination controls every aspect or initiative of social life as well as our own representations. Michel Foucault will remain the most original thinker who interpreted many institutions and categories from this point of view. We should add to this internal critique of classical sociology the growth of respective groups—religious, ethnic, and moral—that cannot be reduced to their social functions.

To sum up, sociology today is dominated by the study of processes of "desocialization" or of "deinstitutionalization" to such a large extent that sociology, as a professional field of teaching and research, has lost ground, as can be easily observed in major bookstores, where cultural studies and especially race relations, gender studies, and, more recently, gay and lesbian studies have increased their presence on the shelves.

In a parallel way, radical sociology, which was based on the explanation of social behavior by nonsocial factors, by the nature of capitalism, colonization, or "patriarchal" society, offers less and less original analyses and limits itself to the—very important—task of uncovering invisible or only partly visible forms of repression, cruelty, or discrimination. Finally, the most attractive research is that which demonstrates the decline or disappearance of traditional forms of sociability, social norms, and moral judgments and the progress of all forms of individualism. These negative conclusions can help to support Burawoy's categories.

Neither economic nor cultural factors can entirely determine social life. Actors who try to link the global economy with specific cultures manifest themselves in a more and more active way. To study them is the main task of public sociology. This field is a wide-open one, except in extreme cases where impersonal, economic, or military forces or uncultural values and practices are completely separated, a situation that corresponds to the clash of civilizations defined by Samuel Huntington. The new critical sociology studies in particular the transformation of moral values into authoritarian regimes. But beyond this critical approach, which refers to a central contradiction between the indestructible logic of domination and the illusory subjectively determined action, it is necessary to substitute a new principle of value orientation for the idea of society, which has been torn into pieces.

We are accustomed to defining this principle in terms of "natural rights" and liberation movements or in terms of achievement or even conformity with a divine message and the like. What is new in our situation is that all transcendental principles have been eliminated from societies that can entirely create or destroy themselves. That makes it necessary to go further than in previous forms of legitimation of "rights" and to recognize that the basic right is for everyone to be considered as a "subject of rights." As a subject of rights, an individual or a category has the right not only to defend his or its identity—a formulation which is dangerously one-sided—but also to be a free and responsible actor in relationship with an environment, an environment that is always loaded with power relations. This "subject" can be built in a negative and destructive way as well as in a positive one. It can define itself as a race, as God's representative, as an elite, and in many other ways that destroy and negate other people's rights. This happens when an individual or a category claims the monopoly of meaningful subjectivity. This is the case when communitarian movements refuse to subordinate themselves to universalistic individual rights that are expressed in particular by the concept of citizenship. This observation allows us to get rid of the superficial critique that the notion of subject is "moralistic" and is an ideology which supports conformity and conservatism. The real meaning of subject is exactly the opposite. It mobilizes universalistic principles against all forms of order and power. But it is true that it can easily be transformed into weapons used by authoritarian elites who claim for themselves the monopoly of the active defense of political, social, or cultural rights. Beyond the claim for citizenship, terror is present. Behind the defense of workers' rights exists the danger of a dictatorship imposed in the name of the proletariat.

Sociology cannot define itself without explicit reference to "rights" that resist all kinds of domination. This statement corresponds to what Burawoy calls the "reflexive dimension of sociology." Actually, the central subject matter of sociology is the study of all forms of resistance to power-loaded transactions and institutions. We cannot define public sociology independently from a direct reference to the recognition of the rights of a subject who is directly or indirectly defined by an opposition to all forms of dependency and domination.

The role of public sociology was particularly important in Europe after World War II and the Nazi regime. Sociology was born again, first of all, as industrial sociology, under the leadership of Georges Friedmann, in many different countries. It criticized the ideology of the scientific organization of work and proposed that analysis focus on the labor movement and class consciousness and the already emerging processes disorganizing the so-called working class.

These social actors create a new type of institution which protects individuals against the state. The American Supreme Court is the best example of the institutionalization of the rights of individuals and categories to defend themselves against markets, financial networks, and authoritarian governments. In societies where basic civic rights are respected, the defense of everybody's capacity to respect other people's rights and freedom leads to new institutional groups. Everybody has the right to be a "subject" and to be recognized as such. This is a result of campaigns of protest, legal measures, or different channels through which "human rights"—not only political but social and cultural rights as well—are defined and defended. This new type of social institution is the field of intervention on which a new classical or professional sociology can be built.

This short description of what sociology is gives a central role to public sociology. It makes clear the difference between, on one side, public sociology and sociology of policies and, on the other, critical sociology. It is possible now to give a synthetic expression of the representation of the sociology I am proposing and to compare it directly with the scheme which has been proposed in a more detailed way by Burawoy.

It is clear that my starting point is the decline of classical sociology, which has presented itself as a professional sociology but has no right to

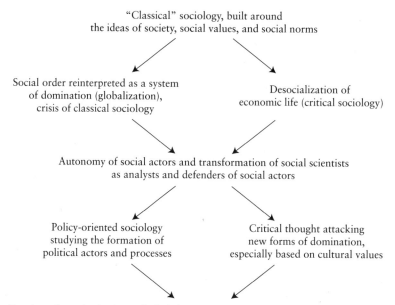

"Classical" sociology, built around
the ideas of society, social values, and social norms

Social order reinterpreted as a system
of domination (globalization),
crisis of classical sociology

Desocialization of
economic life (critical sociology)

Autonomy of social actors and transformation of social scientists
as analysts and defenders of social actors

Policy-oriented sociology
studying the formation of
political actors and processes

Critical thought attacking
new forms of domination,
especially based on cultural values

Creation of new institutions which defend actors against internal or external constraints
New professional sociology

do so because the respect accorded to professional criteria must be applied to all orientations. By way of consequence, public sociology occupies the central place because it is the search for actors. Policy-oriented sociology and critical sociology are two complementary orientations, but they can be considered products of public sociology. Finally, a neoprofessional sociology appears as the study of institutions that are no longer centered on the need of social systems but on the defense of individuals and groups against dominant forces.

Public sociology cannot be reduced to the diffusion of professional studies, even if it is true that the discovery and the study of social problems must always be integrated into "general sociology." Today public sociology is general sociology. One example I consider particularly important is that women's studies is an essential part of general sociology and not a specialized field of studies.

To address any kind of public is, first of all, to speak about "rights" in a way that corresponds to this public's capacities and expectations. At the same time, this does not mean formulating an ideology which is congenial to this public's interests and values. Sociology makes clear the presence, in a given situation and for a certain category of people, of a contention about rights. Sociology studies normatively oriented behavior.

The relative importance of each of the four main orientations in sociology depends to a large extent on the degree of autonomy of social actors in the face of power structures, on the one side, and defensive neoascription, on the other. But we should not close frontiers between various historical and geographical situations, because we can find everywhere examples of high or low levels of actors' autonomy.

The further we are from the most powerful concentration of economic, political, and cultural power, the more we feel that a growing distance will separate a global economy from local or neocommunitarian social life. By way of direct consequence, it is less likely that political and social actors can organize themselves in such a situation. In many cases, a direct confrontation between economic forces and cultural values obliges professional sociology to identify itself with a critical sociology.

In this extreme situation, there is a risk of the self-destruction of a sociology that proclaims that there is no space left for social actors between all-powerful economic forces and the dominated and defensive cultures. Since the breakdown of the Soviet ideology and regime, especially in Danubian and Eastern Europe, it has been extremely difficult to build new institutions and to redefine the field of social sciences. Nationalism was too strong and the economic constraints too tight for social actors to play an autonomous role. In "central" countries, on the contrary, the danger is to take too seriously institutionalized norms and forms of organization without deconstructing them, uncovering domination processes behind rationalization. In intermediary situations, which correspond to many European cases, policy-oriented sociology is most active, and many sociologists become the prince's counselors and abandon professional research.

In many Latin American situations it is not uncommon to observe the convergence of policy-oriented sociology and radical sociology. The danger here is that it will eliminate professional sociology; this solution was frequently used during the first years of the Cold War. The danger has decreased since then, but there is still a strong tendency to mix professional sociology, policy-oriented studies, and even critical sociology into an overall condemnation of situations that are not seriously analyzed.

An optimistic conclusion would be that, once the old definition of sociology as the study of social systems has been left aside, all types of sociology are parts of a general sociology of actors, that is, a public sociology. One consequence of this definition of sociology is that a large number of studies, which describe and analyze situations, often in quantitative terms but sometimes in historical terms as well, should not be considered as part of sociology, even when their quality and usefulness are recognized. That corresponds to an evolution that has progressively relocated, into economic analysis and, first of all, into institutions of economic research, a large number of studies that are more carefully carried out by economists, who, in a parallel way, incorporate more and more social and cultural factors into their analysis.

I consider as extremely positive the fact that Burawoy defines the field of sociology as a combination of four main orientations that are much more than complementary activities—like productions and their diffusion or applications—because this corresponds to important components of sociological knowledge. What makes a general agreement difficult is that each type of sociological research is strongly connected both with a national, cultural, and political history and with the division of intellectual labor, which influences the representation both of sociology and of its frontiers with neighboring social sciences.

In a much more concrete way, the conditions of circulation of knowledge entail great difficulties for real communication. The concentration of a large number of books and other publications in the United States and in London, because of the necessary existence of one international language, can give the impression of a large degree of consensus in the profession. This creates the impression that it is impossible to communicate between majority and minorities and, what is even more dramatic, that results and ideas that are published in other languages must be ignored, because the best of them will find their way to a translation in English. In spite of the fact that many more sociologists than before have a good knowledge of what is going on in different cultural areas, we live, in my opinion, in an intellectual world that seems to be more divided by conflicts and contradictions than it actually is. This is the reason I consider Burawoy's initiative important, even beyond its direct effects.

The present-day situation is certainly much better than during the Cold War, when sociology was forbidden and repressed in many countries where ideology, in its most brutal form, dominated and destroyed sociological research and where a so-called academic sociology was unable or unwilling to perceive the conflicts and processes of change.

One of the main conditions to reach a higher level of communication—at both the international and national levels—is to give priority to public sociology. I mean by that the observation, analyses, and interpretations that are most directly related to social life, as it can be observed, in particular, but not only, by those who want to modify social practices by discovering new forms of organization and decision. There are times in which the need for theory is the most urgent; in other circumstances, radical critique has a high priority. We should consider that today we are so far from understanding many forms of behavior that our most urgent task is to increase the quality of fieldwork. But fieldwork must more and more be directly comparative, and if we use the expression "public sociology" exactly in the way Burawoy does, we must be able to address ourselves to publics that are exterior to our own society. This is no easy task. We must recognize that when people belonging to a certain culture study another culture, their studies are often rejected as inadequate by the people who are directly concerned, even when they recognize the professional quality of these studies.

The specific American situation is that the official ideology of American society is so strongly rejected by academics, first of all teachers and students, that these are eager to discover new aspects of "reality," to take part in reform movements, or to transform applied social sciences into campaigns for solving social problems. I am impressed by the enthusiasm of present-day American youth, which can be explained by their hostility to President Bush's policy in the country and abroad. After so many years of deeply studying minorities, gender problems, or ethnic relationships, they begin to tear into pieces the official image of their society. Their intention is to change society and even to "change life." Today young people mobilize themselves very actively against an administration they consider as reactionary inside and aggressive outside.

As a foreign observer, I was impressed by the silence of American public opinion and especially of academic circles when President Bush decided to attack Iraq without any consideration for the multilateral institutions which had been created by the United States itself. A couple of years afterward, I am impressed by the great diversity of projects elaborated by young sociologists for changing their society. These people are so deeply involved in political and social affairs that their research projects are, at the same time, political. Their "alternative" view of society is based on the results accumulated by professional sociology during two or three generations.

If we sum up these remarks it can be said that sociology is more often a public sociology than a policy-oriented sociology, while critical sociology is largely incorporated into public sociology. It can be useful to make short comparisons with different situations.

The history of European social sciences is quite different from the U.S. case. European social scientists developed strong links with public policy makers during the postwar period, especially with planners and industrial unions. France was a good example of cooperation between social scientists and an elite of civil servants who have general views about society. Weak governments were unable to elaborate and carry out such long-term projects, and their best civil servants and intellectuals together elaborated scientifically based and politically oriented projects. This alliance disappeared when state-led postwar reconstruction was eliminated by the new liberal policies in the 1970s. The efforts made by excellent think tanks like the Club Jean Moulin and, later, the Foundation Saint-Simon had limited results. In Germany, stronger links were maintained between the Social Democratic Party and intellectuals.

If we consider the situation four decades after the May 1968 movement, European students are strongly motivated to deal with world affairs, because they are conscious of the fact that national states are less and less able to control the main processes of change, while American students are attracted by public sociology.

The influence of structuro-Marxist ideas has been deep and lasting in some countries, where it led to radical violent action. The result of this extreme radical participation in clandestine or illegal activities was to reject any kind of participation in political processes, so that sociological analysis has been seriously hampered. In formerly Communist countries, the balance is even more negative because, during a certain period of time, sociologists were compelled to give up social sciences to be able to survive, and Western Europe, after the fall of the Berlin wall, has proved unable to produce elaborate intellectual projects for transforming the formerly Communist countries.

The new generation of American sociologists is more committed to politically and morally relevant research than are their European counterparts, who have been exposed so long and so intensely to ideologies that convinced them that nothing could be done against a mass globalized world subordinated to American hegemony. But this is a problem of temporary differences, and the new generation everywhere is finding its way to fieldwork and initiatives that combine in different ways moral commitments and professional skills.

There is an important difference between the two sides of the Atlantic. Gender studies and feminist critiques have reached a very high level in the United States, while in Europe we find more descriptive studies on inequality and violence, very often inspired by a general Marxist point of view. In spite of the importance of these studies for policy makers, they have limited efforts to create interpretations that could reach the same very high level they have reached in the United States.

The case of Latin American sociology is in a certain sense more similar to the U.S. situation than to the European one. The defeat of critical sociology, which has followed the fall of the Cuba myth and of the guerillas, is everywhere visible, even if the influence of Chavez and Castro is gaining ground. On the contrary, policy-oriented sociology is very active. All of the advisors to Ricardo Lagos, former president of Chile, were sociologists, and Fernando Henrique Cardoso, former president of Brazil, is himself a prominent sociologist. In several countries, sociologists are influential, and some United Nations institutions—like CNUCED (Conférence des Nations Unies pour le Commerce et le Développement)—give a prominent role to sociologists as a reaction against the economic orientation of the "Washington consensus," which is now widely rejected. Public sociology is less visible, except in Mexico, where the political system is blocked and where grassroots democracy is very active. But professional sociology has not progressed very much because many sociologists live in exile, while many others participate in government and paragovernment activities. It can be concluded from this brief comparison that public sociology is stronger in the United States, while Latin American sociologists are more often experts for their government.

A few years ago in France, at the end of a long campaign of public debate on "university and society," the final nationwide meeting voted in support of the idea that the same importance should be given to three kinds of knowledge: basic science, applied science, and committed research. Natural scientists often expressed the idea that the social sciences are as important as any field of scientific research, because the social sciences should fight against social "pathologies" like racism, crime, unemployment, inequality of chances, and the like.

Even if in some places sociology is banned, its place in the university is much wider than it was a half century ago. But it seems difficult to introduce it into campaigns that mobilize public opinion. Radical sociology is losing ground more rapidly in both Latin America and the United States than in Europe. Professional sociology has stronger alliances with economic and political sciences in the United States and the United Kingdom and with philosophy and history in countries like Germany, France, and Italy. These comparisons demonstrate the usefulness of the categories elaborated by Burawoy. The internal differentiation of sociology must be combined with the integration or at least the mutual influence of the four main types of sociological achievements. We have as often heard people who condemn the empirical weakness of radical sociology as we have heard people who criticize policy-oriented sociology as being too often used to defend vested interests, but today public sociology combines more easily critical thought with good empirical studies. Its central role comes from the fact that we no longer believe in philosophies of history or in political doctrines, but we feel it necessary to identify the main "social problems" of our time. Such a goal requires the combination of public sociology and professional sociology, while radical and policy-oriented sociology drift away on opposite sides from the main tendencies of sociological research. But let's not forget that professional sociology is useful for public sociology, not only because it imposes methodological rules, but, first of all, because social theory is based both on empirical research and on more theoretical analyses, which are indispensable to discovering in which sectors of social life "committed" sociology can most probably make clear the nature of social problems and the conditions of politically and morally efficient reform programs.

SHARON HAYS

Stalled at the Altar?

Conflict, Hierarchy, and Compartmentalization in Burawoy's Public Sociology

Like the idealistic graduate students in Burawoy's rendering, I remember well my disappointment upon learning that sociology was not what I had dreamed of while filling out all those graduate school applications—it was not a vibrant and inclusive community of public intellectuals dedicated to social change. I mark that memory with my first American Sociological Association meeting in 1991 in Cincinnati. The U.S. Department of Agriculture was holding a convention in the same hotel, and it broke my heart to discover that I couldn't tell the difference between the two. Through my eyes, the sociologists and the government bureaucrats looked virtually the same, passionless automatons without purpose or inspiration, loaded down with papers, wearing the colorless "professional" uniforms of corporate America, just doing their "jobs." And everyone (including myself) was busily checking name badges, anxious for the opportunity to impress those who were higher up the food chain, ignoring those who couldn't be of any help in furthering one's career. At the end of the first day, I went back to my hotel room and cried.

In the years since, of course, I have learned that the national association contains numerous intellectual communities, many of them deeply dedicated to using sociological understanding to make the world a better place. Yet this face of sociology has remained largely invisible to the casual observer, and all those young graduate students who arrive at their first national meeting still have a hard time finding it, at least without a guide.

79

Thus, Michael Burawoy's efforts to create a national movement for public sociology seem long overdue. In the context of a nation moving to the right and a fragmented discipline already nervous about its identity, one can't help but admire Burawoy's courage and dedication in attempting to carve out an honored institutional space for public sociology. He has been a real trouper for the cause: traveling to community colleges, regional meetings, and elite universities, talking to anyone who would listen, putting himself on the line, welcoming criticism. And I am still applauding his hard work and creativity in organizing the 2004 San Francisco national convention, filled with an almost joyous collective effervescence, brought on by what seemed to many of us the "consensual" uniting of the discipline around the goals of public sociology.

For those of us who can't imagine what sociology would be for if it wasn't for "the public," the flurry of activity generated by that coming-out party for public sociology—the scores of new Web pages, the articles published, and the number of people discussing the nature and importance of public sociology in hallways and meeting rooms—couldn't be more refreshing. Unfortunately, after pondering my own experiences within the discipline, as much as I'm quite sure that public sociology is our future, I'm less certain that Burawoy's speech provides us with a completed road map.

Burawoy's public address is, quite clearly, a politician's speech—designed to build consensus and avoid ruffling too many feathers. The impulse to achieve consensus is surely noble. What worries me is the tendency to accept existing hierarchies within the discipline and merely to insert public sociology among them. This allows the intellectual insularity of the discipline to remain intact, does little to affect the conflicts and status inequalities within it, and, most crucially in this context, opens up the potential for simply *compartmentalizing* public sociology within the discipline—thereby reproducing its second-class status. Without a more generalized commitment to sociology on behalf of the public, I fear, all those young graduate students will still be left wandering around, searching for the special meeting halls where public sociology is the central collective goal.

If we're in the business of building utopias, my first choice, following C. Wright Mills (1959), is that *all* sociologists will identify themselves as public sociologists. Amid our diversity in interests, methodologies, theoretical positions, and social locations there is still hope, I think, that we could come together as a community of intellectuals who are ultimately dedicated to sharing the insights of sociology with the public and contributing to the common good. The road to this utopia requires a broad and inclusive definition of public sociology. Although it might ruffle some feathers and shift the foundations of some existing hierarchies, as a long-term strategy, I'll argue, proclaiming the absolute centrality of public sociology offers a more powerful grounding for consensus building than does an affirmation of existing distinctions in the division of sociological labor.

PROBLEMS OF CONFLICT AND HIERARCHY

Burawoy's analysis, as I understand it, defines public sociology as relevant, accessible, and publicly influential sociology, engaging the central moral and political issues of our time through teaching, activism, the media, and (widely read) written work. Public sociology, Burawoy writes, is one of four interdependent types of sociology, sitting alongside professional sociology, policy sociology, and critical sociology in the disciplinary division of labor.

Professional sociology and its "instrumental" ally, policy sociology, are rightfully at the top of the sociological hierarchy, he argues, since they are the primary producers of sociological research and theory. "Reflexive" critical and public sociology serve as necessary counterpoints, providing the moral and political critiques and popular dissemination for professional and policy work. Burawoy explicitly states that he does not advocate a transformation of sociology that makes all sociology into public sociology (this volume, 31). Rather, he suggests that, given the contemporary importance of public sociology, it deserves explicit recognition, institutional support, and a more honored place within the discipline.

Burawoy's "division-of-labor" argument is intended to displace older, conflict-producing dichotomies—qualitative versus quantitative, micro versus macro, positivists versus interpretive sociologists—with a friendlier vision of interdependent diversity (this volume, 34). Yet, as much as Burawoy's categories are useful in many respects, the division-of-labor argument potentially operates to obfuscate the disagreements and struggles for status that divide us, burying the underlying problems and setting up the possibility that public sociology will be cordoned off as just another form of lowly labor—a mail room job for losers.

If this scenario sounds slightly paranoid, it might be worth reiterating some of the myriad ways in which non-merit-based hierarchies play out within sociology.

As Burawoy suggests, the reason that we have to stage a movement on behalf of public sociology is precisely that the definition of "good" sociology is contested, and of late, public sociology has *not* had a position anywhere near the top (or even the middle) of the profession's ranking system. Generally it is treated as "merely" journalism or "merely" activism, a hobby for tenured faculty members or a side gig for scholars who want to make use of all that extra time they have on their hands. Connected to this is an implicit hierarchical division between scholars and the public—as if the association with "ordinary" people might taint our ability to think clearly.

In the same terms, the movement for public sociology would have been received quite differently if it had been initiated by a woman, a Latino, a black, or a queer theorist. No matter how brilliant the speech writing or how dedicated the organizing, it could not have been effectively set in motion by a professor from Western Missouri State, an untenured sociologist, or a highly energetic freeway flier with a contract to teach introductory sociology at the University of Wisconsin. And, as Burawoy's analysis of global sociology implies, an ASA speech calling for a reawakening of public sociology would have fallen on deaf ears if it had been sounded by a sociologist from outside the United States.

Although Burawoy clearly acknowledges these divisions and hierarchies within the discipline, his overall strategy is to sidestep this problem by emphasizing interdependence and echoing the politicians' favored refrain, "So why don't we all just get along?" This sounds good on the surface. As a strategy for overcoming conflict and inequality, however, it may have the same long-term impact as classic liberalism (without an affirmative action program).

Having spent most of my academic life as an "unprofessional" outsider, it's not hard for me to imagine what Burawoy's speech might sound like (in grossly exaggerated terms) to a hard-working community college professor dedicated to public sociology but regularly reminded of her position at the bottom of the academic barrel: "We, the 'public' sociologists, have come to ask you, the 'professional,' productive, mainstream, money-making, civilized, and superior sociologists to try to be kind to us and make room for us, the lesser, poor, impolite, 'reflexive,' and ideological sociologists. Won't you please, oh powerful leaders, try to find for us a place at the table?"

In other words, an argument that calls for friendship without attacking existing status inequalities, though it might be politic and might even successfully effect change, can also operate to bury conflict, rob social subordinates of their dignity, and let the upper ranks completely off the hook.

Of course, this is not Burawoy's intent. Nonetheless, like most of us, at times he seems trapped in the same disciplinary divisions that define so much of our lives and haunt us all. One indication of this is a set of relatively perplexing—and ultimately telling—contradictions that emerge in his analysis. On the one hand, Burawoy simultaneously valorizes "professional" sociology and, implicitly, degrades it. At the same time, he explicitly renders public sociology as (merely) a handmaiden to professional sociology and yet simultaneously (and quite passionately) implies the intellectual, moral, and political superiority of public sociology.

More specifically, Burawoy calls professional sociology the "heart of our discipline," tells us that it is responsible for supplying us with "true and tested methods, accumulated bodies of knowledge, orienting questions, and conceptual frameworks," reiterates its distinguished ability to garner large research grants, and congratulates professional sociologists for providing "legitimacy and expertise" for sociology as a whole (this volume, 32, 41). For all these reasons, he suggests, professional sociology rightfully belongs at the top of the academic hierarchy. Yet Burawoy also identifies professional sociology as primarily concerned with "instrumental knowledge," links this to the Weberian definition of (formal) technical rationality, and thus implies that professional sociologists are akin to nearsighted bureaucrats who are so concerned with pushing papers that they ultimately forget what the papers are about. As Burawoy points out, the increasing prevalence of this phenomenon is what Max Horkheimer referred to as the "eclipse of reason" ([1947] 1974, 11). (One has to wonder just how many sociologists would proudly associate themselves with the eclipse of reason?)

Following the reverse trajectory, public sociology is, first, explicitly treated as secondary, the "complement" of professional sociology, unable to exist, Burawoy tells us, without the research, legitimacy, and expertise provided by professional sociology (this volume, 24, 41). Yet, on the other hand, public sociology is rendered as the "angel of history," capable of regenerating the discipline's "moral fiber" and ultimately serving as the preeminent defender of "the interests of humanity" (this volume, 23, 25, 55). (Thus, it is not difficult to discern Burawoy's sense of the superior merit of public sociology.)

In all this, it seems to me, Burawoy's road map has the potential for solidifying disciplinary conflicts over knowledge and status rather than building the "synergy" and friendly interdependence he seeks. It appears that Burawoy is hoping to keep all his readers happy—all those critical sociologists who might be unsure of just what position they hold within the discipline, all those professional and policy sociologists who might be nervous that public sociology is attempting to usurp their power, and all those aspiring public sociologists (like me) who most certainly welcome the image of ourselves as the reemerging angels of history. Still, more jittery readers (like me) might still be nervous about exactly what this strategy will accomplish. In any case, Burawoy's categories, insights, and omissions ultimately provide me with important clues as to just what it would take to achieve my preferred utopia.

BRINGING THE "DIVISION OF LABOR" DOWN TO EARTH; OR, WHY AREN'T WE ALL PUBLIC SOCIOLOGISTS?

It's not so much a question of why we should do public sociology; the answer to that question seems obvious—we should do public sociology because it matters. As far as I can tell, if we aren't doing public sociology, we're just talking to each other, and thereby going nowhere. To put it another way, as I say to my students every time they face an essay assignment, "If you haven't said it clearly, in language that your mother can understand, then you haven't said it at all. And if you haven't convinced your mother that what you're saying is worth listening to, then she'll be asleep before you've finished, so you might as well skip the paper and just take a nap yourself."

Of course, I know that some sociologists will disagree with me regarding the importance of social relevance, persuasiveness, and accessibility, but I must admit that I'm still not sure what planet they're living on. After all, it's one thing to be studying microbes or the demise of the spotted turtle and claim that you don't care if the public can understand you because these phenomena are nonetheless relevant for the survival of humans and the planet. This arrogant and paternalistic stand might work if your research involves turtles and microbes—and your primary goal is to *control* your research subjects. But to claim to study society and to say that you needn't bother to make your work relevant or accessible to social members—well, that seems to me just plain insane.

The good news, as far as I can tell, is that the majority of sociologists are not insane. I've been looking for all those sociologists who are completely uninterested in the public or the common good—who dedicate themselves to inaccessible and irrelevant research, who dream of isolation and insularity, who would be pleased to name themselves as mindless bureaucrats obsessed with technique and unable to see the forest for the trees, or who came to sociology because they're money-grubbing careerists who secretly hoped it would offer the tools for making a killing in the stock market. Search as I might, I cannot find them.

Most of the "professional" sociologists I know are not suffering from the eclipse of reason. Most of them know full well that, in the broadest terms, we engage in sociology on behalf of society. Most of them are also relatively good citizens—they vote, read the newspaper, seriously consider issues of the public good, and are genuinely interested in the future of our society and our world. They also know that good sociology can potentially contribute to making better citizens and a better world.[1]

Similarly, most of the "public" sociologists I know actually engage in research, use rigorous methodologies, and participate in theory building. Their talents are not limited to translating the research findings of others, writing in accessible prose, taking media interviews, or engaging in activism. They too recognize that doing good sociology is central to their ability to make a difference in the world. In other words, as far as I can tell, it is neither social commitment nor intellectual seriousness that divides us. So the real question is, why don't all sociologists proclaim themselves public sociologists? What's the holdup?

To bring this down to earth, I've been listening to my colleagues' implicit and explicit answers to this question for some time now. I haven't yet completed the ethnography, and I wouldn't even pretend to have all the answers, but what I hear from those who are critical of public sociology is one or more variations on the following four arguments.

> *Public sociology is not part of our job description.* Engaging with public audiences might be fine, but it's not our job—it's "extracurricular." It's hard enough, they imply, to teach our classes, mentor our students (and often provide them with therapeutic counseling), do our research, try to get published in the mainstream journals, leap through all the hoops required for tenure, manage all those reviews and recommendation letters, and complete all the administrative tasks and committee work involved in department, university, and disciplinary citizenship. We can't be asked to try to be popular, accessible, relevant, and "best-selling" as well, and most of us don't have time to be committed community activists (and some of us don't want to be).

> *Public sociology is not "good" sociology.* Sociology produced for public consumption is dumbed down, merely popular, insufficiently detailed, atheoretical, and/or distorted, one-sided advocacy. We are better than that. We are intellectuals.

Public sociology is not social science. Science requires objectivity and distance; public sociologists, guided by their moral and political interests in a "good society" are, by definition, breaking the rules of good science. Their moral and political commitments, and their engagement with public audiences, public issues, and public interests, will taint the research, pollute the findings, and destroy their ability to objectively assess the operations of society. Science is the search for truth. Public sociology is a popularity contest, an exercise in ideologically grounded activism for a particularistic cause, or a left-wing conspiracy.[2]

Universities will not pay us to do public sociology. (This argument tends to be an extension of one or more of the preceding critical positions.) In order to preserve our standing as a worthy academic discipline, we must identify ourselves as something other than journalists; we must demonstrate our intellectual depth, we must build theory, and/or we must show that we can mimic the natural sciences in methodological rigor.

In order to respond to these criticisms and build the utopia where all sociologists proudly name themselves public sociologists, all we really need, I'll suggest (with hopeful and, perhaps, undereducated idealism), is a broader, more inclusive, more robust, and more fully specified definition of public sociology.

CONSTRUCTING A MORE INCLUSIVE PUBLIC SOCIOLOGY

A crucial insight of Burawoy's analysis is the inclusion of teaching as a form of public sociology. This is the obvious place to start in constructing a broader definition of public sociology. The 70 percent of sociologists who work as academics have regular experience in making sociology public. Arguably, most of the 30 percent of sociology PhDs who work outside universities, mainly in policy research, are also engaged in activities that regularly require them to make their findings accessible and relevant to broader audiences.

Hence, although Burawoy's division-of-labor argument appears to suggest that only a minority of sociologists engage in public sociology, in fact the *majority* of sociologists have a good deal of practice. And, from this experience, the majority of sociologists have also learned that most audiences want to understand not just the practical relevance but also the political and moral implications of sociological insights. Although most of us would argue that sociology can't (and shouldn't) provide absolute "answers" to moral and political questions, we are regularly called upon to engage such questions, and therefore recognize that sociological research will, implicitly or explicitly, be used as a guide. In other words, not only are most of us practicing public sociology in the classroom; whether we like it or not (and public sociologists, of course, are perfectly happy with this), the research we produce is also always "at risk" for being used to influence policy, shape public opinion, or reflect on the moral and political problems of contemporary society. To deny this, or to pretend that politics and morality do not influence the form and impact of our research, is simply to be blind to social reality.

Thus, to name ourselves as public sociologists means, first and foremost, to be more *explicit* and *reflective* about what we are *already* doing. It also means we should push ourselves to be better teachers and better students of society. As any serious teacher-training program will explain, good teaching and good learning require the following: active listening and dialogue, a sense of mutual obligation and accountability, the ability to engage in critical analysis, and an inspired commitment to (relevant, accessible, socially significant) knowledge. From my point of view, this is precisely what it means to be a good "public sociologist."

To respond to those who are nervous about the potentially damaging effects of public sociology, it is also important to point out that embracing public sociology does not mean giving up on standards of merit. For obvious reasons, for instance, it would probably be a bad idea to use one's ability to garner media attention, write best-selling books, or engage in community activism as the appropriate markers of "success." Most of us know that one can gain public acclaim just for being a clever rhetorician, offering snappy sound bites, igniting controversy, or providing an affirmation of popular ideas. It is perfectly reasonable to distinguish, as Mills (1959) did, between "mass" audiences seeking affirmation and amusement and "public" audiences seeking civic engagement and further knowledge of important social issues. We need not feel bound to dumb down our analysis for easy consumption, popularize it to fit the latest fads, or translate it into pure advocacy to satisfy the particular interests of particular publics. What matters are sociological depth, insight, and social engagement, as well as clarity, honesty, and accountability.

With these criteria in place, those critics who worry that public sociology would necessarily be bad sociology should feel a good deal calmer. And to those who worry that the promotion of public sociology is too demanding, an added weight on already busy schedules, I'd suggest that what public sociology actually means is shifting the weight to another foot. That is, our jobs actually offer us a great deal of autonomy, public sociology has a large number of allies, and disciplinary judgments (regarding tenure, research, and teaching) follow from disciplinary commitments. When we think further about busy schedules and "bad" (popular) sociology, it is important to point out that embracing public sociology does, in fact, require us to believe that what we do in the classroom is significant, worthwhile, and (should be) "good" sociology.[3] If we can say this, we are well on the road to (my) utopia.

The critique of public sociology grounded in the belief that scientific objectivity is polluted by public concerns is, I think, the toughest nut to crack. And, reading between the lines, it is clear to me that Burawoy's "professional" category is actually the category of (hard science–inspired) scientific sociology. (Professional sociologists are the methodologically rigorous, grant-getting academics who, Burawoy tells us, provide legitimacy for the discipline.) In the promotion of public sociology, my preference would be to convince all scientists that all research, in the final analysis, is politically and morally motivated, and scientific findings and analyses are always, inescapably, impacted by the political, cultural, and economic systems in which they are embedded. Hence, no human being is able to achieve "objectivity" in the absolute sense. But I'm afraid the science-versus-values debate might be akin to the abortion debate; I could elaborate my point of view until I'm blue in the face and continue to meet with equally strong resistance.

Yet, there is hope. Despite the toughness of this nut, as I've mentioned, most of the "professional," scientific sociologists I know do *not* object to public sociology in the broadest terms—as long as it is good sociology with the appropriate respect for sound methodology, depth analysis, and theory. And it's certainly fair enough to criticize any given public sociologist for being atheoretical, irrational, or methodologically weak—if she or he is. Hence, just as we need a broad and inclusive vision of what counts as public sociology, in this case what is needed is a broader and more inclusive view of what counts as important, social "scientific" research.[4] If we bring the two together, the scientific objectivity objection to public sociology would begin to dissolve.

Finally, regarding universities' willingness to employ us as "public" sociologists, I see very little evidence that universities are relying on singular, absolute, and universal standards for determining the "legitimacy" and value of any given field of study. Historical, cross-disciplinary, and cross-cultural examples suggest that the academy's valuation of sociology is not reliant, for instance, on the discipline's dedication to a narrow definition of science. As much as I recognize that there are a number of complicating factors involved (and I could surely use some research on this point), it seems quite possible that the more sociologists engage in public sociology, the more the "public" will value sociology and sociological insights and the more the academy will value the discipline.

Once such fears are calmed, critiques are clarified, and the intellectual and practical roadblocks to public sociology are cleared away, the only problem that remains is the problem of power. If the discipline of sociology is, at bottom, a competitive field of "rational actors" seeking a spot in the upper ranks of the academic pyramid, then the perpetuation of intellectual insularity and the claim that what we do is so complex that it cannot possibly be understood by publics is a much more useful and clever strategy than public sociology for preserving rigid hierarchies. If the truth be told, I am far more nervous about this possibility than any of the existing critiques of public sociology. But this is a topic for another day.[5]

In my utopia, the public contributions of sociologists would be more explicitly valued, good teaching would have an especially honored place, and direct engagement with multiple publics would be seen as something more than an "extracurricular" activity. We would be committed to training our graduate students in the techniques and importance of public sociology. In no time at all, sociology would become so crucial to public understanding, so much a part of public debate and everyday discourse, that high school students everywhere would be clamoring for its inclusion in their curriculum.

What is crucial, as I've said, is the explicit recognition that sociology is and should be public, that publics are more than simply a handy subject matter, and that, if we want sociology to be something more than a means to a paycheck, we have a serious responsibility to publics. Perhaps my glasses are too rosy, but I also believe, despite all the divisions and hierarchies within our discipline, a collective commitment to public sociology could serve as an extraordinarily powerful foundation for community-building dialogue and debate.

Of course, I may be wrong and Burawoy may be right. Perhaps it is impossible to create a utopia in which all sociologists identify themselves as public sociologists. Perhaps, as Burawoy argues, it is not possible to turn back the clock on the "academic revolution" that valorized a narrow vision of "pure" science as the only worthy form of scholarship (this volume, 31). Perhaps the most that we can hope for is to create one protected space within the division of labor that explicitly understands sociology as "for" (and with) the public, leaving the critical sociologists to dedicate themselves to criticizing other sociologists, leaving the policy sociologists to serve the "kings" (as Mills [1959, 181] put it), and leaving the professional sociologists to imagine their research as outside the public realm, carefully protecting it from the values and politics of contemporary society.

Still, I look around, and, with the exception of a handful of outspoken critics, I believe that the vast majority of sociologists today would understand and agree with C. Wright Mills's (1959, 184) suggestion, "No one is 'outside society'; the question is where each stands within it." I know that Mills is right; I hope that I am too.

NOTES

1. Charles R. Tittle's (2004) critique of Burawoy offers a particularly instructive rendering of professional sociology in this regard.

2. Of course, it could be a right-wing conspiracy, but one doesn't hear this critique. The association of "public" accessibility with "left-wing" activism is, I'd say, a cultural reality worth pondering.

3. To those who would counter that our classrooms are filled with a captive audience, or that our students are undereducated and unsophisticated, I would suggest that the reliance on captivity is simply an excuse for bad teaching, and the fact that we manage to train undergraduates and first-year graduate students in classical social theory and research methods would seem to suggest that audiences can be quite sophisticated—if you push them.

4. As my friends and graduate students know, I have a tough time with the category of "science" and therefore assiduously avoid identifying myself or my own work in these terms. My preference, following Donna Haraway (1988), is for honest, serious, and reliable "situated knowledge." Scientists, of course, are often a very good source for such knowledge.

5. Michelle Lamont's "How to Become a Dominant French Philosopher" (1987) is a good place to start thinking through these issues.

REFERENCES

Haraway, Donna. 1988. "Situated Knowledges: The Science Question in Feminism and the Privilege of Partial Perspective." *Feminist Studies* 14: 575–99.

Horkheimer, Max. (1947) 1974. *Eclipse of Reason.* New York: Seabury Press.

Lamont, Michelle. 1987. "How to Become a Dominant French Philosopher: The Case of Jacques Derrida." *American Journal of Sociology* 93: 584–622.

Mills, C. Wright. 1959. *The Sociological Imagination.* New York: Oxford University Press.

Tittle, Charles R. 2004. "The Arrogance of Public Sociology." *Social Forces* 82: 1639–43.

JUDITH STACEY

If I Were the Goddess
of Sociological Things

Whether measured in attendance or published commentary, no annual meeting theme in the memory of the American Sociological Association (ASA) has struck a chord as resonant and popular with practitioners of the discipline as has "public sociologies" in 2004. A sociologist these days who is not, like Burawoy, "for public sociology" could qualify for endangered species status. Such a creature actually represents an unimaginable species, of course, because sociology is inescapably public. Private sociology, its implied antonym, is an oxymoron. All sociology, whether written or spoken, necessarily addresses a public. The meaningful questions at issue concern which publics sociologists should and should not serve, by what means, and to what ends—questions with an honored ancestry in the discipline, immortalized among them, as Burawoy reminds us, Alfred Lee's "Sociology for whom?" and Robert Lynd's "Sociology for what?"

Building on this august legacy, Burawoy made it his presidential mission to provoke collective disciplinary self-reflection on our diverse, and often contentious, public purposes, powers, and pitfalls. To this end, his presidential address presents his philosophy of sociology in eleven theses replete with a complex four-tab taxonomy of sociological genres (public, policy, professional, and critical) crosscut by two axes of knowledge (instrumental and reflexive) and audiences (academic and extra-academic). Instead of addressing these questions directly, however, let alone quibbling over where Burawoy located my personal public sociological practices and prejudices within his four tabs, I want to endorse the goals of three of his theses and to offer for consideration a number of not-so-modest proposals toward realizing them by revamping institutional structures and intellectual culture in our discipline, and in the academy more broadly. My multipronged, and admittedly utopian, agenda for reconfiguring our discipline "for public sociology" addresses policies and practices in graduate admissions and curriculum; in hiring, teaching, assessment, and reward structures for faculty; and in the rhetoric and culture of sociological writing and discourse. I present these proposals in two sets, the first addressed to the goal of globalizing U.S. sociology, which Burawoy articulates in his ninth thesis, the second to rekindle the endangered public sociological passions and purposes that his fifth and eleventh theses affirm.

TOWARD A MORE COSMOPOLITAN SOCIOLOGICAL IMAGINATION

Just as the United States exercises global imperial power, our national discipline enjoys global dominion over professional sociology internationally. English is the lingua franca of international sociology, and publishing in U.S. academic journals and presses represents the primary means of professional legitimation for sociologists in many parts of the world. In his ninth thesis, "the articulation of national and global sociologies," Burawoy calls for remolding the global division of sociological labor to address, and where possible to redress, the disproportionate influence that U.S. sociology exerts over other national sociologies. "Only in the U.S.," Burawoy maintains, do "we have to invent the term 'public sociology' as an antidote to a powerful professional sociology!" (Burawoy 2004, 106). He urges dialogue between the highly professionalized discipline in the United States and practitioners of other national sociologies, where public sociology is often taken for granted and professional sociology much less developed.

Accordingly, and laudably, the 2004 program featured a greater number of international voices and themes than ever before, more than doubling the number of registrants from outside the United States over the prior year.[1] I was disappointed, therefore, when I participated in the U.S. regional session of a Ford-sponsored thematic series in international public sociology, to find that all of the invited speakers were from the United States and none undertook to reflexively locate U.S. sociology within an international context. This was a missed opportunity, in my view, because, as in most asymmetrical relations, subordinates know more about dominants than vice versa. The oversight, moreover, seems

symptomatic of the national insularity and parochialism that characterize U.S. culture, our educational system, and even sociology. In the service of Burawoy's ninth thesis, therefore, I propose that we undertake
initiatives to deparochialize our discipline by structuring international
exchanges, representation, and knowledge not only into meetings and
conferences, but into our journals, departments, and graduate programs. To this end, I offer the following set of proposals:

1. Establish formal "sister" department relationships between sociology departments in the United States and complementary
   departments at universities in other nations in order to institutionalize diverse forms of transnational academic alliances and
   exchange. Sister departments would establish, and perhaps even
   mandate, regular exchanges of their faculty and graduate students
   and would undertake collaborative research, conference, and
   teaching projects.

2. Allot permanent faculty full-time-equivalent positions in U.S.
   sociology departments (and ideally throughout our universities)
   for the regular appointment of visiting international scholars,
   particularly from Global South nations. In addition to offering
   courses and colloquiums of their own, visiting faculty would
   team-teach with regular members of the host department.

3. Expand affirmative action admissions and support policies in
   graduate and postdoctoral programs in sociology to include
   recruitment of international candidates, again particularly from
   Global South nations.

4. Revise doctoral degree requirements in sociology programs to
   require that all doctoral candidates demonstrate at least reading
   facility in a second language and that they participate in at least
   one research project with an international component.

5. Mandate substantial international representation on all future
   ASA program committees as well as on the editorial boards of
   our professional journals, university presses, and research grant
   review panels.

6. Devote an ASA annual meeting, as well as symposia in our
   journals and professional newsletters, to analysis of the current
   and appropriate place of U.S. sociology in its global context.
   Participants in such efforts should be nationally diverse in order
   to cross-fertilize emic with etic views.

TOWARD A MORE ENGAGED AND ENGAGING DISCIPLINE

"Locating the sociologist," Burawoy's fifth thesis, laments "the mismatch of her or his sociological habitus and the structure of the disciplinary field as a whole." I share Burawoy's disgruntled view that "it is as if graduate school is organized to winnow away at the moral commitments that inspired the interest in sociology in the first place." We characteristically recruit to our graduate programs students whose sociological imaginations and commitments to social justice were awakened in engaging and provocative undergraduate courses treating subjects like race, gender, family, work, crime, drugs, sexuality, revolutions, popular culture, cities, and social movements. But then our doctoral programs proceed immediately to muzzle these interests, typically front-loading the curricula with mandatory courses in statistics, quantitative methods, and classical theory that allow little if any time or encouragement for students to pursue their substantive and public passions. Too many times over the past quarter century, I have witnessed the emotional toll that this disjuncture exacts from new graduate students, generating disillusion and disaffection with the discipline and the academy, often culminating in withdrawal from both. Likewise, I have too frequently shared Burawoy's unhappy experience observing junior faculty being well advised strategically by senior colleagues to defer pursuing their avid interests in public sociology until after they have successfully jumped through the increasingly daunting and dehumanizing professional hoops that patrol the path to tenure. "Better to indulge the commitment to public sociology from the beginning," Burawoy exhorts us, "and that way ignite the torch of professional sociology." Hear! Hear!

I have more reservations, however, about the whiff of chauvinistic disciplinary self-aggrandizement that I detect in the tripartite division of the social sciences that Burawoy identifies in his final thesis, "sociologist as partisan." I suspect that few sociologists, or even many economists and political scientists, for that matter, would quarrel with his claims that U.S. economics "depends on the existence of markets with an interest in their expansion" and that "political science depends on the state with an interest in political stability." Anointing sociology, however, as the branch of knowledge that, through its dependence on civil society, represents "the best possible terrain for the defense of humanity" is certainly tendentious, not to speak of insulting to several of our social scientific siblings with legitimate claims to this humanist terrain.

Through a rhetorical sleight of hand that attributes his disciplinary selection criteria to space limitations, Burawoy explicitly excludes from his social science cartography "such neighbors as geography, history, and anthropology" and neglects even to acknowledge the existence of psychology. Yet, several of these exempted disciplines could certainly mount robust competitive or, better, complementary claims to representing "the interests of humanity—interests in keeping at bay both state despotism and market tyranny." And surely the intellectual traditions of two of these—anthropology and history—value reflexive and critical over instrumental forms of knowledge more strongly than is true of sociology in the United States.

Rather than compete with neighboring social science disciplines to occupy vanguard status in defense of humanity, I would make common cause with colleagues in as many of these as possible, as well as with those in the humanities and the rest of the liberal arts and sciences. Collectively we should challenge those increasingly market-dominated, career-focused, reward structures, and excessively professionalized cultures in the academy that reproduce norms and forms of disciplinary insularity inimical to public sociology and public intellectual life more broadly. Here I am far less interested than Burawoy seems to be in fortifying what I take to be atavistic disciplinary borders or in nurturing a distinctive (but to my mind an incoherent) sociological identity. In short, I unapologetically subscribe to the view that Burawoy unfairly labels the "genetic fallacy" about the atavistic boundaries of the nineteenth-century disciplinary division of intellectual labor (see Stacey 1999). I judge these boundaries to be anachronistic, not, as Burawoy maintains, "just because they were created at a particular moment of history," but precisely because they are no longer congruent with "their ongoing and changing meaning and the interests they represent." The alternative to defending the nineteenth-century borders, in my view, is not to embrace the "positivist fantasy" of a unified social science but to foster creative disciplinary reconfigurations, cross-fertilizations, and renovations designed to better nurture public sociologies and public intellectual life.

At the crux of such an agenda, I would place measures designed to combat ever-escalating and, I believe, anti-intellectual "standards" that judge scholarly merit overwhelmingly by the quantity and imprimatur of academic publications. In the interest of intellectual vitality and the conservation of trees, I seek a substantial shift in concern from the quantity to the quality, originality, and significance of the publications. To effect such a shift, we need a bracing "structural adjustment program" to provide intellectual relief and inspiration to the overworked American academic. Thus, if I were the goddess of sociological things,[2] I would radically expand the three-pronged mission of the new ASA task force that has been established to institutionalize public sociologies. Here are some, perhaps immodest, suggestions in that vein:

1. Declare a rotational moratorium on academic publishing by all full-time faculty members in each department. At staggered intervals of perhaps one year out of every three, departmental faculty would be precluded from submitting any work for publication in a peer-reviewed academic journal or press. My rationale for this proposal is to reap the creative fruits of intellectual crop rotation. Just as medieval farmers replenished depleted soil by periodically allowing fields to lie fallow, I hope to rejuvenate intellectual life and creativity within the academy and beyond by imposing on scholars a periodic mandatory recess from productivity norms and practices governed by the goal of academic publication. A direct counter to the Chaplinesque assembly-line model of scholarly productivity that has come to dominate academic hiring and promotion standards, such a structure would facilitate broader, more adventurous, less instrumental reading, learning, teaching, reflection, and writing.

   My proposed moratorium on publication does not extend to more popular venues and genres. Therefore, it would enable scholars to devote more time to writing "for public sociology." It would also free up time for faculty who wished to actively pursue Burawoy's call to "cultivate a collaborative relation between sociology and journalism" (this volume, 57). Such faculty might choose, for example, to develop their public communication skills by enrolling in courses in journalism, as Barbara Ehrenreich recommended during the 2004 ASA meetings, or perhaps in creative writing, media studies, or documentary filmmaking.

2. Abolish the rank of associate professor, replacing the three-tiered tenure-track system of status-differentiated ranks and titles with a two-tiered system that distinguishes only between tenured and untenured professors, as is the practice in most U.S. law schools. The current anachronistic, hierarchical titles misleadingly imply distinctions in occupational function where none exist. In the U.S. academy nothing but a title distinguishes

the work performed by full and associate professors. Likewise, assistant professors do not "assist" either of the former, and they perform the identical professorial labors but for their exclusion from participating in promotion reviews of more senior colleagues. The vestigial middle-tier rank of associate professor serves principally the task of fortifying invidious academic status "distinctions" in Bourdieu's sense, imposing hidden (and not so hidden) injuries on psyches, collegiality, and department morale.

Equally unfortunate and counterproductive, the post-tenure distinction in rank imposes the arduous tax of a second full-scale promotion review on candidates, colleagues, administrative and clerical staff, and once again trees. This superfluous promotion review process functions like a fraternity initiation or public humiliation ritual, and to what substantive effects? On the one hand, ironically enough, the labor-intensive review process itself represents a massive drag on productivity—for the candidates who must prepare their statements and dossiers and for senior faculty and administrators within and external to the department who participate in assessing these. On the other hand, associate professors are already "lifers" whose security of employment is not at risk and who, again ironically, are more likely to remain in a department in which they receive a negative than a positive review for promotion to the rank of full professor. Does anyone genuinely believe that the prospect of being promoted from one tenured rank to the next encourages scholars to produce a higher quality of research, publication, teaching, or service, or that a negative promotion review has a constructive effect on future scholarship? At best, it promotes a greater quantity of publications, fostering instrumental and strategic approaches to research and publication over taking intellectual risks or engaging in public sociology.

3. Expand the charge of the new ASA task force for public sociology, or perhaps establish a broader commission, to develop model disciplinary guidelines for promotion to tenured rank and for post-tenure merit reviews that directly counter assembly-line standards of productivity. The central goals of these guidelines would be to promote the quality over quantity of publications, to value contributions to public sociology in addition to academic achievements, and to foster greater intellectual

breadth and creativity. In addition to developing incentives and professional standards for distinguishing "good from bad public sociology," such as mandatory disclosures about sponsorship and remuneration for intellectual activities, the guidelines should suggest ways to make such contributions "count" as valued elements rather than altruistic digressions (typically considered under the comparatively denigrated rubric of "service") from intellectual work. The guidelines also should devise more flexible review timetables and incentives tailored to the demands and practices of distinct disciplinary profiles of scholarly research and intellectual production. Scholars could negotiate longer intervals between reviews, for example, to conduct research that requires major time investments in language acquisition or other new skills, lengthy periods of immersion in field research, or publishing books rather than articles. To arrive at these guidelines, the commission should initiate and preside over a broad disciplinary dialogue by inviting ideas, input, and proposals from all of the ASA sections and the membership at large and holding town hall plenary sessions for this purpose at annual regional as well as national association meetings. Draft guidelines should then be submitted to the membership for deliberation before final proposals are offered for formal adoption.

Clearly, however, this cannot be a project for sociology in isolation. Just as history proved Trotsky correct about the impossibility of sustaining socialism in one country, no major reforms of promotion, tenure, and merit standards can be achieved in a single discipline. Sociology could take the lead here, however, in advocating for a major overhaul in academic culture and practices along these lines. Such a project would itself represent an exemplary form of public sociology, a collective commitment to "sociology as partisan."

4. Allocate permanent faculty full-time-equivalent positions in U.S. sociology departments (and ideally throughout our universities) for the regular appointment of public intellectuals, such as featured plenary speakers at the 2004 ASA meetings Paul Krugman, Barbara Ehrenreich, Mary Robinson, Arundhati Roy, and Fernando Cardoso, to serve as full-time or part-time visiting professors for periods of one to four semesters. As with the proposal for positions for visiting international scholars I

advanced above, these visiting faculty would team-teach with regular members of the host department as well as offer courses and colloquiums of their own.

5. Institute a regular system for local, cross-disciplinary exchanges of faculty between departments and programs on the same campus. All faculty members would be required to spend at least one year out of perhaps every six participating in intra-campus faculty exchanges, literally "changing places" with col-leagues in neighboring fields by swapping offices, teaching obligations, and committee responsibilities. Cross-disciplinary team-teaching should be facilitated as well.

6. Mount a major campaign to revamp writing standards in the discipline to encourage scholars to compose more engaging, accessible prose. I seek to combat the deadening, hermetic, humorless, impersonal rhetorical style that pervades our aca-demic journals—a style succinctly coined "academese." In addition to discouraging this dialect's characteristically lavish displays of superfluous jargon, I target the ubiquitous use of the passive voice as a particular mission of my teaching and men-toring. The passive voice, despite its possible utility as a treat-ment for insomnia, often evades authorial accountability and camouflages fuzzy thinking, as any good instructor of introduc-tory writing composition can confirm. Too many insecure aca-demic apprentices seek refuge in the scientistic expository voice. However, genuine intellectual authority does not emanate from the head of an omniscient, invisible, value-free author, let alone from that of an unaccountable one.

I wish to see our journal publications become literally and unapologetically more "journalistic." The anonymous review-ers of an ethnographic article I recently submitted to one of our "flagship" journals offered me numerous constructive criti-cisms. I do not include among these, however, one reviewer's complaint that "the writing suggests an essay rather than a research report." An essay is indeed what I wrote and, in my view, what more of us should be writing and reading in our journals. While "essay" literally connotes human effort, a "report" implies a positivist belief in the transparency of repre-sentation—"nothing but the facts, ma'am," pure research find-ings gathered and conveyed unsullied by human intervention.

Likewise, I urge my doctoral students to try to write books rather than dissertations. I believe the discipline should explicitly advocate preparation of and incentives for lucid and lively communication in our graduate programs and publications. Handing a copy of Howard Becker's *Writing for Social Scientists* to new graduate students, as is the practice at the University of California, Santa Barbara, might be an easy first step.

Sociologists who embrace Burawoy's eleventh thesis, and I count myself among them, must sign on to a daunting, countercultural mission both within the discipline and far beyond. I believe we must engage in a form of disciplinary cultural crusade to unseat the false god of value-free social scientific knowledge and to install in its place the grail of intellectual integrity. Self-reflexively acknowledging our values and our stakes in the knowledge we seek and that we "essay" to convey, we should teach the public the distinction between virtual sociology (see Stacey 1997) and sociological virtue. While I have neither desire nor prospects to become a goddess, the public contributions that committed sociologists can make are no small things.

NOTES

1. A total of 144 non-U.S. participants registered for the 2004 meetings, compared with 50 in 2003, 68 in 2002, and 95 in 2001. This does not include registration among regular ASA members from outside the United States.

2. With all due apologies to Arundhati Roy.

REFERENCES

Burawoy, Michael. 2004. "Introduction" to "Public Sociologies: A Symposium from Boston College." *Social Problems* 51:103–106.

Stacey, Judith. 1997. "Virtual Social Science and the Politics of Family Values." In *New Locations: The Remaking of Fieldwork and the Critical Imperative at Century's End*, ed. G. Marcus. Santa Fe, NM: School of American Research.

———. 1999. "Ethnography Confronts the Global Village: A New Home for a New Century?" *Journal of Contemporary Ethnography* 28 (6): 687–97.

PATRICIA HILL COLLINS

Going Public
Doing the Sociology That Had No Name

For years, I have been doing a kind of sociology that had no name. With hindsight, the path that I have been on seems clear and consistent. In the early 1970s, as a teacher and community organizer within the community schools movement, I did some of my best sociology, all without publishing one word. For six years, I honed the craft of translating the powerful ideas of my college education so that I might share them with my elementary school students, their families, my fellow teachers, and community members. My sociological career also illustrates how the tensions of moving through sociology as a discipline as well as engaging numerous constituencies outside sociology shaped my scholarship. This impetus to think both inside and outside the American sociological box enabled me to survive within the discipline. Early on, I recognized that I needed to create space to breathe within prevailing sociological norms and practices. I wrote "Learning from the Outsider Within: The Sociological Significance of Black Feminist Thought" to create space for myself as an individual, yet that article simultaneously generated dialogues with a broad range of nonsociologists (Collins 1986). Similarly, writing *Black Feminist Thought* (Collins 2000) for social theorists, for sociologists, for feminists, and for ordinary people—in particular, African American women whose lives I hoped to influence—was an exercise in the energy that it takes to engage multiple audiences within one text. When colleagues tell me how much the ideas in that one book have traveled, I realize the importance of connecting scholarship to broader audiences. With hindsight, I see how important my years spent working in the community schools movement have been to my subsequent sociological career.

Over the years, my personal engagement in speaking with multiracial, multiethnic audiences from many social class backgrounds, citizenship categories, genders, sexualities, and ages has taught me much. As a professor, discussing my ideas with diverse groups at colleges, universities, community centers, academic conferences, and social activist arenas has improved my scholarship. Take, for example, how different audiences engaged the ideas in *Black Sexual Politics* (Collins 2004). Writing a book is one thing—talking with different groups of people about what I had written was an entirely different experience. My generic lecture title, "Introduction to *Black Sexual Politics*," fails to capture the wide range of talks that I actually delivered. The African American community residents in Tulsa, Oklahoma, who came out to their local public library to hear the version of the talk that I prepared for them had different reactions than the college students and faculty on the beautiful campus of the University of California, Santa Barbara, who encountered the same ideas, yet in a vastly different format. At times, I had to fall back on pedagogical skills honed during my days teaching seventh- and eighth-grade students, the case when I addressed a lively group of African American and Latino high school students in Louisville, Kentucky. How different their reactions were to the ideas in *Black Sexual Politics* than those of the audience at the feminist bookstore in Cambridge, Massachusetts. The list goes on. I realize how diverse American society is, let alone how rich the tapestry of global cultures and experiences outside U.S. borders. Writing for and speaking with multiple publics has been challenging, but also worthwhile.

Despite this history, I initially found Michael Burawoy's ideas about public sociology unnerving (this volume). I certainly like Burawoy's model and think that it interjects a much-needed breath of fresh air into some increasingly stale sociological debates. At the same time, I'm not completely comfortable with it. Apparently, I had been *doing* public sociology without even knowing it. Moreover, I was not alone. Despite my inability to classify them as public sociologists, many other sociologists had also made the decision to "go public."

On the one hand, I should be happy that the type of sociological practice that has so long preoccupied me is now gaining recognition. What has long been "out" now has a rare invitation to attend the party within American sociology, which has not been particularly inclined to changing its ways. Most certainly individual sociologists have been at the forefront of many progressive issues, yet they do not constitute the center of the discipline of American sociology. On the other hand, I question whether this new visibility for public sociology is inherently good for practitioners of public sociology as well as for public sociology itself. What are the potential challenges that accompany Burawoy's gutsy move?

WHAT'S IN A NAME?

One challenge facing public sociology concerns the way in which naming it will help or hurt its practitioners. Is naming public sociology inherently beneficial? Most people assume that institutionalizing public sociology will be a good thing. Naming public sociology should help legitimate it within the discipline. Perhaps. Yet as mental patients, escaped slaves, runaway brides, and prisoners remind us, institutionalization need not be good for everyone. It all depends on where you stand. Once a set of practices is named, and thereby placed in its classificatory cell within an institution, those practices can become even more difficult to do. In this spirit, I wonder how discussions about public sociology will assist sociologists who currently practice public sociology? We assume that naming will elevate the status of current practitioners, but it may instead install a permanent and recognizable underclass that now carries the stigmatized name of public sociology. Stated differently, will doing public sociology emerge as a new form of tracking within the discipline?

As an ideal type, public sociology seems glamorous. Yet who actually does this kind of sociology? Current practitioners of public sociology are typically not housed in premier institutions, nor do many of them come from privileged groups. I suggest that individuals who are most likely to commit to public sociology have had experiences that provide them with a distinctive view of social inequality. African Americans, Latinos, new immigrant groups, women, working-class and poor people, lesbian, gay, bisexual, and transgendered (LGBT) people, and others who remain penalized within American society and their allies may gravitate toward a sociology that promises to address social issues that affect the public. If not predisposed before entering sociology, individuals from these groups and their allies may develop a public sociology perspective as a result of their sociological graduate training.

Many graduate students choose sociology because they are attracted to the vision of an until-now-unnamed public sociology that they encounter in their undergraduate classrooms. Most do not enter graduate programs to become professional or policy sociologists. For many, graduate training resembles a shell game—they look under one shell for the public sociology prize that they anticipated; yet when they pick up the shell, nothing is there. The real prizes, they are told, lie under the remaining three shells of professional, policy, and, to a lesser extent, critical sociology. They are pressured to choose among types of sociology and to leave behind the idealism of public sociology and the "you'll-never-get-a-job-if-you-keep-that-up" stance of critical sociology. Fortunately, my graduate training differed. I was encouraged to be an independent thinker, and I took my professors at their word. My own path within sociology certainly reflects this predisposition to focus on the recursive relationship between doing and naming.

I often wonder how I managed to carve a path for myself by doing a sociology that had no name. For me, this is not a new question, but rather one that has shaped my entire career. Being an African American woman in overwhelmingly white and male settings, as well as carrying my working-class background into situations that routinely privilege the cultural (and actual) capital of middle-class families, has been frustrating yet immensely helpful. I am used to not belonging, to being stared at as the one who must introduce myself to yet another sociological clique at the American Sociological Association (ASA) in order to put my colleagues at ease. Because I belong to groups that garner less value within American society, I hold ideas about democracy, social justice, color blindness, feminism, and a long list of social practices that differ from those of the mainstream. I stand in a different relationship to power relations, and as a result, I hold a distinctive standpoint on those relations. Being committed to principles that are larger than myself has not been easy. I am the one who has been denied jobs for which I am qualified because I do not do the kind of sociology that is valued. Doing public sociology either will make you strong or might kill you. Would naming the kind of sociology that I have been doing have made these struggles any easier?

Perhaps. Yet at the same time, being classified under the banner of public sociology may foster a kind of sociological ghettoization, primarily because those who gravitate toward public sociology may already hold subordinate status within the discipline itself. Public sociology can thus become a convenient tool for getting African Americans, Latinos, women, community college teachers, and the like to do the service work of the profession, this time not just spreading sociology's mission to students, or serving on endless committees because their "perspective" should be represented, but also by explaining sociology to multiple publics. In this endeavor, would time remain to "do" public sociology in its most robust form? Or would a legitimated public sociology be reduced to a service arm of the discipline, with the "real" sociology of professional sociology still holding sway? Is public sociology a "sociology of and for the Others," namely, all those people who cannot make it within other ideal types of sociology? If so, then the irony of having those who have struggled so mightily to become sociologists serve as the public face of sociology, with the sociological center remaining intact, becomes especially poignant.

Beyond this issue of how legitimating public sociology via naming it might not necessarily help its current practitioners, the act of naming might also shift the very mission of this kind of sociology. I envision the spirit of public sociology as resembling historian Robin D. G. Kelley's notion of a "radical imagination"; or the tenets of "magical realism" invoked by Lani Guinier and Gerald Torres as part of their project to transcend the limits of current thinking about race and democracy; or even sociology's own C. Wright Mills's clarion call for a new "sociological imagination" (Kelley 2002; Guinier and Torres 2002; Mills 1959). In my own work, I draw upon these ideas via the concept of visionary pragmatism within African American women's oppositional knowledge, a creative tension that links visions for a better society and pragmatic strategies of how to bring it about (Collins 2000).

Public sociology resembles these activities. It constitutes a constellation of oppositional knowledges and practices. If American society were just and fair, if the American public were fed, clothed, housed, educated, employed, and healthy, there would be no need for public sociology. Its very existence speaks to the need to *oppose* social injustice yet also to be proactive in creating a democratic and just public sphere. Naming public sociology strives to enhance the stature of these oppositional knowledges and practices by carving out spaces within the boundaries of an established discipline in ways that legitimate the public sociology that already exists and, perhaps, catalyze more. Naming aspires to redefine public sociology as no longer being a subordinated, submerged way of doing sociology and seeks to elevate its stature.

Yet, in the American context, making the shift from outsider to insider knowledge may change the ethos of public sociology. Ironically, despite good intentions, naming public sociology may step on existing land mines of defining the purpose and practices of oppositional knowledge as well as the social location of insiders and outsiders who produce such knowledge. Naming public sociology, and thereby opening the doors to the valid question of defining its distinguishing features, can catalyze endless debates about boundary making. A subtle shift can easily be made from doing an unnamed, messy, and thus incorrigible public sociology to talking about public sociology in ways that shrink its possibilities. Public sociology can easily become yet another fad, a nugget of commodified knowledge that privileged sociologists can play at just as a cat toys with a mouse. What comforting procrastination—one remains ethically honorable by paying lip service to public sociology while never having to take a stand by actually doing it. I can see it now—legions of dissertations analyzing the contributions and failures of public sociology versus dissertations that *do* public sociology. Better yet, what would the "Introduction to Public Sociology" course look like? Which sociological worthies would make the cut to be included on the required reading list and which would be left outside to stare at a closed door?

WHAT'S IN *THIS* NAME?

Another challenge confronting public sociology concerns its chosen name. Is this a good time for the discipline of sociology to claim the term *public*? Is this the best name for this work, even as we persist in doing it? After over two decades of sustained assault on public institutions in the United States, throwing in one's lot with the sinking ship of anything "public" may seem suicidal. Let's just paint a big target on sociology, some professional and policy sociologists could argue; sociology will become viewed as a field for losers.

In the United States, the privatization of public power seems ubiquitous (Guinier and Torres 2002). In the 1980s and 1990s, social policies dramatically reconfigured the meaning of *public* generally and the social welfare state as the quintessential public institution. Current efforts to privatize hospitals, sanitation services, schools, and other public services and attempts to develop a more private-sector, entrepreneurial spirit in others by underfunding them—public radio, public television, subcontracting specific services via competitive bidding—illustrate this abandonment and derogation of anything public. Deteriorating schools, health care services, roads, bridges, and public transportation, resulting from public failure to fund public institutions, speak to the erosion and accompanying devaluation of anything deemed "public." In this context, *public* becomes reconfigured as anything of poor quality, marked by a lack of control and privacy—all characteristics associated with poverty. This slippage between lack of privacy, poor quality, and poverty affects the changing meaning of *public*.

Much of this push toward privatization in the United States has covert yet powerful racial undertones. When African Americans and Latinos among others gained expanded rights, individuals and groups with power increasingly abandoned public institutions. Take, for example, the legacy of the 1954 *Brown* decision that outlawed racial segregation in public education. Thurgood Marshall, Derrick Bell, and other civil rights activists had no way to anticipate how a new color-blind racism would effectively stonewall school integration initiatives. The early trickle away from public schools by middle-class white parents who founded private white academies so that their children need not attend racially integrated public schools opened the floodgates of white flight from public institutions of all sorts. Public schools, public health, public transportation, and public libraries are all now devalued in the face of market-based policies that say "privatization will shield you from rubbing elbows with the public." These new social relations signal a distinct reversal—the public sphere becomes a curiously confined yet visible location that increases the value of private services and privacy itself. Public places become devalued spaces containing Latinos, poor people, African Americans, the homeless, and anyone else who cannot afford to escape. In this context, privacy signals safety; control over one's home, family, and community space; and racial homogeneity—all qualities that can be purchased if one can afford them. This version of privatization dovetails with Lani Guinier and Gerald Torres's notion of the privatization of power. If private spaces are better, then shouldn't private entities run the public itself?

In this political context, naming this sociology *public* sociology inherits this history and these social issues. What does it mean for sociology to claim to be for and about the public at this historic moment? Will this be perceived as sociology for the dispossessed, the displaced, and the disadvantaged? Despite Burawoy's efforts to generate much-needed dialogue that is designed to reinvigorate sociology, I suspect that those currently privileged within professional, critical, and/or policy sociology will express far less enthusiasm for an increased emphasis on public sociology than the internal integrity of doing public sociology might suggest. Following public sociology into the realm of the public

raises too many uncomfortable questions about the discipline of sociology's merit, value, purpose within contemporary American society.
Currently, the term *public* invokes neither populist nor democratic sensibilities. Rather, it means *popular* (as in popular versus high culture)
and, more ominously, inferior. Let the diverse public in and your discipline suffers. Let public sociology in and your scholarship deteriorates.
Is sociology ready for that?

I certainly hope so. The social justice sensibilities of public sociology
constitute one of its defining features. Caring about the public, seeing
all of the others not as devalued entities that one must "mentor" or
"help" but rather as potential partners for the betterment of society
itself provides a core vision or ethos for this kind of work. People want
ideas that matter both to them and within society itself. Public sociology suggests a recursive relationship between those inside the profession and people who are engaged in efforts to understand and challenge
prevailing social inequalities that now characterize an increasingly
devalued public. In this regard, if public sociology is unprepared to
jump into the controversies that surround the term *public,* then this
may not be the best name for it.

CAN WE ALL GET ALONG?

A third distinctive challenge confronts public sociology in the United
States. Now that public sociology has a name, when it comes to its relationship with professional, critical, and policy sociology, I wonder, can
we all get along? American sociologists familiar with the circumstances
that catalyzed the 1992 riots in Los Angeles might remember these
words from motorist Rodney King. King's videotaped beating by members of the Los Angeles police department was shown around the
world. The court decision that exonerated the police also catalyzed several days of rioting, when Angelenos burned down entire city blocks
because they couldn't envision living in Los Angeles the way it was. The
media loved to broadcast King's query, "Can we get along?" His plea
reified American assumptions that talking things through will yield a
fair solution for everyone, that better evidence yields stronger public
policy, and that if we just put our heads together and let rational minds
prevail, we should be able to solve this mess.

However, can it ever be this simple? I have great difficulty imagining
a mahogany conference table with representatives of the Los Angeles

police force, African American, Latino, and Korean grassroots community groups, mayoral staff, the Los Angeles chamber of commerce, church folks, representatives of the Justice for Janitors and Bus Riders unions, and other members of the Los Angeles community putting aside their differences with an "oops-let's-try-this-again" mentality. Most of us would recognize that the historical power relations in Los Angeles that created many of these groups in the first place make such a scenario unbelievable. The groups themselves are involved in a continually shifting mosaic of hierarchical relationships with one another—sometimes they operate as friends, other times as enemies, and often they have little knowledge of what the others are actually doing. Despite my incredulity about such a meeting, if it did occur, at least the people around that conference table would recognize that the knowledge they brought to the mahogany conference table grew directly from the power relations that got them there. They would know that they could not achieve a new vision for Los Angeles without taking power differentials among themselves into account, let alone among those segments of the public that did not get invited to the meeting.

I wonder whether sociologists would have the same sensibility, if they even saw the need for such a meeting in the first place. Burawoy's four-cell typology gives the impression of parallelism among professional, policy, critical, and public sociology, yet it is important to reiterate that Burawoy proposes a Weberian *ideal-type* framework. These four types have never been nor are they expected to be equal to one another. Therein lies the problem. Unless sociology itself expands (the old Reagan policy of creating a bigger pie so that public sociology can cut a piece), creating space for public sociology means taking away from the space of the other three. Will they move over to make room at the mahogany table? Or do professional, policy, and critical sociology see public sociology as the interloper in a game of musical chairs?— because they occupied the three subdisciplinary seats when the music stopped, poor public sociology is left permanently standing.

This is the rub—in the U.S. context in the post–World War II period, professional and policy sociology have exercised imperial authority within American sociology in ways that obscure public sociology. One would think that critical sociology resists these impulses, but when it comes to the privatization of power, practitioners of critical sociology promise more than they deliver. Critical sociology often talks a good game, yet when it comes to the types of institutional change required to let in sufficient numbers of the unruly public, the intellectual blinders of many progressive sociologists keep them from delivering the goods. For example, the ideas of color blindness and gender neutrality that underpin conservative agendas of the Right seem eerily similar to arguments on the left that race and gender-based identity politics basically destroyed a progressive, class-based politics. They too long for a color blindness and gender neutrality that will uphold a class-based agenda. Yet this failure to engage race and gender as a route to rethinking social class has limited critical sociology's contributions as a vibrant force within American society. Just as it took Hurricane Katrina in 2005 to jolt the American public into seeing the realities of race and class in the United States, so too were critical sociologists caught off guard.

As the sociological pie shrinks, in large part because the demonization of the public outside sociology occurs via race- and gender-based bashing of large segments of the American population, fighting over crumbs within the discipline mimics behaviors that are as American as apple pie. Professional and policy sociology have well-established constituencies and do make important contributions. Critical sociology may have long contested the ideas of professional and policy sociology, yet it too has its well-established constituencies who can be just as resistant to a fully actualized public sociology as their well-heeled counterparts. Why should any of these three ideal sociological types cede territory to the upstart of public sociology, especially one that may contain disproportionate numbers of less desirable people? Given the derogation of anything public in the American setting, public sociology faces an uphill battle in finding its place at the sociological table.

WHY DO PUBLIC SOCIOLOGY?

Given these challenges, why would anyone willingly choose public sociology? When I've shared Michael Burawoy's typology of professional, policy, critical, and public sociology as four ideal types of sociology with some of my students, or even simply summarized its ideas, their eyes light up. There's the aha factor at work—"Public sociology is the kind of sociology we want to do," they proclaim. They resonate with the name *public sociology*. Wishing to belong to something bigger than themselves, they know implicitly that doing public sociology constitutes intellectual labor placed in service to broader ethical principles. They are drawn to the concept of a reenergized public where every individual truly does count. By positioning itself in solidarity with ethical principles of democracy, fairness, and social justice, public sociology seemingly offers a path away from provincial careerism and back toward the sociological imaginations that many students felt they needed to check at the graduate school door.

Yet the inevitable questions that come next speak to their pragmatic concerns. "Where do I go to study it? Do the top sociology programs offer a degree in it? Can I get a job doing it?" they query. Moving quickly through the preliminaries and homing in on the promises of mentoring and role modeling, they shift to the next set of questions: "How did you come to do public sociology?" they ask. "You appear to be successful. Can you teach me how to become a public sociologist?"

I don't fault the students. Their questions stem from the disjuncture between one set of promises within American sociology to place the tools of sociology in service to solving social problems and actual sociological practices that must attend to the realities of car loans and mortgage payments. Unlike students of the past, contemporary students are much more cognizant of the fact that the bill will come due one day. So they feel pressured to choose wisely. Professional and policy sociology may position them to better pay off their student loans—what can critical sociology deliver, or worse yet, public sociology? They confront the contradiction of wishing to garner the moral capital of supporting social justice initiatives without taking personal risks such as having articles rejected from top journals or being denied their dream job. Can one truly work for social justice from the comfort of a cushy job with tenure? Derrick Bell labels this impetus "ethical ambition" and offers reassurances to his readers that it is possible to be ethical and successful at the same time (Bell 2002). I sincerely hope that he is right, but I also know that the vast majority of people who actually do public sociology receive few perks and even less praise.

I suspect that people work at public sociology for very much the same reasons that some individuals become dancers, actresses, singers, painters, or poets—training for their craft may be part of their passion, but they would find a way to dance, act, sing, paint, or write even if no one paid them. The ardor of artists provides a template for the passion for social justice that many sociologists bring to their intellectual work. American pragmatism and its grand entrepreneurial spirit strive to stamp out this passion for justice, raising the question of whether there is even any room for public sociology sensibilities within American sociology anymore. Yet visitors from other national sociological traditions at the 2004 ASA meeting on public sociology remind us that public sociology not only exists but also holds a much larger place in their sociological vision than it does in the United States. It may be more difficult to see public sociology here, in the center of a major world power, but the stakes are too high not to.

When I look back and try to map my involvement in public sociology, I realize that, as with love, I found it in unlikely places. For example, I love social theory—no secret there. But with hindsight, I recognize that the reason that I so appreciated early sociological theorists is that they all seemed to be doing public sociology, or at least that is the way I was introduced to their work. Despite our current efforts to objectify, deify, freeze, and squeeze Karl Marx, Max Weber, Georg Simmel, Émile Durkheim, W. E. B. DuBois, and other classical social theorists into ossified boxes of their "most important contributions that you will need to know in order to get a job," I read the works of these theorists as public sociology. I remain inspired by their commitment to bring the tools of sociology to bear on the important issues of their time. The public need not have been their direct audience—given literacy rates of the late nineteenth and early twentieth centuries, few could read their work—yet so much of what they did was on behalf of bettering the public. They talked to one another because they wanted to understand and better society.

Contemporary American sociology has moved away from this kind of energy and excitement. Yet because public sociology demands that we consider the major issues of the day and that we bring tools of sociological analysis and empirical research to bear on them, it promises to breathe new life into sociological theory as well as the discipline overall. Despite the challenges facing public sociology, as well as the difficulties that I have encountered in my career doing it, I would choose it all over again. At this point in my career, what we call it matters less to me than knowing that I am not alone in choosing this path.

REFERENCES

Bell, Derrick. 2002. *Ethical Ambition: Living a Life of Meaning and Worth.* New York: Bloomsbury.

Collins, Patricia Hill. 1986. "Learning from the Outsider Within: The Sociological Significance of Black Feminist Thought." *Social Problems* 33 (6): 14–32.

———. 2000. *Black Feminist Thought: Knowledge, Consciousness, and the Politics of Empowerment.* New York: Routledge.

———. 2004. *Black Sexual Politics: African Americans, Gender, and the New Racism.* New York: Routledge.

Guinier, Lani, and Gerald Torres. 2002. *The Miner's Canary: Enlisting Race, Resisting Power, Transforming Democracy.* Cambridge, MA: Harvard University Press.

Kelley, Robin D. G. 2002. *Freedom Dreams: The Black Radical Imagination.* Boston: Beacon.

Mills, C. Wright. 1959. *The Sociological Imagination.* New York: Oxford.

POLITICS AND THE PROFESSION

WILLIAM JULIUS WILSON

Speaking to Publics

In his thought-provoking essay, Michael Burawoy stated: "Public sociology brings sociology into a conversation with publics, understood as people who are themselves involved in conversation" (this volume, 28). Public sociology's input into this conversation is based not only on empirical research findings but also on insights gained from the development of conceptual frameworks and the elaboration of theoretical perspectives. As Carol Weiss (1993) of Harvard University points out, although high-quality data are useful and establish credibility, of equal importance is the sociological perspective on processes, entities, and events. Participants in the public and policy arenas can benefit from an understanding of the forces and conditions that shape actions and from the structures of meaning derived from sociological concepts, theories, and research (Weiss 1993, 37). In other words, public sociology can provide what the late Morris Janowitz (1970) called "enlightenment."

But this enlightenment emanates from the activities of professional sociology, which "supplies true and tested methods, accumulated bodies of knowledge, orienting questions, and conceptual frameworks" (this volume, 32). As Burawoy points out, professional sociology provides the expertise and legitimacy for public sociology. Moreover, many professional sociologists contribute to public sociology.

We often overlook or are not aware of ways in which professional sociologists have effectively engaged the public. Indeed, the public discourse on issues such as persistent poverty, urban planning, and criminal justice has changed because of thought-provoking ideas from professional sociology. Theories of class conflict and mobility have influenced government policies in education, social services, and community development. Concepts such as participatory decision making, labeling, and concentration effects have been incorporated in public and policy discussions concerning criminal justice, mental health, and poverty (Weiss 1993). "One would not have to be a public sociologist to contribute to public sociology," states Burawoy. "One could do so by being a good professional, critical, or policy sociologist" (this volume, 44).

Moreover, it is important to consider Carol Weiss's argument that sociological conceptions more than discrete data sets have influenced the way actors in the policy arena think about social issues. Sociology provides fresh perspectives for policy makers, journalists, and the public at large, advances new insights on causes and effects, and challenges assumptions that are widely held and taken for granted (Weiss 1993, 48).

Likewise, although sociologists can produce excellent documentation on the incidence, frequency, and intensity of a condition, they are also able to demonstrate that the world works in ways that might not be considered by public opinion leaders (Kingdon 1993). In other words, sociologists' knowledge of the way the world works enables them to make better cause-and-effect connections than can most observers in the public arenas.

However, some of the best sociological insights never reach the general public because sociologists seldom take advantage of useful mechanisms to get their ideas out. Most academic journals are not accessible to the general public. As the late James Coleman pointed out in an article in *Newsweek,* it is "extremely important for sociology to demonstrate its utility to society if it's going to be viable in the long run" (quoted in Kantrowitz 1992, 55). And Herbert Gans (1997) maintains that "sociology's support from the general public . . . depends in significant part on how informative that public finds sociology, and what uses it can make of the discipline's work."

Nonetheless, some sociologists argue that it is good that our research draws very little attention from the media and policy makers because it insulates the discipline from outside pressures to pursue certain research topics. As Burawoy puts it, many professional sociologists "fear public involvement will corrupt science and threaten the legitimacy of the discipline as well as the material resources it will have at its disposal" (this volume, 41). There may be some merit to this argument. However, if sociologists are concerned about the present and future state of the discipline, this argument is shortsighted. Why? Simply because the more sociology is ignored by the media and policy makers, the less attention it receives as an academic discipline and therefore the more removed it is from the decision-making arena, the fewer students it attracts, and the more difficulty it has in obtaining funding for research from private foundations and government agencies. Accordingly, the issue is not whether we should be concerned about attention from the media and policy makers; the issue is how to get such attention. To the extent that public sociology engages the public in ways that Burawoy envisions, it can generate media attention and in the process provide professional sociology the kind of public recognition that is so vital to maintaining its position as an important social scientific discipline.

It is essential to emphasize, as does Burawoy, that "there should be, and there often is, respect and synergy" between professional and public sociology. "Far from being incompatible, the two are like Siamese twins" (this volume, 41). In this connection, we ought to consider how the discipline of economics speaks to publics on the basis of knowledge derived from professional economics.

The field of economics has certainly not suffered from all the media attention it has received over the years and from the efforts of internationally known economists to engage the public, including Nobel Prize winners such as Gary Becker, Robert Solow, Joseph Stiglitz, and the late James Tobin. Examples of other prominent economists who make an explicit effort to reach or make their work accessible to the public include Princeton economist Paul Krugman, even before he became a *New York Times* columnist; Alan Krueger, another outstanding Princeton economist; Laura Tyson, formerly of the University of California, Berkeley, and now the dean of the University of London School of Business; Richard Freeman of Harvard; and John K. Galbraith of the University of Texas.

As we think about ways to spread our messages and insights to a broader general audience, we ought to keep in mind the success of these economists in engaging the public. Their writings and insights have ranged from regular columns in magazines such as *Business Week* and the *Economist* to occasional columns and op-ed articles in the *New York Times, Wall Street Journal, Washington Post, Los Angeles Times,* and other influential newspapers.

However, this is not to suggest that sociologists have not had some success in reaching the public through the print media. As Michael Burawoy points out, "We can locate sociologists who write in the opinion pages of our national newspapers, where they comment on matters of public importance" (this volume, 28). Indeed, I feel that a very important mechanism for bringing sociological insights into the public arena is op-ed articles, a medium used successfully by some outstanding sociologists, including Christopher Jencks, Orlando Patterson, and Theda Skocpol of Harvard; Alan Wolfe of Boston College; Todd Gitlin of Columbia University; Andrew Cherlin of Johns Hopkins; and Seymour Martin Lipset of the Hoover Institution and George Mason University. It would not be fair simply to refer to this group as public intellectuals because they all are outstanding scholars in their own right. And their sociological insights are compelling enough to interest the media. But aside from being first-rate scholars, these sociologists have another thing in common—they know how to write and do not rely on academic jargon to communicate their ideas.

Stilted, ponderous, jargon-laden language will all but ensure that one's writings will not penetrate beyond a narrow academic field of specialization. It amuses me to hear someone dismiss a book written by a sociologist as journalistic simply or solely because it is accessible to the general public. Also, it is commonly and falsely assumed in the academic world that if a book is accessible to a broad audience, including the media, it is likely to be ignored by academics. This is a concern voiced frequently by scholars, especially younger, nontenured scholars who would like to reach a wider audience with their writings but feel that their peers would censure them. I think this is a legitimate concern that ought to be a topic of any serious discussion on the social organization of the discipline of sociology.

And I would suggest that we begin that discussion by noting that some of the most important and influential books in our discipline are among those that are accessible to the general public. I have in mind books such as David Riesman's *The Lonely Crowd* (1950), Herbert Gans's *The Urban Villagers* (1962), Gerald Suttles's *The Social Order of the Slums* (1968), Robert Bellah and colleagues' *Habits of the Heart* (1985), Daniel Bell's *The Coming of Post-Industrial Society* (1973), Seymour Martin Lipset's *Political Man* (1960), Richard Sennett and Jonathan Cobb's *The Hidden Injuries of Class* (1972), and Arlie Hochschild's *Second Shift* (1989). All of these books were among the fifty-three titles that Herbert Gans identified as best sellers by sociologists—that is, books, excluding textbooks, which have sold at least fifty thousand copies—in a 1997 *Contemporary Sociology* article. They collectively represent what Burawoy calls traditional public sociology. They qualify as books that "are read beyond the academy, and they become the vehicle of a public discussion about the nature of U.S. society—the nature of its values, the gap between its promises and its reality, its malaise, its tendencies" (this volume, 28). For the purposes of his study, Gans defined sociologists as "authors with graduate degrees or teaching affiliations in sociology, or social scientists from related disciplines, particularly anthropology, whose books have been adopted as sociological because their concepts and methods are . . . often cited or widely read by sociologists and their students" (Gans 1997, 131).

As Gans notes, the books on his list of best sellers tend to be among the "most readable." Not only have they been discussed widely by academics; they have drawn the attention of educated lay readers in the general public as well. I draw several conclusions from a careful reading of many of these outstanding books, namely, that clear, intellectually rigorous, thought-provoking, and creative arguments will draw a wide readership both within and outside academia, especially if such arguments focus on issues that are high on the public agenda.

It is important to remember that the media are constantly looking for fresh ideas, creatively developed and thoughtfully presented. As Burawoy points out, "Journalists may carry academic research into the public realm" (this volume, 28). If such ideas receive attention in the academic community, they are even more likely to attract media attention. Indeed, as a general principle, I think it is fair to say that scholars whose work is ignored by the academic world will receive little attention in the media.

The real challenge, therefore, is to produce works that seriously engage both the academic and nonacademic communities. On the one hand, if the work is too technical and not accessible, however creative, it is unlikely to be discussed in the media. On the other hand, if it is accessible but not thoughtful or intellectually rigorous, it will be ignored in the academic community. In short, cogent arguments that resonate with both a lay audience and the academic community are more apt to draw media attention.

If the work of a public sociologist attracts both media and academic attention, it is much more likely to represent good as opposed to bad public sociology. "We must encourage the very best public sociology," states Burawoy. "Public sociology cannot be second-rate sociology" (this volume, 58). I feel that an important indicator of whether public sociology is first-rate or second-rate is whether it seriously engages both the public and academic communities. We cannot have a public sociology that is ignored by the academic community. The canons of professional sociology have to extend to public sociology.

Herbert Gans's comments (1997, 135) are appropriate in this regard. He states: "Finally, that I could find only 53 books that have sold over 50,000 since the 1940s suggests that the discipline still has a long way to go before it makes a significant impression on the general public. How it can best do so is a subject for another article, but it should not do so by attempting to publish bestsellers. Sociologists ought to publish intellectually and otherwise useful work, empirical and theoretical, that adds to our own and to the public understanding of society."

The growth of public sociology could result in clearer writings in professional sociology. As more and more sociologists accept the challenge of clearly conveying formal ideas in writing so that educated laypersons will find them readable, the more likely it is that lucid writing will become a cherished norm throughout the discipline. In particular, a stronger emphasis on public sociology will tend to encourage students to write clearly and, in the process, rely less on sociological jargon. And we would be able to demonstrate even more firmly that rigor is not sacrificed by clarity of expression.

But clear writing would receive an enormous boost if graduate students and young nontenured faculty were centrally involved in the quest for public sociology. In this connection, I am reminded that when I participated in a plenary session titled "Speaking to the Public" at the 2004 American Sociological Association meetings, I responded to a student's question about the appropriate time to become a public sociologist by stating that it would be wise for her to wait until she receives tenure. My reasoning was that given the social organization of the discipline, young scholars would be penalized in the tenure process by engaging in public sociology. Burawoy forcefully addresses this issue in his essay. He states:

> How often have I heard faculty advise their students to leave public sociology until after tenure—not realizing (or realizing all too well?) that public sociology is what keeps sociological passion alive. If they follow their advisor's advice, they may end up a contingent worker, in which case there will be even less time for public sociology, or they may be lucky enough to find a tenure-track job, in which case they have to worry about publishing articles in accredited journals or publishing books with recognized university presses. Once they have tenure, they are free to indulge their youthful passions, but by then . . . they may have lost all interest in public sociology, preferring the more lucrative policy world of consultants or a niche in professional sociology. Better to indulge the commitment to public sociology from the beginning, and that way ignite the torch of professional sociology. (this volume, 40)

If one has the future of the discipline in mind, this is sound advice; however, if an individual graduate student were to follow Burawoy's firm suggestion, chances are good that she would be jeopardizing her professional career given the current norms of the discipline. Just as professional sociology needs to closely examine the lack of rewards that encourage clear writing, so too should it look closely at the absence of incentives for students who want to pursue public sociology. If, as Burawoy's article suggests, public sociology is the lifeblood of professional sociology, then every effort should be made to ensure that the younger members of our discipline are free to undertake research and writing that clearly speak to publics.

REFERENCES

Bell, Daniel. 1973. *The Coming of Post-Industrial Society: A Venture in Social Forecasting.* New York: Basic Books.

Bellah, Robert, Richard Madsen, William M. Sullivan, Ann Swidler, and Steven M. Tipton. 1985. *Habits of the Heart: Individualism and Commitment in American Life.* Berkeley: University of California Press.

Gans, Herbert. 1962. *The Urban Villagers: Group and Class in the Life of Italian-Americans.* New York: The Free Press.

———. 1997. "Best-Sellers by Sociologists: An Exploratory Study." *Contemporary Sociology* 26: 131–35.

Hochschild, Arlie. 1989. *Second Shift: Working Parents and the Revolution at Home.* New York: Viking.

Janowitz, Morris. 1970. "Sociological Models and Social Policy." In *Political Conflict: Essays in Political Sociology,* ed. M. Janowitz. Chicago: Quadrangle Press.

Kantrowitz, Barbara. 1992. "Sociology's Lonely Crowd." *Newsweek,* 3 February: 55.

Kingdon, John W. 1993. "How Do Issues Get on the Public Policy Agendas?" In *Sociology and the Public Agenda,* ed. W. J. Wilson, 40–50. Newbury Park, CA: Sage Publications.

Lipset, Seymour Martin. 1960. *Political Man.* New York: Doubleday.

Riesman, David. 1950. *The Lonely Crowd: A Study of the Changing American Character.* With N. Glazer and R. Denny. New Haven, CT: Yale University Press.

Sennett, Richard, and Jonathan Cobb. 1972. *Hidden Injuries of Class.* New York: Knopf.

Suttles, Gerald. 1968. *The Social Order of the Slum: Ethnicity and Territory in the Inner City.* Chicago: University of Chicago Press.

Weiss, Carol. 1993. "The Intersection of the Sociological Agenda and Public Policy." In *Sociology and the Public Agenda,* ed. W. J. Wilson, 23–39. Newbury Park, CA: Sage Publications.

LYNN SMITH-LOVIN

Do We Need a Public Sociology?

It Depends on What You Mean by *Sociology*

Social psychology is an interdisciplinary, theoretically driven field. As it has developed within sociology, it probably comes closer to following a neopositivist, hypothetical-deductive "natural science" model than most other substantive domains within our discipline. It has both deductive and inductive methodological traditions, but it is very much basic science. Therefore, as a social psychologist, I might be expected to take a fairly traditional, conservative position on the fourfold division of sociological labor that Burawoy (this volume, 34) proposes—professional, critical, policy, and public sociology. I have a clear taste for instrumental rather than reflexive knowledge; that's the type of knowledge contained in Burawoy's professional and policy quadrants.

Yet when Michael gave one of his warmly received talks advocating public sociology at a local colloquium series last year, I had no argument with his simple message: that all four sociological activities are interrelated, mutually reinforcing, and mutually dependent. He said that sociologists should be encouraged to develop publics that are defined by our sociological knowledge. We should attempt to have some positive impact on those publics with our acquired knowledge, and not all of this impact should be guided by who is willing to pay us (his low blow to policy sociology). Who could argue with that? He pointed out that public sociology *needs* the other quadrants to produce knowledge. He was openly respectful and conciliatory toward professional sociology. I found little with which to disagree. Indeed, it seemed like the least intellectually controversial talk I had ever heard Burawoy give. Who could quarrel with the idea that sociologists should be encouraged to participate actively and openly in civic life? Who would say that our knowledge should not be used to improve the lot of others, when it is relevant to their (potential) interests?

I found it a little odd that someone with Burawoy's intellectual history spent so little time dealing with the power dynamics in the discipline. The allocation of scarce resources to different lines of action would be a thornier issue. In his talk, we all sounded like one big, happy, mutually appreciative family. It seemed that he wanted to spend his presidential year encouraging unity, positive participation, and mutual respect. I was with him all the way. When I was president of the Southern Sociological Society, I tried to devote my fifteen minutes of fame to a similarly integrative purpose (using my own knowledge base from the sociology of emotions, social psychology, and social ecology to develop a set of behavioral principles for productive interaction within the discipline) (Smith-Lovin 1999).

As Burawoy's presidential year developed, however, I began to see how the public sociology movement would impact the discipline. Burawoy's more complete statement of his argument in his presidential address makes the elements of purpose, power, and resource allocation clearer. Now, I think that I have something with which to argue.[1]

Burawoy is urging sociologists to develop, aid, and be shaped by social movements. He wants us to participate in a consensus-building enterprise where we and our publics become one. So long as this proposal is urging individual sociologists to become involved in civic life, to put their knowledge to work, I think it is admirable. But, clearly, Burawoy goes a step further and wants this value-laden activity to be embraced within the disciplinary structure itself. He wants it to become an integral, respected part of what we do as sociologists. While he acknowledges that professional sociology may maintain a hegemonic grasp over disciplinary structures, he clearly wants us to embrace public sociology as a legitimate, rewarded activity. He speaks approvingly of moves to give it journal space, to reward it in the context of sociological careers, to give it legitimacy as a part of the discipline, and to devote organizational resources to it.[2] I have three points of disagreement with this broader institutional/organizational argument. I think that they are based on a somewhat different definition of what sociology is and some disagreement about the structural features that will maintain sociology's integrity and progress.

SOCIOLOGY FOR WHAT? SOCIOLOGY FOR WHOM?

Burawoy (this volume, 33–34) quotes these classic titles to remind us that others have used the ASA presidency to argue for morally motivated involvement in civic affairs. But then he goes further and says that to pose these questions is to answer them, "since few would argue for a hermetically sealed discipline, or defend pursuing knowledge simply for knowledge's sake." He assumes that social change motivates most people to enter sociology and that academic motivation is difficult to sustain without civic involvement.

The latter is an empirical question. We could try to answer it (avoiding the common pitfalls of social desirability and projection of our own 1960s historical climate to the more conservative students of today). But one might argue that why students come to sociology is only the start of a process of education. Many come to avoid more mathematical/formal studies or because they think we will lead them seamlessly to a career in social work: they don't always know what they are getting into. Burawoy and I agree completely that our educational job is to take students from where they start. We need to create a dialogue between our accumulated sociological knowledge and their own experiences so that they are both excited and illuminated by a new understanding of their world. Unlike Burawoy, I would argue that the discipline is in real trouble if students cannot be motivated to explore sociological ideas without involvement in movements involving an outside public. Furthermore, everything that we know about the power of institutions and the progress of the discipline argues that the necessity of social movement involvement is unlikely.

But these are minor issues, in a way. The real crux of Burawoy's push for a public sociology is not its ability to inspire students. It is his assumption that knowledge for knowledge's sake is a vacuous exercise.

Notice that when Burawoy asks, "Sociology for whom?" he asserts that the question answers itself. He supports this assertion by creating a (false) parallel between two positions that "nobody" would support (this volume, 33): "a hermetically sealed discipline" and "knowledge . . . for knowledge's sake." Well, yes and no. He is right that we would not argue for a hermetically sealed discipline, because to do so would be unsociological. Our understanding of institutions and organizations within a larger social system would make the idea logically unsupportable. We know that we are not immune from our own theories. Furthermore, widely held values about the benefit of individual civic participation would reject isolation, even if it were possible. (Some of us might like to be a bit more hermetically sealed from some of the current social trends, but we are not optimistic on that point.) But mixing the straw man of a hermetically sealed discipline with valuing basic scientific knowledge is effective but misleading rhetoric.

I would, indeed, argue for knowledge for knowledge's sake. I entered sociology because I thought that some "puzzles" were intriguing. The process of doing research to answer them was gratifying.[3] It helps to understand things, even if there is no immediate avenue to change them. When I saw an organization of which I was very fond experiencing the natural consequences of growth through size and differentiation, I found it personally useful to recognize that what was happening was a shift from mechanical to organic solidarity, even though I was unable to convince the participants that it was not a set of individual failings that was leading to their decrease in experienced community. Perhaps I have this orientation because much of social psychology is this way. It helps you *understand* why people are behaving the way that they are, even if you don't have enough control over the situation to change it. Maybe I'm more interested in a scientific sociology than a public one—how 1950s of me![4]

Or maybe I'm just very skeptical of our ability to predict what knowledge will be useful in the long run. I remember a trip to Kitt Peak Observatory outside Tucson, Arizona—a beautiful mountaintop overlooking the sparsely settled Sonoran Desert, with shapely white buildings housing an array of telescopes. It's a beautiful temple of basic science. On a tour of the facility, the young astronomy student who was leading the group was accosted by an older fellow. The visitor was angry that we had spent so much government money to build not one but *seven* telescopes. He asked why private enterprise could not have done such a thing and demanded to know what *use* had come of the endeavor. The young man stumbled, not used to such hostile questions in such a lovely, uncontroversial place. He didn't have much of an answer. I'm sure that a more experienced professional, used to congressional questions, could have come up with a long list. There are many occasions when understanding the world around us has led to discoveries that are widely, importantly useful in the long run.

But I've always thought that trying to justify things like astronomy by pointing to useful side benefits is false advertising. I like my basic science for the same reason that I'm an environmentalist. I don't support it because there may be some beneficial cure lurking out there in an endangered species. I support it just because I think it is uplifting and *human* to want to know more about how things work. And I enjoy the environment that exists outside of our manipulation.

While it would appear that Burawoy and I disagree fundamentally on knowledge for knowledge's sake, I want to note one indication that we are not so far apart as his rhetorical stance would indicate. Both of us bemoan the declining support for high-quality, widely available public education. We are privatizing everything from universities to scientific research. The state (with its politics) and corporate actors (with their global reach and profit motive) have growing control over the generation and communication of knowledge. The increasing use of an underclass of temporary workers to teach our students has undermined the academic institution.

Burawoy focuses primarily on the hegemonic influence of elite professional sociologists within this system. He is right. We are the privileged ones who continue to benefit as the institution strays from its central goals. He thinks that the ability to engage in public sociology should be extended downward in this hierarchy and not just reserved for a lucky few. I, in turn, worry that a system that was devoted to generating knowledge—both through research and through dialogue with students—is too far from hermetically sealed. I worry that the academy is no longer able to follow its own logical structures in the search for new insight. Instead, it is pushed and pulled by the need to raise money in directions that are unproductive for anyone except powerful outside actors. I would prefer a societal value of knowledge for knowledge's own sake. And, while not hopeful, I think this is more likely than public support for a spawning ground of social movements. If we want to play politics as one of our core activities, we will have to compete in the political marketplace for popularity and power. We need to accept that we might not win. The consequences of losing are catastrophic.

I want to be clear that I am *not* encouraging sociologists to keep their heads down and avoid civil engagement in their personal lives. I fully embrace the academic freedom and respect for divergent ideas that come with an institution that has as its primary goal fostering creativity and understanding. Any attempt to limit that range of ideas (or an individual's desire to apply them in whatever ways she or he sees fit outside the academy) would be antithetical to my view of professional academia. But Burawoy (in my reading, at least) wants more: he wants us to embrace public sociology as a full, legitimate enterprise within the discipline, as part of our professional structure. This expansion of our goals would imply something rather different.

ACCOUNTABILITY, LEGITIMACY, AND CUMULATION

While Burawoy (this volume, 59n7) defines *public sociologist* as a brand of public intellectual who limits public commentary to areas of established expertise, he is clear that the public sociologist is accountable to his or her designated (or created) publics. To the public sociologist, truth value is not empirical, established through standards of peer review, but is established through the consensus that is formed as a result of dialogue with a public. This reminds me of a cartoon that I have on my office door at Duke: under the label "Scientific Privatization!" it has a series of panels with various "publics" proclaiming "findings" with which most scientists would not agree.[5] If we take as the core enterprise of sociology the accumulation of knowledge about social processes, the accountability to publics is a problem for a scientific sociology. (We, as sociologists, do not overlook that knowledge is a socially constructed product of an institution. That institution contains social actors that operate according to all of the processes that we study. But to give up the goal of generating intersubjectively stable knowledge is to fundamentally change what we are about.)

I fear that I edge over into what Michael would characterize as the "despotic" control of the discipline by professional sociology. I argue that critical, policy, and public sociology must all be judged (at least within the context of the discipline) on what they contribute to the cumulation of knowledge. I think this because I consider that cumulation to be the core enterprise of sociology. Notice that this is very different from saying that critical, policy, or public sociology is bad, irrelevant, or useless. Rather, I acknowledge that critiques have often pushed overly staid research programs into new areas. The feminist critique of status attainment is my personal favorite (e.g., England 1999). I acknowledge that policy studies can be excellent basic science that just happens to be paid for by someone outside the academy. Here, the SIME/DIME (Seattle-Denver Income Maintenance Experiment) study of the effects of an income maintenance program on family and work behavior is my favorite (Groeneveld, Tuma, and Hannan 1980). Public sociology has its own successes. Arguably, the entire subfield of social movements has its roots in the engagement of students in the civil rights and antiwar activism of the 1960s (e.g., McAdam 1988).

Burawoy goes further than these appreciative bows to the evolution of our thought, however. He seems to imply that we should actively encourage, promote, and reward public sociology within the context of the discipline. He suggests that we incorporate it into our institutional structure. He wants to encourage its practice among those who do not have the personal leisure to engage in such civic engagement as a non-work activity. He, if I read him correctly, would have our "decentralized participatory democracy" (this volume, 54) of a discipline expanded to include the publics which we develop or aid through activity driven by our individually held values. He does argue that we will limit our commentary (and presumably our disciplinary support) to areas of "established expertise" (this volume, 59n7). But one need not spend much time on the ASA council to discover that there is fierce disagreement about the scope of our expertise and how to apply it. Are we against the boycott (or blacklist) of the Israeli academics, or do we support the Palestinians in their subjugation under Israeli occupation? Do we oppose the war in Iraq? Based on sociological knowledge, or principles that are quite independent of that knowledge?

Was a sociologist doing public sociology when he expressed his deeply felt religious beliefs that his town should not extend marital benefits to gay partnerships? Were the sociologists who later opposed hiring him because of those statements justified (because of *their* publics)? Or were they discriminating against a public sociologist (since he had never been charged with treating gay students unfairly)?[6] With effort and institutional support, I believe that we can respect widely divergent values and opinions on the part of our colleagues. I firmly believe that less powerful members of the academy, like students and temporary workers, should be extended that respect. I encourage colleagues to engage in public debate and can tolerate the fact that they sometimes argue for positions that I find troubling, mostly because I recognize that I am a creature of my own social position and *I* could be wrong. I encourage a free exchange of ideas. I encourage civic engagement. But I find it difficult to imagine developing a serious, meaningful institutional system that would train people for, encourage, and reward political activism when we do not agree on the value positions that are endorsed by that activism.

The fact that we *seem* relatively homogeneous in our values is a function of homophily (McPherson, Smith-Lovin, and Cook 2001): we interact more with those who agree with us. And, as Burawoy notes in his first thesis, we have a strong ideological identity relative to the rest of American society's politics *at this particular point in history, when our discipline is dominated by baby boomers who chose the discipline during the protests of the 1960s.* But to assume that we will encourage and reward *all* public sociologies is to assume that we will be even more value-free than a traditional conception of science. Is the sociologist organizing the neo-Nazis to reinforce their white racial identity due the same respect and promotion as the one who is protesting the Iraq war? If we reward value-promoting activity without discrimination among causes, it seems that we have truly abdicated our responsibility as moral beings.

Shifting the burden of proof onto the relevance of our professional knowledge for the issue at hand could be the answer to this quandary. But I suspect that the debates fostered by this exercise would make the traditional tensions in our discipline—the tensions between quantitative and qualitative, deductive and inductive, basic and applied, programmatic and critical—pale in comparison. If we have difficulty agreeing on what we know, how shall we agree to what it is relevant?

Furthermore, there is the question of who does the evaluating. Since, Burawoy suggests, the truth standard of public sociology is consensus with our developing publics, sociologists would effectively be giving a substantial part of the discipline's evaluative structure over to a force outside our own boundaries. We would be driven not just by the availability of research funding (the nasty underbelly of both professional and policy research) but by the popularity contest of the public domain. Burawoy (this volume, 43, table 3) acknowledges this problem with his pathology of faddishness. I just see it as more endemic to the inclusion of public sociology as an integral part of our discipline.

THE STRUCTURAL INTEGRITY OF THE DISCIPLINE AND OUR ABILITY TO SUSTAIN OURSELVES

Given my despotic professional stance, Burawoy and I agree on his last two theses. We both think that sociology has something very powerful to say, something that is very distinctive from the other social science disciplines. We both care deeply that this perspective and the knowledge that informs it survive in the face of challenges from the state and the market (and their academic representations in political science and economics). We both believe that sociologists should use their knowledge in the civic arena when possible to create a public (or publics) that share some of this sociological understanding. We differ considerably in our judgments of what institutional forms will promote these goals.

Burawoy envisions a discipline energized by engagement with publics, suffused with moral fervor, motivated to do the science of sociology by a perceived social need and a hope of political impact. I see that path leading to fracture, conflict, and distraction. In earlier work, I have made an ecological argument based on McPherson's (1983; McPherson, Popielarz, and Drobnic 1992) evolutionary ecological model of affiliation. If we have more ties to those beyond the boundaries of our discipline, and fewer strong ties to those within, the center will not hold. If we are accountable to publics, if dialogue with publics is our procedure, and if consensus arrived at with publics is our truth standard, then ties outside the discipline will be many. Difficult judgments about the legitimacy (e.g., the relevance of sociological knowledge) of public sociology will create many negative interactions within the discipline. If we use journal pages (as have *Social Problems, Social Forces,* and *Footnotes*) to showcase issues that divide us rather than insights that can contribute to our general knowledge base, we will fracture rather than cohere. Furthermore, it is unrealistic to expect continued public support for such an endeavor. If citizens do not want to pay taxes for us to educate students and to develop a cumulative body of knowledge, they will be even less enthusiastic about supporting us to develop contentious publics.

I think that we *need* the core mission of cumulating knowledge. We need to be able to judge our contributions based on that relatively traditional, conservative, professional goal in order to sustain the legitimacy and internal consensus that allow us to sustain the discipline. If we widen the scope of our enterprise to make public sociology a full partner, I fear that we will lose the institutions that allow us to promote academic freedom. And then individual civic action will be less possible, not more.

So, I guess I am more in favor of that "hermetically sealed" straw man than I thought. I think that an ivory tower allows individuals unprecedented freedom of thought and discovery. Without the first column of Burawoy's fourfold table (the professional science and the critical theoretical commentary that pushes it onward), I fear that society would lose a great deal. I, unlike Burawoy, see the connections to the outside as holding more threat than promise. We need mutual respect and tolerance for each other's political positions, but integrating their expression into the institutional structure of our discipline is counterproductive to his goals and mine.

NOTES

1. Before beginning counterarguments, however, let me reaffirm my admiration for the general points outlined above, which came through so clearly in Bura-

woy's verbal presentations. That call inspired young people in the audience to an extent that surprised me. Perhaps they saw his agenda more clearly than I did!

2. There is an irony here. The public sociology movement purports to aid the less powerful and broaden our "conversation" to include a wider range of people. But its actual operation has been to privilege people (like me) who are getting the opportunity to publish about our opinions and values. Like the new journal *Contexts*, public sociology actually seems to take us away from an open, peer-reviewed process and toward a platform where some people and their values are privileged. Journal space is definitely being taken up by public sociologists (often senior scholars, invited and not reviewed) and taken away from the young scholars who are trying to get their ideas out.

3. Specifically, I was amazed that society could convince women to have children, even in a modern structure where those women so obviously suffered disadvantages because of their childbearing. There were many implicit assumptions buried in that question (about the position of women in the social structure, my own privileged position as a woman with quickly opening options, etc.), which became apparent to me as I studied sociology. And Miller McPherson, my husband and colleague, who takes a more evolutionary approach to social forms, has since pointed out to me that if there were anything that was selected for over our evolutionary history as biological beings, having offspring would probably be it. At any rate, my first major publication (Smith-Lovin and Tickamyer 1978) was a study of the interrelationship of women's work, fertility behavior, and sex role attitudes. We were astonished to find that in our data women's fertility influenced work and attitudes, with very little impact in the other directions. Thus, we found out one of the key benefits of scientific study: it teaches us that all people are not like us and that we need systematic observation to open our views to encompass a wider system than the homophilous local environment that shapes our own beliefs and values.

4. I should note that social psychologists have made contributions that could count as public sociology, so I am not taking this position to avoid irrelevance for my field. Charlan Nemeth (1983) shows how minority opinion is valuable for opening up the framing of problems and allowing more creative solutions, even when the minority opinion is itself not substantively useful. Exploration of token effects (Kanter 1977 and those who built on Rosabeth Moss Kanter's work) has led to useful new strategies for incorporating minorities into establishments without high personal cost to the newcomers. Experimental research on power-dependence structures has led to theoretical generalizations that can be useful in designing stable, productive exchange systems (Molm and Cook 1995).

5. Some examples: "That species can just move to some other habitat." "There is no evidence for global warming!" "Evolution never did happen—not in my family anyway." "Being gay is just a lifestyle choice." "Mercury poisoning is really not such a big deal." There is a similar cartoon of a mock *Scientific American* cover proclaiming "We give up!" and announcing headlines such as "The Earth Is Flat After All." There is a little guy in the bottom corner of my cartoon that speaks in the artist's voice: "Will real science be there when you need it?"

6. I refer here to the late Clifford Clogg and his public statements in State College, Pennsylvania, and to debates among faculty, students, and alumni that

occurred at the University of North Carolina, Chapel Hill, when they considered hiring him away from Pennsylvania State University.

REFERENCES

England, Paula. 1999. "The Impact of Feminism on Sociology." *Contemporary Sociology* 28: 263–67.

Groeneveld, Lyle P., Nancy Brandon Tuma, and Michael T. Hannan. 1980. "The Effects of Negative Income Tax Programs on Marital Dissolution." *Journal of Human Resources* 15 (Autumn): 654–74.

Kanter, Rosabeth Moss. 1977. *Men and Women of the Corporation.* New York: Basic Books.

McAdam, Doug. 1988. *Freedom Summer.* New York: Oxford University Press.

McPherson, Miller. 1983. "An Ecology of Affiliation." *American Sociological Review* 48: 519–32.

McPherson, Miller, Lynn Smith-Lovin, and James M. Cook. 2001. "Birds of a Feather: Homophily in Social Networks." *Annual Review of Sociology* 27: 415–44.

McPherson, Miller, Pamela Popielarz, and Sonja Drobnic. 1992. "Social Networks and Organizational Dynamics." *American Sociological Review* 57: 153–70.

Molm, Linda D., and Karen S. Cook. 1995. "Social Exchange." In *Social Psychology: Sociological Perspectives,* ed. K. S. Cook, G. A. Fine, and J. House. Boston: Allyn & Bacon.

Nemeth, Charlan J. 1983. "Reflections on the Dialogue between Status and Style: Influence Processes of Social Control and Social Change." *Social Psychology Quarterly* 46: 70–74.

Smith-Lovin, Lynn. 1999. "Core Concepts and Common Ground: The Relational Basis of Our Discipline." *Social Forces* 79: 1–23.

Smith-Lovin, Lynn, and Ann R. Tickamyer. 1978. "Nonrecursive Models of Labor Force Participation, Fertility Behavior, and Sex Role Attitudes." *American Sociological Review* 43: 541–56.

ARTHUR L. STINCHCOMBE

Speaking Truth to the Public, and Indirectly to Power

In his *Speaking Truth to Power* (1979), Aaron Wildavsky mainly empha-sizes speaking so that one might be heard in policy circles. But the sub-title (*The Art and Craft of Policy Analysis*) suggests that the truth of a policy (or other public) analysis is central to its function. Thus a true answer to "How can we get out of Iraq and Afghanistan?" is still the one Amitai Etzioni once gave on Vietnam: "Get on boats." But speaking that way does not get heard in the circles of power, nor is it acceptable pub-lic discourse. My politics are closer to Michael Burawoy's than to Wil-davsky's. But Wildavsky's point is that discourse has to be shaped by qualities of all parties to the discourse. I will argue that we do not have enough truth to offer, to shape that discourse so that it will improve pol-icy or the public's understanding of their situation. More specifically, we must tend to our job of getting enough truth of the kind that can bear on the future, which is what is relevant to public discourse. I will argue here that that is so difficult that we should not be distracted much by con-tributing to public discourse, and that what we do along that line is not likely to be much use to the public.

I have devoted most of my intellectual life to the very great difficulty of figuring out what is true, rather than what will be heard. So I am in the upper left box, the "professional sociology" box, of Burawoy's dia-gram of sociology writ large; I am mostly a "technician." One of my early books (Stinchcombe [1968] 1987) was on how to build theory, a toolbox for keeping one's logic clear. More recently I have written on how to build methods (Stinchcombe 2005). It's pretty tame stuff for a left social democrat. Even when I used those methods to teach how to run socialist steel plants in democratic countries in South America (Stinchcombe 1974), neither socialists, nor South Americans, nor steel managers read it. The "professional" truths in it about organizational sociology had a brief flurry of interest only in Norway. Perhaps it had too long of an appendix on method at the end and too short an ethnographic narrative on the sorry state of Latin American bureaucracy. Its outer signals to the reader were clearly technical, numerical, and a bit mathematical. But I was trying very hard with all that apparatus to get it right. And I definitively failed at public sociology before I gave it up. William H. Whyte's *Is Anybody Listening?* (1952) at least showed me that the capitalists were not doing well at public discourse either.

The deep problem with public or policy sociology is the same as the problem of economics: its truths must be truths about the future. Little public discourse is about the past. But facts about the future are absent to both disciplines. The economists are satisfied to follow Euclid when he shows that the angles of a triangle sum to two right angles, now and in the future as in the past. But Euclid turned out to be wrong, too, as Einstein showed. There is no use doing rational action, individual or collective, to change the past.

Economics starts with the presumption that all action is directed toward the future, as rational action must be. Since economists suppose everybody knows the future sufficiently to act in their neoclassical way, they do not feel uncomfortable being pretty positive about their ability to understand that future. But this is not the case for sociology: Seymour Martin Lipset had a minor career project to show that sociologists and other social scientists were almost always actually wrong about the future. But the economists and Euclid have been right in one thing: only theory could address the future, since empirical research on the future was and, I predict, will be impossible. Only by theory empirically based on the past can we know, for example, whether training the chronically poor is likely to make them employable. But the American belief that education always works is not a well-grounded theory. Similarly, it is theory that tells us whether raising the minimum wage will produce more unemployment, not any careful analysis of future unemployment rates.

A public sociologist is more likely to use investigation to show how miserable it is to be chronically poor or that it has happened to more African American single mothers and their children than to white mar-

ent may need people competent in abstract discourse is ten-
eloped in my work on formality [Stinchcombe 2001].)
ication of such a theory to summers was diverted by Bernstein
 public sociologist before we knew the causes of class differ-
terns of discourse, or why the middle classes made money on
earch there was assumed, because of the firmness of our belief
where schools are responsible for teaching abstraction, that
 to poor people's failure to learn would be found in schools,
mers. It did not encourage educational sociology to learn
ntellectual effect of the other four-fifths of students' waking
ough estimate for the United States) outside school.

se do not know whether this line of work would pay off in
edge nor whether my speculations about the line of theoriz-
ght work to figure it out would actually say anything about
tures. I certainly could not sell it now as an essay to *Atlantic*
or to the National Science Foundation as a grant proposal—
quire too much ruminating first. And it is even more prob-
ether it would lead to building cultures of abstract discourse
sing projects for poor single mothers to make part of their
gue.

t here is that the puzzle I have outlined above has been there
ature since the 1970s, with a lot of evidence in its favor. But
have a strong belief in idle curiosity about well-established
d an ivory tower to protect us, we will not have any truth
t causes social gaps in test scores to contribute to public dis-
d in this case, I would argue, a more powerful tradition of
ublic intellectualism in Britain provided an alternative career
in and an alternative to solving the puzzle that he did so
cate. The long gap before volume 4 of his *Class, Codes, and*
ernstein 1991) shows some of that. Burawoy is trying to pro-
alternative careers for sociologists.

us look briefly and very sketchily at possible remedies, sug-
he above puzzle. Let us suppose that the figure of about half
uch teaching time (in some sort of social structure), at least
or and the African American population, would be required
er turns out to be the real problem. One place to look for
bay for overtime teaching is at that being wasted on the crazy
licy of the United States. It is now arming so as to fight a
var in space against a very advanced and massive military
where, that is, to fight the next Cold War, wherever and
t appears.

ried mothers and their children. They will show that in the past, especially the recent past, more of the chronically poor end up in prison or
jail or are killed by their lover. This gives human interest to inequality of
income and of life chances of children. But it does not tell us whether the
poor in Norway or Sweden (where they are a lot better off than the
American chronically poor) will be enough happier in the future to be
worth the price. And, even if it is worth the price, it does not show us
that social democratic governments will become more prevalent. When
Christopher Jencks et al. (1972) suggested that giving poor families more
money rather than more education would increase total happiness, we
do not know enough about the future to say whether they were right.

As far as we can tell, the increase in the average income over the last
few decades has not increased people's reports of happiness in surveys.
But this fact does not tell us anything either, because we do not have a
theory of the relationship between reports and some measure of "true
happiness." Lenin of course had a different answer than Swedish social
democrats about "What is to be done?" In the cross-section, richer people report they are happier, but over time greater riches do not seem to
work. So how can we know enough about the future to contribute to
controlling it through discourse relevant to individuals or policy relevant to public discourse about the government? And the few participants in public discourse who do not talk about the future will not be
glad to know about our confusion on as elementary a subject as what
makes people happy.

TRUTH ABOUT THE FUTURE

One fact about the past is that the gap in achievement test scores
between African Americans and whites has been about a standard deviation since World War II. Another fact is that, on the Armed Forces
Qualification Test, used in World War II, the achievement test score of
African Americans has increased about a standard deviation when re-
administered recently, so that they are now equal to the whites of about
six decades ago. So whatever we did over the last half century was
enough to close the gap. It did not close it because whatever it was we did
that increased test scores was apparently done to whites as well as blacks.

The most obvious thing we did to both races was to increase average
years in school by about four years, or about half again as many as the
eight that was common then. So one policy bet would be to give African
Americans the time equivalent of six more years in school (or other

environments that expose the children to reading, writing, history, and mathematics). We know that achievement scores for African Americans can be increased, because we have done it. The crude data suggest that education as measured in years may contain the cause of that increase and that it apparently takes a lot (sixty years maybe) of whatever that is to have an effect as big as the gap. But do these data show anything about the future? Hardly. A median years-in-school for African Americans of about eighteen, half again as much, while holding the whites at a median of around twelve is not likely to be our future.

To see the trouble here, and why it is a trouble in public discourse, I will go back to my argument (Stinchcombe 1997) that Charles Tilly has taught us to study historical changes as "a sequence of futures." Social forces produce a vision of the future that makes some ways of affecting the future (e.g., in Tilly, petitioning Parliament) seem real. That changes what is rational politics, and so changes politics. That is, for more or less rational people and corporate groups to act, they must have a view of the future and of how that future might rationally be changed. But the main lesson of history, "It was different in the old days," is a consequence of people having had a different picture of the future. Since that picture changed over time and was different between places, so the course of history was different between times and places. To change our future in light of the facts above, we have to know in considerable causal detail how the change in scores came about, and how the racial gap in achievements came about.

For example, Barbara Heyns (1978; for similar but not identical recent results, see Alexander, Entwisle, and Olson 2001) many years ago satisfied me that most of the gap in achievement scores did not develop during the school year but instead before children entered school (this seems, from other evidence, to be much less true if they participated in Head Start) and during the summers after they entered. Rich and poor children learn at about the same speed as members of the other group in the year that they had started with the same score. For example, if a student starts grade ten at a reading level of the average eighth grader, he or she will learn as much during the tenth grade school year as the average eighth grader did during the eighth grade school year and will be ready in the spring to start the junior year learning as a ninth grader. (Note that, as Alfred Binet already knew, the standard deviation of achievement within both races as measured in year-equivalents increases with year in school, which undermines many statistical treatments.) But poor and African American students will then, on the average, unlearn a part

---

of that (or, in the recent results, no while the richer and whiter studen ences are where a student starts th back, stabilizes, or keeps learning o

The argument is complex, even m run socialist steel plants. And no one future in which summers were a diff to school more hours per day, or mo one that distributed the extra time d classes. So there has been lack of in research along the same lines, and n als, sociological or not, about how to

This lack of an imaginable fut whether the causes involved are d though the preliminary evidence is starting school and during summers tion. Imagining a future of homes a African American children will learn dren learn from their homes and ne does not hold homes and neighborh more subtle and abstract words, n answers, and more useful mathemat because we rely on participants in p so collectively we do not get intere imagined future. It is some comfort citations to Heyns's early work have

My argument is that if we do n Heynses, our Stinchcombes, and our towers with tenure and without que not too often), we will never know. T differences between the rich and p between poverty and low outside-sch is probably along the lines laid out 1991). He emphasizes the difference and concrete ("context dependent") dle classes and teachers use more ab their teaching *and home life* expose c words, more subordinate clauses and and quantitative reasoning. Nothing i choice standardized test question. (A

---

or govern
tatively de

The app
becoming
ences in pa
it. What re
in a future
the remed
not in su
about the
hours (my

I of cou
new know
ing that m
possible fu
Monthly,
it would r
lematic w
in the ho
mother to

My poi
in the lite
unless we
puzzles, a
about wh
course. A
scholarly
for Berns
much to l
Control (
mote such

Now l
gested by
again as
for the po
for whate
money to
military p
strategic
engine el
whenever

If we could uproot this dogma from our Defense Department's generals and admirals and their supporters in Congress, we would have lots of money left over after expanding the precollege education budget by half, especially if it were for only half of the school population, and to pay interest on our national debt. We then need a theory of how extreme and unlikely scenarios of the future get so deeply embedded in a bureaucracy and its institutional support and how these scenarios get enormous resources to carry out preparation for a science fiction future. We need sociologists to see the social basis of what C. Wright Mills (1956) called the military's "crackpot realism," which otherwise may be the future of most U.S. federal government spending. I do not have evidence, nor a good theory, about the degree of crackpot realism in the future. I have only idle speculation about how we might get expensive, unlikely scenarios forever.

THE UNTIDY CLASH OF THEORY, EVIDENCE, AND POLICY

If it is true that only theory, not facts, can deal with the future and that much public discourse is about what sort of future we ought to have, how can we get out of the box of the institutionalized rigidity in our imagined futures?

So our second general puzzle is how views of the future get institutionalized in bureaucracies and in the relationships bureaucracies have to their suppliers, their legislative monitors, and how they get stably isolated from other discourse, from evidence on how well their plan works, and so forth. Many bureaucracies in many countries have created such isolated dogmatisms, or reestablished them after a period of heresy, purged opponents within, and the like. A typology of some of such isolated dogmatisms was embedded in Max Weber's sociology of religion in *Economy and Society* ([1924] 1968). But that rough typology and the understanding of its mechanisms have not been much improved by our opportunities to study the processes in the Nazi bureaucracy (except that it was "banal"), the Stalinist bureaucracy, or the reestablishment of orthodoxy in the Catholic Church since Vatican II.

Then before going public, we need to analyze why we are so eager to accept that this is someone else's business, not that of us sociologists, so we let disciplines further to the right of most sociologists have a monopoly on our military future and on the general sociology of bureaucracies' knowledge of (scenarios of) that future. The other disciplines have not theorized bureaucratic intellectual isolation much. I have myself written a lot on bureaucracies while hardly touching the topic (but see indirect discussion in Stinchcombe 1995).

Poking around in the nooks and crannies of comparative bureaucratic history to develop a theory will not get us a popular public, nor much discourse except to say that Eichmann was not really banal, but evil, or that abstinence propaganda may not have worked very well in spite of a couple of millennia of bureaucratically organized propaganda, but that it might work in our future, or that who knows about India, China, and Russia as nuclear powers fifty years from now? But this last is my point: we have no serious way to investigate that future. We have no serious way to investigate how much good sense there may be in all those classified documents or what social supports there are for increasingly fanciful scenarios or whence comes lack of investigation about whether the theories in those scenarios are any good.

The U.S. Army listens to the rare military sociologists we produce, like Charles Moskos. But combat troops and the strategic planners listen less. And we have no believable truth to tell them about how to make bureaucracies think (cf. Taylor 1984; Espeland 1998). Consequently we have nothing to tell public audiences about how to free up money from Star Wars to close the race and class gaps in academic achievement test scores, even if we knew how to close them.

If we had a bit more truth about what children do during the summer, or what massive extra years of schools would produce, embedded in a solid theory of what test results measure that produces higher wages and less unemployment, we might build a public sociology that had some truth in it. If we would bother to build such a theory, we might avoid a future filled with punishing more and more schools for failing to close that gap. Otherwise we have wind, and a vague feeling that the Japanese understand these things better than we do; but we, and perhaps they, do not know what it is that they understand.

And without a solid theory of why generals and people similarly situated believe they know all about the future, we will not understand why public sociology has nothing to say about our biggest public policy, strategically killing people on a very large-scale some long time in the future.

CONCLUSION

My bet (and fear) is that public sociology will fit David Riesman's (Riesman and Glazer 1950) description of the "indignant" political participant: high in affect, low in competence. Burawoy is excepted, of course. But that for me is because Burawoy is curious and is ensconced in the great ivory tower in the Berkeley Hills, at least during the day.

Further, as he well knows, I will tell him if I think he is wrong, and he will do me the same favor, whatever puzzle I happen to have been working on. That is the true definition of the ivory tower, with the necessary proviso that neither of us can punish the other for disagreeing. The normative key is that no curiosity is satisfied by a bad answer. The market for bad answers on editorial pages, in advertisements, and as rationalizations of our foreign policy is evidently infinite. That is the pot public sociology proposes to stew in. Even in the ivory tower, deans measure our teaching by what easily fits in the mind of a sophomore, the government by what easily fits in the mind of a bureaucrat. In both cases, occasionally a lot will fit. We can hope that those few in public discourse or bureaucracies will set the tone for the rest, but the democracy of teaching evaluations is more likely, in my vision (not a theory, yet) of the future.

There needs to be sociology with theory that is empirically solid enough to deal with the future, a public sociology later, with gentle peer pressure against saying things to the public that are provably false about the past or present, so that are unlikely guides to the future. In that gentle peer group, incompetent contradiction is valueless.

Enough truth to make a contribution to changing our view of the future and its possibilities is hard work. For a sociological theory to be solid enough to analyze even the rough outlines of the future is terribly hard work and, so far, nearly always fails. Public sociology may make us correct our course in the face of obvious failure, and may even help us guess what we did wrong. But evidence on why the war on drugs does not work, why we could improve African American achievement scores by a standard deviation over a half century but can't do it now, why abstinence propaganda does not work but abstinence in the early modern West European late marriage pattern worked wonderfully (as far as one can tell from the low illegitimate birth rate), why Japanese militarism was not reconstructed as soon as MacArthur was out of the picture while American militarism is flourishing—all are scarce. If we do not know why some things work and some do not, we have very little truth to offer in a public discourse about major public policies or about individual future lives.

REFERENCES

Alexander, Karl L., Doris R. Entwisle, and Linda S. Olson. 2001. "Schools, Achievement, and Inequality: A Seasonal Perspective." *Educational Evaluation and Policy* 23 (Summer): 171–91.

Bernstein, Basil B. 1971–74. *Class, Codes, and Control.* 3 vols. London: Routledge and Kegan Paul.

———. 1991. *Class, Codes, and Control: Structuring Pedagogical Discourse.* Vol. 4. London: Routledge and Kegan Paul.

Espeland, Wendy Nelson. 1998. *The Struggle for Water: Politics, Rationality, and Identity in the American Southwest.* Chicago: University of Chicago Press.

Heyns, Barbara. 1978. *Summer Learning and the Effects of Schooling.* New York: Academic Press.

Jencks, Christopher, Marshall Smith, Henry Acland, Mary Jo Bane, David Cohen, Herbert Gintes, Barbara Heyns, and Stephen Michelson. 1972. *Inequality: A Reassessment of the Effect of Family and Schooling in America.* New York: Basic Books.

Mills, C. Wright. 1956. *The Power Elite.* New York: Oxford University Press.

Riesman, David, and Nathan Glazer. 1950. "Criteria for Political Apathy." In *Studies in Leadership: Leadership and Democratic Action,* ed. A. Gouldner, 505–59. New York: Harper and Brothers.

Stinchcombe, Arthur L. (1968) 1987. *Constructing Social Theories.* New York: Harcourt, Brace and World. Repr. Chicago: University of Chicago Press.

———. 1974. *Creating Efficient Industrial Administrations.* With Zahava Blum and Rene Marder. New York: Academic Press.

———. 1995. "Lustration as a Problem of the Social Basis of Constitutionalism." *Law and Social Inquiry* 20 (Winter): 245–73.

———. 1997. "Tilly on the Past as a Sequence of Futures." In *Roads from Past to Future,* C. Tilly, 387–409. Review essay. Lanham, MD: Rowman and Littlefield.

———. 2001. *When Formality Works: Authority and Abstraction in Law and Organizations.* Chicago: University of Chicago Press.

———. 2005. *Logic of Social Research.* Chicago: University of Chicago Press.

Taylor, Serge. 1984. *Making Bureaucracies Think: The Environmental Impact Statement Strategy of Administrative Reform.* Stanford, CA: Stanford University Press.

Weber, Max. (1924) 1968. *Economy and Society: An Outline of Interpretive Sociology.* Vols. 2 and 3, ed. G. Roth and K. Wittich. New York: Bedminster Press.

Whyte, William H. 1952. *Is Anybody Listening? How and Why U.S. Business Fumbles When It Talks with Human Beings.* New York: Simon & Schuster.

Wildavsky, Aaron. 1979. *Speaking Truth to Power: The Art and Craft of Policy Analysis.* Boston: Little Brown.

DOUGLAS S. MASSEY

The Strength of Weak Politics

As a member of the Council of the American Sociological Association, I argued a few years ago that the American Sociological Association (ASA) should *not* take official positions on political issues. I lost that battle, but I continue to believe that sociologists are more likely to advance the political causes they care about if they separate their collective dedication to social science from their individual commitments to political action. Sociologists should—indeed must—speak forcefully on important issues whenever they have something to say, but they should do so as individuals and not collectively as a profession. The only issue on which we have a legitimate right to speak as a profession is the science and practice of sociology. The ASA thus has an *obligation* to make itself heard in debates about research funding, professional ethics, scientific integrity, and academic freedom; and it is perfectly legitimate for the ASA to empanel a committee of sociologists to consider the state of scientific knowledge on a particular issue, even one with major political ramifications. But in my view, it is inappropriate and counterproductive for sociologists to opine politically as a profession.

I come to this conclusion as a politically active sociologist who has been deeply involved in a variety of contentious public issues—immigration politics, human rights, socioeconomic inequality, racism, prejudice, and discrimination—and one who has strong feelings about the need for greater social justice, both in the United States and around the world. Nonetheless, I remain firm in my belief that the best way to advance the causes I care about is for the ASA to establish itself as a nonpartisan scientific organization dedicated to the highest professional standards. Its primary mission should be to promote outstanding training, research, and practice within the profession.

NONPARTISANSHIP IN PRINCIPLE

I offer three reasons for the ASA to adhere to this seemingly narrow scientific mandate rather than taking broader political positions in public debates. First, effective policy requires an accurate understanding of the social structures, group processes, and individual behaviors that one seeks to modify through political action. As the recent application of neoliberal economic policies to countries throughout Latin America has shown, when political actions are based on faulty understandings and dubious assumptions, the "cure" that follows is often worse than the "sickness" originally diagnosed (Massey, Sanchez, and Behrman 2006). The road to hell is, unfortunately, very often paved with good intentions.

Achieving an accurate understanding of the social world requires a willingness to admit that one's own views might be misguided or just plain wrong. Sociological knowledge is not revealed truth. It is established through reason and facts and the bringing to bear of logical arguments and empirical data. Reasonable people may evaluate the accumulated evidence and make independent judgment about what, for the moment, may be construed as sociological "truth." It is only over time that concepts and theories evolve through constant empirical testing and consensual evaluation to reflect social reality more accurately and thereby provide a firm basis for political action.

A logical corollary of maintaining an open mind and a healthy respect for logic and data is a tolerance of opposing viewpoints, even those that may be personally noxious. By tolerance I don't mean acquiescence to or even acceptance of views one finds troublesome, but a willingness to hear the argument through, debate its merits openly and objectively, and evaluate its claims against logic and evidence. Whenever a professional organization such as the ASA adopts a position on a political issue, it lends its professional stamp to one particular version of the truth. But equally qualified and well-intentioned sociologists often disagree on the relative merits of the politics surrounding a particular issue, and adopting one position over another necessarily marginalizes those holding a dissenting view and implicitly questions their legitimacy as moral actors and sociologists.

The way to overcome arguments one does not like is not to suppress or marginalize them—either organizationally, by staking out an "official" sociological position, or individually, by shaming those with opposing views and ridiculing their ideas—but rather to address them openly and demonstrate their inconsistency with empirical facts and/or logical deductions. Suppression only stifles inquiry, chokes off debate, and makes an accurate understanding of society less rather than more likely.

Examples of the downside of mixing politics with science are what happened to Daniel Patrick Moynihan after the leak of his infamous report on the black family (see Rainwater and Yancey 1967); to Oscar Lewis following the elucidation of his culture of poverty hypothesis (Ryan 1976); and to Arthur Jensen after his analysis of black-white test score differentials (Gould 1981). As I have noted elsewhere (Massey 1995), the personal vilification heaped upon these scholars for expressing heterodox views had a chilling effect that dissuaded a whole generation of sociologists from undertaking research on the roots of intergroup differentials with respect to touchy subjects such as family dissolution, unwed childbearing, poor test performance, criminality, and other antisocial behaviors. I believe the absence of research by liberals on these issues during the 1960s and 1970s helped pave the way for the conservative ascendancy of the 1980s and 1990s.

A second reason for keeping the ASA politically neutral is that a reputation for impartiality and objectivity greatly enhances the value of the statements that the association *does* choose to make on questions of public import. A good example is the controversy over efforts to change the U.S. welfare system by placing lifetime caps on the receipt of federally subsidized income transfers. Many sociologists wanted the ASA to go on record opposing the legislation, but to do so would have presumed that sociologists really know whether prevailing welfare policies, on balance, help or hurt poor families, a very complex issue involving moral as well as scientific judgments. Taking a principled stand for or against proposed legislation might have indeed reflected the political sentiments of a majority of sociologists, but as noted above, it would have marginalized and ostracized others, and more seriously, it would have undercut the power and legitimacy of any *statements of scientific fact* the ASA might care to make.

Suppose it is the case, for example, that a working majority of sociologists agree, based on accumulated scientific research, that generous welfare payments neither increase unwed childbearing nor lower maternal employment. Sociologists can agree that this conclusion is consistent with the evidence and still disagree about the advisability of proposals for welfare reform. Whatever one's beliefs about welfare reform per se, the information is clearly relevant as input to the debate, and if the information is perceived as objective and scientific, it might well assuage the fears of conservatives who worry about welfare's disincentive effects.

If the ASA had already gone on record to oppose welfare reform on political grounds, however, such statements of scientific fact would lose their power and persuasiveness to objective observers. Indeed, they would quite logically become suspect in the minds of many. If the ASA has already announced its political position in advance, then the presentation of any facts that happen to be consistent with that position will, very appropriately, be discounted in most people's minds. If one wants objective scientific facts to play a role in political debates, then professional organizations presenting those facts need to remain above the fray. If a scientific consensus exists about a set of findings relevant to a divisive political issue, it is quite appropriate for the ASA to report this fact; but it is equally important to let each sociologist and member of the public make up their own minds about which side of the debate ultimately to support.

A third advantage to maintaining the ASA as a scientific rather than a political organization is that by establishing best practices and standards, it provides sociologists with a means to build professional respect and scientific prestige and, hence, the legitimacy to weigh in on debates as individuals. Once a field has established a canon of accepted methods, theories, and practices, it is up to each sociologist to meet those standards so that his or her work is viewed credibly and taken seriously by other sociologists, even those who may not share the same political beliefs. In this way, respect and prestige earned as a social scientist can be turned to advantage in the political arena when a sociologist participates in a public debate individually or as a member of a partisan advocacy group. If an individual sociologist has met the highest standards of the profession and has achieved recognition for doing so (winning prizes, being elected to professional office), then it provides him or her greater intellectual leverage as a political participant. A letter of protest signed by Nobel laureates carries far more weight than one signed by a cross section of scientists from a particular discipline.

ORGANIZATIONAL PRACTICE

I have witnessed the payoff to political nonpartisanship personally through my experience as president of the Population Association of America (PAA), which is one reason I supported a similar policy of political neutrality when I served as president of the American Socio-logical Association. The PAA is the leading professional association of demographers in the United States. It is by nature interdisciplinary, containing, in addition to sociologists, members who are economists, statisticians, geographers, historians, anthropologists, and biologists. Its membership spans the political spectrum, from conservative free-market economists such as Gary Becker at the University of Chicago (see Becker 1993) to radical feminist economists such as Nancy Folbre at the University of Massachusetts (see Folbre 2002). Perhaps because of this diversity of disciplines and viewpoints, the PAA has a long-stand-ing and strict policy of *not* taking formal positions on political issues.

Although the PAA works hard to remain nonpartisan, it nonetheless has an extremely active public affairs program and maintains a remark-ably visible profile in Washington, DC, especially given its small size (fewer than three thousand members). On its own and in collaboration with other nonprofit organizations, such as the Population Resource Center and the Population Reference Bureau, each year the PAA spon-sors numerous briefings before elected representatives and executive policy makers on topics of public interest. Typically a team of three to five prominent demographers is assembled and each person makes a fif-teen- to twenty-minute presentation drawing on personal knowledge and research findings to address controversial issues such as population aging, marriage and divorce, single parenthood, infant mortality, racial inequality, immigration, and social stratification.

I have personally participated in many PAA-sponsored briefings on the subjects of immigration, segregation, discrimination, and interna-tional development, and I have seen how eager public officials are to receive objective information and conclusions based on sound research. I know from personal conversations with policy makers and legislators how well received and respected the PAA is on Capitol Hill and by exec-utive agencies. Its political nonpartisanship gives it widespread access and legitimacy in the corridors of power, and this access enables PAA members to bring the results of their social scientific research directly to bear on political issues in a very tangible and constructive way, yielding policy outcomes that most liberal sociologists would favor. I believe the political influence of the PAA and its individual members is significantly enhanced because of the association's recognized political neutrality and its hard-earned reputation for scientific integrity. In my opinion as a former president of both organizations, I believe the PAA has more clout in Washington than does the ASA, despite its much smaller size.

PERSONAL EXPERIENCE

In my own career as a sociologist I have consciously sought to separate my work as a social scientist from my behavior as a political actor. Before I opine politically I want to get the social science done correctly and at the highest possible level. I write proposals for competitive peer review for grants to support research on topics of interest to me as a sociologist, such as immigration, segregation, education, and stratification. With whatever support I am able to garner, I carry out empirical research in collaboration with colleagues, postdocs, and students to build theories and test hypotheses using the best available methods and the most reliable data I can muster. I then collaborate with my colleagues to write up the results in scientific papers and submit them at the earliest possible opportunity to peer-reviewed journals. The latter step is especially important because we all, as human beings, are blind to our own weaknesses and naturally inclined to be critical of facts that contradict our preconceptions while accepting of those that confirm them. The peer-review process, while not perfect, provides a check on self-delusion and, over the long run, produces a more accurate and better understanding of the social world.

Once a paper is published in a peer-reviewed journal, I feel I have earned the right to disseminate its findings widely and, where appropriate, bring them to bear in ongoing public debates. After all, it's not just me who thought the paper was good—it also passed by a set of reviewers and an editorial committee. If a paper's results are especially relevant to some salient political issue, I often work with the public affairs office at my university to prepare a press release, or alternatively, I prepare an op-ed article for a major newspaper. Sometimes the press release produces no interest from reporters and yields little more than a short item in the back pages of a regional newspaper. At other times, however, the press release or the op-ed article generates tremendous interest that translates into front-page stories in multiple newspapers as well as interviews on television and radio and hours spent in give-and-take with reporters.

Once I have published a significant number of studies in refereed journals on a particular topic, I begin to feel more confident and justified in trying to elucidate "the big picture" for a more general audience. This I accomplish in one of two ways. I may write an extended article for a magazine such as the *American Prospect* or *The Nation* to outline my take on a social problem and bring the results of my research to bear in suggesting policy actions. If I believe that the subject requires a fuller treatment, however, and a more permanent place in the public dialogue than a single article can afford, I attempt to weave together the disparate strands of my published research into a book-length treatment for a general audience. As with articles in popular magazines and newspapers, books generate attention and publicity when they are published; but unlike articles they have a longer shelf life and provide a continuing basis for discussion, debate, and policy formulation over the years.

I can cite two personal examples of how my seemingly narrowminded dedication to social science has led to concrete political outcomes that would not have occurred had I taken a more "political" route from the start. Like many sociologists, I am deeply troubled by the persistence of racial prejudice and discrimination in the United States, especially as they affect African Americans in U.S. housing markets. The 1968 Fair Housing Act, in theory, prohibited racial discrimination in the rental and sale of housing in the United States, but because of a compromise brokered to overcome a southern filibuster, the act's enforcement provisions were diluted and federal authorities were largely disempowered from acting directly to identify and prosecute instances of housing discrimination.

During the 1980s, civil rights activists and liberal legislators became increasingly aware of the deficiencies of the Fair Housing Act, and many bills were submitted to bolster its enforcement provisions. As a member of the ASA, I could have written a resolution condemning racial discrimination in housing and calling on the association to support these bills. I might have presented my resolution to attendees at the annual business meeting and probably would have received a favorable ratification from the floor. The resolution might then have gone as a referendum to the entire membership, and I suspect that the ASA would have voted to go on record as opposing racial discrimination in housing markets and calling for more vigorous enforcement of fair housing laws.

But so what? With all due respect to my colleagues in the profession, the political clout of the ASA on Capitol Hill is minuscule. Inside the Beltway, the sad reality is that few people pay any attention to the political stands collectively taken by sociologists. I doubt that a working majority of legislators would ever have even learned that the ASA had taken an official position on amendments to strengthen the Fair Housing Act. Personally, I might have felt very self-satisfied and "politically correct" to have sponsored the formal resolution to burnish my antiracist credentials, and ASA members might have felt very virtuous for having voted for it. But what really would have changed? I suspect very little.

Instead of going the political route, beginning in 1984 I pursued a social scientific route. I began by obtaining competitive support from the National Institute of Child Health and Human Development to study the causes and consequences of segregation in U.S. cities, and using this support as a foundation, I was able to leverage additional funding from the Hewlett and Guggenheim Foundations. From 1985 through 1995 I published several dozen refereed articles on the patterns, determinants, and effects of segregation among Latinos, blacks, and Asians in U.S. metropolitan areas, many coauthored with my colleague Nancy Denton, who served as a postdoctoral research associate on the project.

After we outlined our theoretical and methodological approach (Massey 1985; Massey and Denton 1985), our first major study on the levels, trends, and patterns of segregation was published in the *American Sociological Review* in 1987 (Massey and Denton 1987). Concurrent with its publication, we worked with the University of Chicago's News and Information Office to prepare a press release. Much to our surprise, the fact that blacks continued to be more segregated from non-Hispanic whites than other groups proved to be big news around the country. The fact that two decades after the Fair Housing Act little progress toward racial integration in housing had been made became a front-page story, with articles appearing in newspapers such as the *New York Times, Los Angeles Times, Philadelphia Inquirer, Dallas Morning News, USA Today,* and many other dailies, including the *Washington Post,* where the story was read by the chief of staff for Representative Henry B. Gonzalez, then chair of the House Subcommittee on Housing and Community Development, which happened to be planning hearings on legislation to strengthen the Fair Housing Act.

Congressional staff members quickly tracked us down, and in January of 1988 Nancy and I found ourselves invited to Washington, DC, by Representative Gonzalez to offer testimony on behalf of a bill that was debated and ultimately passed in August 1988 as the Fair Housing Amendments Act. This act has been called "the most important development in housing discrimination law in twenty years" (Schwemm 1990). It eliminated provisions of the 1968 act that had discouraged victims from filing suit, increased the risks and penalties to would-be discriminators, expanded the federal government's powers of investigation and adjudication, and granted greater authority to the attorney general to pursue cases on behalf of individual plaintiffs. After testifying, Nancy and I received handwritten notes of thanks from Representative Gonzalez, who said "how grateful we all are for your great contribution."

Between 1988 and 1992 Nancy and I continued to move forward our research agenda on segregation, focusing increasingly on the unique situation of African Americans. A series of articles published in peer-reviewed journals developed a new multidimensional model for measuring segregation (Massey and Denton 1988a); showed that black segregation was not mitigated by suburban residence (Massey and Denton 1988b); introduced the concept of "hypersegregation" (Massey and Denton 1989); and demonstrated how black hypersegregation led directly to concentrated neighborhood poverty (Massey and Eggers 1990) and thereby acted forcefully to perpetuate black disadvantage over time and across the generations (Massey, Gross, and Eggers 1991).

By 1992, Nancy and I felt the time had come to tie everything together in a book-length treatment that would offer a comprehensive argument outlining segregation's pernicious effects on the status and well-being of African Americans. By writing a book, we hoped to have a more enduring influence on the debate then raging about the causes and consequences of the "urban underclass." Our efforts culminated in early 1993 in the publication of *American Apartheid: Segregation and the Making of the Underclass,* which went on to win the ASA's Distinguished Publication Award and the Population Section's Otis Dudley Duncan Award.

In the years since the book's publication, Nancy and I, both together and apart, have been invited to address numerous civic groups, fair housing organizations, congressional committees, governmental commissions, and academic audiences of all sorts. The book's most concrete policy impact, however, occurred early in the Clinton administration after the new secretary of Housing and Urban Development (HUD), Henry G. Cisneros, read it and followed up by assigning it to be read by assistant secretaries and senior staff members at HUD. He then brought me and Nancy to Washington to deliver a tutorial on segregation and fair housing enforcement to senior officials in the Office of the Secretary. During 1993 and 1994, under Secretary Cisneros's leadership, HUD worked to implement virtually all of the policy recommendations we laid out in the last chapter of *American Apartheid,* yielding a tangible increase in fair housing enforcement and record settlements in discrimination cases.

This kind of success in bridging social science and social policy is not confined to the realm of segregation, however. Another topic of personal interest—both academic and political—is immigration to the United States, especially from Mexico. Since 1982 I have codirected, with Jorge Durand of the University of Guadalajara, a large research project to compile and analyze data on documented and undocumented Mexican migrants (reviewed in Durand and Massey 2004). As with the work on segregation, we began by securing funding from the National Institute of Child Health and Human Development to anchor the project and then added supplementary funding from the Hewlett, Mellon, Sloan, and Russell Sage Foundations to expand our work into ancillary domains.

Our first book, *Return to Aztlan: The Social Process of International Migration from Western Mexico* (Massey et al. 1987), presented a detailed quantitative and qualitative analysis of the origins and development of migratory flows from four specific Mexican communities. In subsequent years, Jorge and I have worked with students and postdocs to publish dozens of additional articles in peer-reviewed journals in an effort to expand scientific understanding of the complex process of Mexico-U.S. migration. Our research has shown that migration stems from economic development rather than its absence (Massey 1988); that migration is determined more by market inefficiencies in sending regions than by wages in receiving areas (Massey and Espinosa 1997); that migration from Mexico historically has been circular (Massey and Singer 1995); that migrant remittances contribute importantly to Mexican development (Durand et al. 1996); that interpersonal connections between migrants and nonmigrants yield social capital that perpetuates international migration over time (Massey and Phillips 1999); and that because of social networks migratory flows tend to build up a self-perpetuating momentum over time (Massey and Zenteno 1999).

As with the project on racial segregation, along the way Jorge and I prepared press releases and endeavored to write accessible articles for magazines (see Durand and Massey 2001) and op-ed pieces for newspapers (see Massey 2000). By late 2001 we decided to tie these disparate studies together to construct a comprehensive model of the workings of the Mexico-U.S. migration system in order, first, to describe and evaluate the effects of U.S. immigration and border policies and, second, to offer a scientifically grounded agenda for immigration reform. The end product was *Beyond Smoke and Mirrors: Mexican Immigration in an Age of Economic Integration* (Massey, Durand, and Malone 2002), which also won the Otis Dudley Duncan Award from the ASA Population Section and received an honorable mention for the Thomas and Znaniecki Award of the Section on International Migration.

Once again, attention generated by the book resulted in a series of congressional briefings, public presentations, and popular publications on immigration policy that culminated in the introduction of reform legislation by Senators Edward Kennedy and John McCain in the spring of 2005. As this legislation was being drawn up, I was asked to make a presentation in Washington, DC, to staff members responsible for crafting the legislation and various interest group representatives who had input into its writing. I was startled to learn that many of those working on the legislation had read *Beyond Smoke and Mirrors* and were trying to figure out how to enact the recommendations we made in the book's last chapter. The legislation was introduced on May 12, and I was called to testify in support of it before the Senate Judiciary Committee's Subcommittee on Immigration on May 26. As of this writing, the final disposition of the proposed legislation is unknown, but if it does become law, it will improve the lives of millions of people on both sides of the border and could save the lives of hundreds who die needlessly each year while attempting to enter the United States without authorization.

WHEN LESS IS MORE

The foregoing personal and professional experiences reaffirm my belief that, for sociologists contemplating action on behalf of a cherished political cause, less can often be more. By abjuring daily involvement in the ongoing politics of race and immigration and not seeking to drag the ASA into taking a position on specific pieces of legislation, I was able to build a record of scientific research that was much more effective in advancing the causes I believed in, outstripping what I could have possibly achieved had I authored ASA resolutions on behalf of these causes or personally picketed in front of the Capitol or White House.

My experiences also illustrate the three reasons outlined at the outset for why the ASA should maintain a nonpartisan stance. By not taking sides in the immigration debate, the ASA was able to organize a credible, well-received briefing on the subject before Congress by me and other sociologists (see Ebner 2005), and to disseminate our research findings to a wider public (see Alba, Massey, and Rumbaut 1999). By defining best practices, specifying appropriate methodologies, and managing the process of peer review, the ASA created a framework within which I could screen my work for flaws and weaknesses and build credibility for my findings. Finally, by creating systems of reward and recognition for scientific achievement and professional accomplishment, the ASA enabled me to accumulate the professional status and respect to be

taken seriously when I opined on politically controversial subjects. Ultimately, as sociologists, that is all we have a right to ask.

REFERENCES

Alba, Richard D., Douglas S. Massey, and Rubén G. Rumbaut. 1999. *The
Immigration Experience for Families and Children.* Washington, DC: American Sociological Association.

Becker, Gary S. 1993. *A Treatise on the Family: Enlarged Edition.* Cambridge,
MA: Harvard University Press.

Durand, Jorge, William Kandel, Emilio Parrado, and Douglas S. Massey. 1996.
"International Migration and Development in Mexican Sending Communities." *Demography* 33: 249–64.

Durand, Jorge, and Douglas S. Massey. 2001. "Borderline Sanity." *American
Prospect,* 15 September.

———. 2004. *Crossing the Border: Research from the Mexican Migration Project.* New York: Russell Sage Foundation.

Ebner, Johana. 2005. "ASA Holds Hill Briefing on Immigration." www.asanet
.org/public/immigration.html.

Folbre, Nancy. 2002. *The Invisible Heart: Economics and Family Values.* New
York: New Press.

Gould, Stephen J. 1981. *The Mismeasure of Man.* New York: Norton.

Massey, Douglas S. 1985. "Ethnic Residential Segregation: A Theoretical Synthesis and Empirical Review." *Sociology and Social Research* 69: 315–50.

———. 1988. "International Migration and Economic Development in Comparative Perspective." *Population and Development Review* 14: 383–414.

———. 1995. "Review Essay on *The Bell Curve: Intelligence and Class Structure in American Life,* by Richard J. Herrnstein and Charles Murray." *American Journal of Sociology* 101: 747–53.

———. 2000. "To Study Migration Today, Look to a Parallel Era." *Chronicle
of Higher Education Opinion,* 18 August: B4–B5.

Massey, Douglas S., Rafael Alarcon, Jorge Durand, and Humberto Gonzalez.
1987. *Return to Aztlan: The Social Process of International Migration from
Western Mexico.* Berkeley: University of California Press.

Massey, Douglas S., and Nancy A. Denton. 1985. "Spatial Assimilation as a
Socioeconomic Outcome." *American Sociological Review* 50: 94–105.

———. 1987. "Trends in the Residential Segregation of Blacks, Hispanics, and
Asians." *American Sociological Review* 52: 802–25.

———. 1988a. "The Dimensions of Residential Segregation." *Social Forces* 67:
281–315.

———. 1988b. "Suburbanization and Segregation in U.S. Metropolitan
Areas." *American Journal of Sociology* 94: 592–626.

———. 1989. "Hypersegregation in U.S. Metropolitan Areas: Black and His-
panic Segregation along Five Dimensions." *Demography* 26: 373–93.

———. 1993. *American Apartheid: Segregation and the Making of the Underclass.* Cambridge, MA: Harvard University Press.

Massey, Douglas S., Jorge Durand, and Nolan J. Malone. 2002. *Beyond Smoke and Mirrors: Mexican Immigration in an Age of Economic Integration.* New York: Russell Sage Foundation.

Massey, Douglas S., and Mitchell L. Eggers. 1990. "The Ecology of Inequality: Minorities and the Concentration of Poverty, 1970–1980." *American Journal of Sociology* 95: 1153–88.

Massey, Douglas S., and Kristin E. Espinosa. 1997. "What's Driving Mexico-U.S. Migration? A Theoretical, Empirical and Policy Analysis." *American Journal of Sociology* 102: 939–99.

Massey, Douglas S., Andrew B. Gross, and Mitchell L. Eggers. 1991. "Segregation, the Concentration of Poverty, and the Life Chances of Individuals." *Social Science Research* 20: 397–420.

Massey, Douglas S., and Julie A. Phillips. 1999. "Engines of Immigration: Stocks of Human and Social Capital in Mexico." *Social Science Quarterly* 81: 33–48.

Massey, Douglas S., Magaly Sanchez R., and Jere R. Behrman, eds. 2006. "Chronicle of a Myth Foretold: The Washington Consensus in Latin America." *Annals of the American Academy of Political and Social Science* 66. Thousand Oaks, CA: Sage Publications.

Massey, Douglas S., and Audrey Singer. 1995. "New Estimates of Undocumented Mexican Migration and the Probability of Apprehension." *Demography* 32: 203–13.

Massey, Douglas S., and René Zenteno. 1999. "The Dynamics of Mass Migration." *Proceedings of the National Academy of Sciences* 96 (8): 5328–35.

Rainwater, Lee, and William L. Yancey. 1967. *The Moynihan Report and the Politics of Controversy.* Cambridge, MA: MIT Press.

Ryan, William. 1976. *Blaming the Victim.* New York: Vintage.

Schwemm, Robert G. 1990. *Housing Discrimination: Law and Litigation.* New York: Clark Boardman.

FRANCES FOX PIVEN

From Public Sociology to Politicized Sociologist

I define the term *public sociology* broadly, as the uses of sociological knowledge to address public and, therefore, political problems. This simple and sweeping definition means, I think, that public sociologists treat public problems as the important part of our research agenda, and it also means that we communicate our findings to the political constituencies who are affected by those problems and can act on them in politics. I am in favor of these uses of sociology. However, I think some self-scrutiny is called for about the social and political influences to which we ourselves are subject when we act as public sociologists.

The current preoccupation with public sociology comes easily to our field. After all, it is, in a way, a return to our roots. Sociology was born in the mid-nineteenth century out of the self-consciousness about the social environment forced on thinkers by the public problems, the disorder, and the disturbances evident in urbanizing and industrializing societies. In the United States, our first sociologists were associated with reform organizations trying to cope with the problems of poverty, deviance, and conflict evident in the growing cities. Later, in response to an insurgent labor movement, we developed a sociology of labor and industrial relations. And later still, as the civil rights, feminist, and anti-war movements gained momentum, we developed sociologies of race, gender, and peace studies.

As the discipline matured and sought status and position in the academy, it elected as its forebears, its founding fathers, the European theorists whose work was most clearly marked by a preoccupation with the upheavals of industrial society. Karl Marx, Max Weber, and Émile Durkheim were all preoccupied with public and political problems. Durkheim became for a time the most influential in American sociology, and in the post–World War II period he is often regarded as the more conservative theorist. But it was Durkheim's brilliant stroke to challenge reigning psychological or genetic theories of human behavior with the bold assertion that society existed and that it was a palpable influence on human behavior. He could see society and feel its weight precisely because traditional modes of social organization were changing, because the world around him was in tumult.

Inevitably a field framed by these influences continued to be at least in part a public sociology. One way that was expressed is in the study of social problems. In the aftermath of World War II, leading sociologists tried to institutionalize and formalize the field, staking out a distinctive academic identity by elaborating sociological methods, primarily the methodology of the survey, and by scrutinizing our founding fathers to delimit a distinctly sociological theoretical framework. But even while this was the main tendency, a feisty faction arose and broke away from the American Sociological Association to establish the Society for the Study of Social Problems. And for a time in the 1950s and 1960s, the best place to look for a lively public sociology was among those who were studying social problems and the public policies oriented to solving them.

However, the preoccupation with social problems itself became institutionalized and formalized as something that came to be called policy science. Policy science took as its distinctive field of study the policy interventions that would ameliorate social problems. It undertook to identify and measure the social conditions considered problematic, to identify and measure the ostensible causes of these conditions, and to evaluate the impact on these problematic conditions of alternative policy interventions. And because the interventions, real and imagined, were usually government policies, so was the public, real and imagined, the government agencies and the policy networks that presumably influence government.

In this pursuit of a science of policy, sociologists came to define for themselves a rather narrow and largely technical role. Perhaps in reflection of the status anxieties natural to a relatively new discipline, we tended to define for ourselves a role as technical experts. Or perhaps it was, as Neil Smelser argues, that "adherence to the model of positive science, as methodologically sound, and as therefore supportable on the grounds that they [the causal relations posited by the models] are legitimately scientific," was a strategy to blunt criticism from donor agencies and other government officials (Smelser 1988). In any event, our preoccupation was with the methodologies that would produce verifiable data about the cause-and-effect relationships of policy interventions. And the methodology that was overwhelmingly favored, perhaps because the statistics it required lent us an aura of expertise, was multivariate analysis. We did, to be sure, see problems in our policy science endeavors. But these problems were mainly methodological. The big challenge was to deal with the complexity of the real world, with the multiple variables and the multiple chains of intersecting causation, in a way that made possible the necessarily simple cause-and-effect relations entailed by our policy analyses and recommendations.

The early critiques of policy science, for example, by Michael Polanyi and Michael Oakeshott, questioned the capacity of social science to provide the knowledge necessary to intervene purposefully in a complex and fluid society. It was a critique of central planning, of the Soviet model, to be sure, but it was also a critique of the aspirations of the American New Deal, and the critique had influence on American sociology (Merton 1968). The core argument was that the simplification demanded by empirical research into the cause-and-effect relations that shaped social and economic life was inevitably incommensurate with the actual complexity and fluidity in the real world. More recently, the thread of this argument has been taken up by the left in the name of "local knowledge," a social science of sorts that eschews abstract models and quantification in favor of contingent and complex assessments of action in specific settings (see Schram 1995; Toulmin 2002; Flyvbjerg 2001; Scott 1998). There *are* problems of methodology and reliable knowledge, and they are serious, to be sure. But they are not the biggest problems on which this variant of public sociology has stumbled and compromised itself.

The bigger problems have to do with our social environment, the sociology of the public sociologists. We sought position and influence in the institutional world of government, foundation, research institute, and university. We wanted funding for the ever-more-elaborate research projects we designed. How could it be otherwise? We too were subjects of the Durkheimian insight that society molds its members. Just so did the incentives made available by the evolving institutional world of policy science influence us. We might not like to say so, and there may have been those who resisted, but who remembers them now? Public sociologists of the policy science variant were for hire. We sought out patrons, and inevitably we fell under their influence.

This means we were influenced by the understandings of the social world that our patrons wished to cultivate, about why some people commit crime, or why some people are poor, or why some families become dysfunctional. Our research methodologies grew more and more sophisticated and came closer to satisfying what is commonly regarded as the Weberian injunction about separating fact and value. But all of this sophistication—our ever-more-careful research designs and our ever-larger research projects—was put to work investigating causal relations dictated by the interpretations, the story lines, advanced by our patrons. That was our problem as policy scientists, and it still is.

During the more liberal administrations of the Great Society era, policy scientists included institutional variables in their exploration of the causes of crime, or poverty, or unemployment, or out-of-wedlock births. To be sure, there was still much talk and much study of the culture of poverty, for example. But there was also attention to the influence of labor markets, school systems, institutional patterns of discrimination, and so on. A policy scientist could find work investigating the great sociological idea that society and its institutions shaped behavior. In the 1970s, with the rising influence of business and the populist right, that changed, albeit not all at once.

It has become a commonplace to say that the right-wing mobilizations that began in the 1970s were fueled by new ideas. In fact, the ideas were not so much new as a revival of nineteenth-century laissez-faire, a celebration of markets and market "law," coupled with the castigation of government policies that interfered in the direct relation between the individual and the market. This market doctrine was again coupled, as it had been historically, with the religious doctrine positing a direct relation between the individual, God, and God's law. The metaphorical parallelism is striking and may help underpin the peculiar political alliance between religious fundamentalism and business interests who profess a market fundamentalism, at least when it comes to government policies aimed at supporting mass publics. But if the ideas were old, the apparatus constructed to promulgate them was new. Very rapidly, beginning in the early 1970s, and with die-hard business conservatives in the lead, a vast apparatus of foundations, think tanks, periodicals, associations, media outlets, and university bastions was created. It was something like a political party, but a political party devoted more to popular education than to elections. In any case, there was another instrument for elections, the Republican party, and by the late 1970s the quasi party was beginning to dominate the actual Republican party, which was gaining ground in Congress. Then, in 1980, Ronald Reagan won the presidency.

These developments meant that policy scientists had new patrons, and with new patrons came new interpretations, new story lines about the causes of social problems. The revelatory slogan was "personal responsibility." Now problems like crime or poverty or unemployment or out-of-wedlock births reflected the characteristics of particular communities or families and the flawed patterns of socialization for which they were responsible. Gone from the picture, from the research model, were the big institutional arrangements, labor markets or patterns of corporate investment, for example, and the bearing of government tax and spending policies on those patterns. Now the focus was on "the pathological black family, the dysfunctional, disorganized culture of poverty, and eventually the dangerous, nearly subhuman 'urban underclass'" (Reed 2004). Even more perniciously, a new causal model gained favor, the model of perverse effects that identified the causes of these social problems as the result of earlier misguided and too-generous policy interventions.

Did the findings support these models? Well, yes and no. The findings were decidedly mixed. In any case, we all understand that the very complexity of the social world that had chastened the ambitions of some policy scientists makes possible all sorts of multivariate correlations. In a complex and fluid society, almost anything can be correlated with many things. And, of course, correlations do not establish causality. In any case, communities, families, local cultures, all these do indeed matter in the complex shaping of human behavior. But to fasten on the findings misses what I think is the main point. The important consequence of all of this policy science was not in providing scientific knowledge as the basis of policy innovation. The intended changes in policy direction were, in fact, clear from the outset. The importance of the research was that it singled out for study those policies that the new patrons wished to change and endlessly sought to associate the policies with problems like poverty or unemployment or single-parent families or out-of-wedlock births. Whether the correlations were statistically compelling or not, and mostly they were not, the very fact that all of this research was being produced reiterated, and by reiterating underlined, the dominant story line about personal responsibility instead of collective responsibility that justified the new policy directions and also provided the story line with the gloss of scientific legitimacy. Wittingly or unwittingly, at least some public sociologists had served the new political elites instead of the public.

So, if we are to follow Michael Burawoy's compelling call for public sociology, I think we have to reflect critically on our relations with the public. We should in fact try to reconstruct these relations, by breaking out of the too-comfortable pattern of treating government as our patron and speaking directly to the public. This is easy to say, but the first question it raises is, which public? American society is sharply polarized; indeed, world society is sharply polarized. Bitter conflicts simmer in the United States and rage in the open throughout the world. The corruption of democracy and the ensuing loss of legitimacy by governmental authorities in the United States are, in fact, what make the uses of sociologists and sociology by the American government so problematic. Not so long ago, we took for granted that the American government represented, in a flawed way to be sure, a kind of societal consensus, or at least a majority consensus. However imperfectly, this was a democracy. No attentive person thinks it is that simple now. So, we have to ask, just who is it we serve when we serve government?

If public sociology is to thrive, we have to recognize not one public but many publics, and once we acknowledge the sharp divisions in our society, we have to decide which publics we want to work with. I propose as a guideline that we strive to address the public and political problems of people at the lower end of the many hierarchies that define our society. That means we devote our attention and our knowledge skills to the expressed needs of the poor and the working class rather than to the comfortably well off, to racial minorities and especially African Americans, to women more than men, to those without legal residence instead of those with legal residence and citizenship, to the marginalized and down-and-out of all descriptions. And not just in the United States. We also, when our skills allow, ought to regard the teeming multitudes around the world as our public, especially the hundreds of millions of people elsewhere whose traditional livelihoods are being destroyed by the depredations of international capitalism, which importantly means American capitalism. Their felt problems should become our sociological problems. If we do this, then public sociology becomes a dissident and critical sociology. Maybe there was a time when this was not necessary. Now it is.

Hah, you will think this is adolescent romanticism! It simply is not going to happen, for the straightforward reason that there are few job descriptions that match my injunction and hardly any research grants, and without jobs and research grants there won't be career awards like articles and books published, prizes received, promotions conferred, and so on. Alas, there is truth in all that.

Still, before you dismiss my injunction out of hand, consider the possibilities for sustaining a dissident public sociology. It's always instructive in examining action options to consider the places we live and work. Most of us work at colleges and universities. We are accustomed to thinking of these institutions as peripheral compared, say, to the mass-production industries. Maybe they once were, but no longer. The institutions of postsecondary education are huge, and in fact, more people are involved in universities and colleges, whether as staff or students, than in the manufacturing sector.

If we sometimes underestimate the importance of the institutions in which we play a large role, the organized right certainly does not. Over the past thirty years, right-wing groups have been engaged in a long march through the institutions. And they have been successful in most of these institutions. Large media corporations fell into the hands of right-wing moguls, and any who couldn't be simply bought were brought in line with a campaign of intimidation. Journalists became terrified of being called "liberal" or "pink" and, more recently, of being charged with a lack of patriotic ardor. The Corporation for Public Broadcasting has been in the news of late because the Bush acolyte who now heads it has been pulling his weight, especially targeting *NOW*, the program formerly hosted by Bill Moyers. But *NOW*'s bold critiques of public policy have been an exception. Most of public broadcasting was tamed years ago.

Or think of the churches. The mainline Protestant churches as well as the Catholic Church provided key support to the movements of the 1960s, especially the civil rights and antiwar movements. A combination of direct attacks by the right and the bleeding of their congregations by the growing fundamentalist churches seems to have tamed them as well.

The organized right did not ignore the universities. And some inroads were made, mainly through right-wing support of university centers and faculty positions in law and economics. But despite the furor aroused by the National Association of Scholars a couple of decades ago, and the recent upsurge of attacks on particular academics, all of which seemed to be coordinated by David Horowitz, the right has made few inroads in higher education, at least so far, and even fewer inroads in academic sociology. That is the main reason that Michael Burawoy can comment, "Over the last half century the political center of gravity of sociology has moved in a critical direction while the world it studies has moved in the opposite direction" (Burawoy 2005; this volume, 26). I am not really sure why we have so successfully defended the university. Perhaps the very features of the ivory tower that we sometimes criticize—namely, its elaborate rules and privileges and its wide areas of faculty governance—have been more useful than we usually acknowledge. Whatever the reason, however, we should rejoice that we work in institutions where we are largely protected from the bully tactics of the organized right, at least so far.

But while the universities and colleges offer us some protection, they are far from a perfect environment for nurturing a dissident sociology. Like most institutions, they encourage conformity to whatever it is that went before, to whoever it is that is above us in the hierarchy. So, we have to try to create our own environment, an environment that encourages criticism and dissidence and allows us to devote our intelligence and our time to understanding the problems of the world's majorities. How to do this? Well, if as social subjects we respond to incentives and rewards, we should begin to construct those systems of rewards, and perhaps of sanctions as well. We should use our conferences to honor the best dissident public sociology, and to criticize those sociologists who we think are contributing, by the kind of work they do, to misery and subjugation. We should create alternative journals that publish refereed articles of the best dissident public sociology. Above all, we should make sure we have comrades who support us when we need that support, as we surely will if we are sharp enough and critical enough.

We should also seek out alternative constituencies. We are accustomed to doing research for government agencies. Now we should try to cultivate the relations that will allow us to do research for unions, advocacy organizations, and community groups. And we should explore more participatory research methods with these groups, methods in which the subjects become partners in the design and conduct of the research. Such organizations are not likely to be able to fund the massive research project to which some of us have become accustomed. So be it. We will be able to do good research anyway.

Finally, I think we have to reevaluate the philosophical basis of our endeavors, and do this in writing, with theoretical sophistication. The scientific ideal, the injunction to emphasize the positive science in social science, was always too simple-minded in its treatment of the fact and value distinction. And the best sociology, the sociology of the great thinkers in our field, was, in fact, inspired by the moral and political concerns they confronted in their place and in their time. Now, in our place and in our time, moral and political concerns are overwhelming. Our political system moves toward theocracy, our government undertakes preemptive war and torture and creates concentration camps, our public policies push the planet toward an environmental tipping point, a wholesale assault is under way by the right on critical thinking and science, and wealth concentration spins out of sight while the earnings of most people stagnate and even their pensions are robbed, by the companies they work for, and perhaps by the government as well.

How can we not be critical and dissident public sociologists?

REFERENCES

Burawoy, Michael. 2005. "2004 Presidential Address: For Public Sociology." *American Sociological Review* 70: 4–28.

Flyvbjerg, Bent. 2001. *Making Social Science Matter: Why Social Science Fails and How It Can Succeed Again.* New York: Cambridge University Press.

Merton, Robert. 1968. "Role of the Intellectual in Public Bureaucracy." In *Social Theory and Social Structure,* R. Merton, enlarged edition, 261–78. New York: The Free Press.

Reed, Adolph. 2004. "Reinventing the Working Class: A Study in Elite Image Manipulation." *New Labor Forum* 13 (Fall): 22.

Schram, Sanford. 1995. *Words of Welfare: The Poverty of Social Science and the Social Science of Poverty.* Minneapolis: University of Minnesota Press.

Scott, James C. 1998. *Seeing Like a State.* New Haven, CT: Yale University Press.

Smelser, Neil. 1988. "Introduction." In *Handbook of Sociology,* ed. N. Smelser, 15. Beverly Hills, CA: Sage Publications.

Toulmin, Michael. 2002. *Return to Reason.* Berkeley: University of California Press.

FALSE DISTINCTIONS
CONCEPTUAL RESERVATIONS

IMMANUEL WALLERSTEIN

The Sociologist and the Public Sphere

The debate about the proper role of the sociologist or any other variety of scientist/scholar/intellectual in the public sphere is perpetual, repeatedly insistent, and totally unresolved. Political authorities are never happy if intellectuals offer them reasoned resistance and are seldom happy if intellectuals decline to support them in what they consider fundamental issues of value and policy. Intellectuals are never happy if they are pressed by public authorities or anyone else to espouse positions that are not theirs and are seldom happy if public authorities do not take cognizance of what intellectuals consider to be important findings or evaluations that they make or could make. And there are always organizational structures (religious structures, revolutionary movements, defenders of abstract rights) that insist that their values take precedence over those of public authorities and that therefore intellectuals who agree with them, or are members or supporters of these structures, ought to challenge public authorities when the values of these organizations are impaired in some way or are unfulfilled.

It is a minefield to find one's way amid these conflicting pressures. Some intellectuals have resolved the issue by avowing allegiances and operating in function of them—whether it is allegiance to a state or to a movement or to a church. Others have resolved this issue by trying to effectuate a radical separation of what they do as intellectuals/scientists/scholars (the search for scientific/scholarly truth) and the uses public authorities or their opponents make of the knowledge claims of the intellectuals. The shorthand name of this latter position is "value neutrality."

The two classic explications of these positions, familiar to most sociologists, are those of Max Weber and Antonio Gramsci. Weber, operating in an intellectual milieu (Wilhelmine Germany) in which the dominant academic figures of the universities espoused a position of fundamental support for the German state, resisted this position by making a claim for the virtue of value neutrality as the underpinning of sound scholarship. Gramsci, operating in an intellectual milieu (early-twentieth-century Italy) in which, in his view, intellectuals used the cover of value neutrality to support the liberal, bourgeois state, made the claim that one should be an "organic intellectual," that is, one who puts talents at the service of the social movement opposing the liberal state.

The problem with being an organic intellectual, whether committed to a social movement or to the state or to any other organization, is that those who are in leadership positions in the public arena tend in the long run to be pragmatists who pursue intermediate objectives and who therefore often change, are obliged to change, their short-range political positions. And the organic intellectual who is committed to supporting a given organization is called upon to follow the swings of position at the expense of intellectual consistency or even honesty. This is a good part of what explains the frequency with which such organic intellectuals become disillusioned and break intellectually and politically with the groups to whose support and direction they have been committed.

The alternative classical position is equally discomforting for the honest intellectual. The problem with espousing value neutrality is that it is intrinsically impossible to keep one's values from entering one's scientific/scholarly work. These values enter automatically at so many levels: at the level of the fundamental epistemology with which one approaches one's work; at the level of the choice of the objects of research; at the level of the choice of relevant evidence; at the level of the interpretation of the findings; at the level of the presentation of the findings. And all this becomes even worse in the frequent instances in which there are overt attempts to constrain the intellectual/scientist/scholar by those who control the material conditions of existence or the funding of research, which thereby accentuates the scientist's/scholar's dependence on presumed values. Weber himself understood this dilemma and therefore the limitations of value neutrality quite well, although this is less true of most of those who cite him as an authority on this question.

So, if it is almost impossible to be honest in the position of an organic intellectual and it is equally almost impossible to be honest in the claim of being value-neutral, what possible position is available to the intellectual in relation to the public realm? I should like to outline what seems to me the only reasonable stance. I believe the scientist/scholar has three functions that can never be evaded. They are linked functions, and sequential, but nonetheless each function involves a quite different task. The first function is that of seeking the most plausible analysis of the issues being investigated, both in detail and in their total context. I call this the intellectual function. The second function is that of evaluating the moral implications of the realities being investigated and effectuating a substantively rational choice.[1] I call this the moral function. And the third function is to analyze the best way of effectuating a realization of the moral good as the intellectual has analyzed it. I call this the political function.

I have said that scientists/scholars can never evade performing all three functions, however much they claim they can do so, and are doing so. This is the trap of the false claim of value neutrality, which asserts that the scientist/scholar is capable of isolating (and should perform only) the intellectual task and allow others (or oneself at other moments of time) to perform the moral and political tasks. In making this claim, one is burying (and thereby denying) the implicit moral and political choices that are in fact being made. But hiding them (from others and from oneself) does not mean that they are not being made. It simply means that it becomes much more difficult openly to discuss these choices and therefore to discuss the implications these choices have for the validity of the intellectual work being done or not being done.

Whereas espousing value neutrality seems to emphasize the intellectual task at the expense of the other two, it is not true that the organic intellectual is doing the opposite and being holistic. In fact, the organic intellectual is simply privileging the political task and hiding the fact that the intellectual and moral choices are being tacitly made, but once again hidden from view, and therefore one cannot openly discuss them, nor evaluate the degree to which the political choices are affecting the validity of the intellectual and moral choices.

How can one openly and sensibly engage in all three tasks? I have said they are sequential. I believe that the starting point is and has to be the intellectual task—the attempt to throw light upon, to analyze, the social reality under investigation. This is neither a micro nor a macro choice. This is neither a quantitative nor a qualitative choice. Micro/macro and quantitative/qualitative are simply dimensions of possible methodological tools that require ad hoc decisions as to their utility and validity in light of the issues under analysis and the data that are reasonably available or can be constructed to do the research. What is crucial is that all such analyses, whatever their immediate objective, be placed in the appropriate large-scale spatial context and the long-term temporal context (not merely the past but the relevant future) that is appropriate for the analysis.[2]

The intellectual analyses are no doubt always affected by one's moral predilections and one's political preferences. And whenever these predilections are not self-evident, the scholar/scientist should feel under the intellectual/moral/political obligation to make these presuppositions clear. Nonetheless, intellectual analyses have their own logic and therefore their own relative autonomy. They are offered in the public sphere to the criticism of one and all and have to be reasonably robust, defensible logically, and historically plausible. They are to be sure always tentative and open to revision, but that does not mean that they are incapable of being taken as sound and momentarily true, meaning that the results may be employed by others in their subsequent analyses as presumptively correct and as evidence that reinforces the analyses of subsequent scientists/scholars.

Advocates of value neutrality would probably assent to this last paragraph but then say that this is where the responsibility of the intellectual stops. But it seems to me obvious that it never stops there. Anything that foresees a trend line foresees situations in which there are choices to be made. And the intellectual cannot afford to neglect not merely to indicate the likelihood and nature of such choices but also to indicate the moral implications of making one choice rather than another. The intellectual can do this only by invoking the sense of, appreciation of, the "good" (and not merely of the "true"). The scientist/scholar can argue that this is not her or his function, but then what is happening is that the reading of the implications of these choices is left to others and the intellectual analyst has merely acceded in advance to their evaluations and recommendations. The intellectual has not thereby avoided making the choices but has simply done so passively rather than actively. The intellectual remains responsible for the moral evaluations that are passively made as a result of the analyses.

Of course, there is the question of the basis on which we are to make our moral choices. This is not an intellectual question, in the sense that empirical analyses or theoretical syntheses lead one inevitably to particular moral choices. Moral choices are the outcome of one's moral philosophy (or, if you prefer, one's religious beliefs). And as we are all aware, there is a wide range of avowed moral philosophies. We can discuss them with each other, debate them, but we can never arrive at a decision which is in some analytic sense the true one (even if many, if not most, people are convinced that the one they hold is the only possible correct choice).

Nonetheless, moral choices are neither random nor accidental. They are the result of our moral education and our reflection. And the world is better off if there is interactive reflection on the fundamental issues under debate. Here intellectuals/scholars/scientists can play a useful role, by clarifying the assumptions about reality that are hidden in the moral philosophies, and subjecting these assumptions about reality to standard scholarly/scientific analysis to see how plausible they are. In doing this, intellectuals may, at least, root out false debates and narrow the divergences about moral issues to what are really differing moral options. This will not end debate, even fierce debate, but it may make it somewhat more reasonable and therefore somewhat more amenable to possible social (that is, historical) compromises.

Nor does the game stop there. Once the intellectual has opted for the good—whether actively or passively—the next question is how one can arrive at the good. This is what we mean by a political task. The good is not a self-realization; it is the outcome of human choices. And the most superficial look at human history tells us that our collective choices have not always been for what we ourselves would define as the good. This is surely true for what lies ahead. Political choices are always being made. And once again the intellectual who has made the analysis and then perhaps indicated the moral choice among the real alternatives is deceiving him- or herself and the world in claiming that these choices are somehow not the responsibility of the analyst. As with the moral function, avoiding the assumption of responsibility for the political function is opting nonetheless for a political choice, but doing so passively and, one might add, surreptitiously. The political function is still being performed.

Political choices are, as anyone who has ever been active politically over long periods of time knows, by no means self-evident. We are all always puzzling why political choices that seem to us not merely desirable but in our view ones that should have been appealing to large majorities of the population are somehow not made. We cannot understand how bad choices continue to prevail. Here, too, the intellectual/scholar/scientist can play a useful political role. He or she can use the analyst's skills to attempt to answer the puzzles and thereby to help in the political process by pointing to alternative strategies and tactics that are more promising in realizing the good, as he or she has defined it in considering the moral options.

It is not necessarily that the intellectual/scholar/scientist is a better political analyst than the full-time politician/activist. It is that he or she may have a bit more psychological distance from the previous strategies/tactics employed, a bit less involvement of ego in maintaining the failing policies of the past, and therefore a slightly more "objective" analysis. In any case, political decisions are seldom individual ones. They are made by groups (whether self-defined or latent), and the group loses nothing (and potentially gains much) if the intellectual/scholar/scientist adds his or her analyses to the public debate.

So, here we have it: the inescapable succession of tasks for the intellectual/scientist/scholar and the clear distinction nonetheless among the three tasks. None of them can be subordinated to the others. All are always being done, whether actively or passively. And doing them actively has the benefit of honesty and of permitting open debate about substantive rationality.

Notice two things about the successive tasks, as I have outlined them. They are not a prescription for particular modes of analysis, particular moral preferences, or particular political strategies or objectives. They remain the role of the intellectual/scientist/scholar no matter what views he or she holds. The tasks are there but will be performed differently whether one is, in the conventional sense, of the left, center, or right, however these terms be defined; whether one's morality is religious or secular; whether one's intellectual analyses are based on methodological individualism or world-systems analysis, or indeed anything else.

The second thing to notice is the meaning therefore of public sociology. I am not enamored of the term. It has the flavor of something special, a sub-branch of sociology, something one does part of the time alongside whatever else one does. I am trying to make the case that all sociologists—living, dead, or yet to be born—are, and cannot be other than, public sociologists. The only distinction is between those who are willing to avow the mantle and those who are not. And, in general, openness in science/scholarship is far more productive of useful results than engaging in work with hidden premises and preferences. We can never come close to a more universal universalism, a more plausible historical social science, a more reasonable accommodation of multiple readings of the good, and therefore ultimately a democratic political system if there is not greater openness in our public discussion. And in this activity, intellectuals/scientists/scholars cannot be, should not be, the laggards.

NOTES

1. *Substantive rationality* is, of course, Weber's term. However, for English users, it must be noted that this is a bad translation of the original German *Rationalität materiell*. Weber was referring to the ancient distinction of Greek philosophy between the formal and the material. Weber, in effect, and in detail if one reads him carefully, was asking us to take seriously the relevance to our own work of material as well as of formal rationality.

2. I refer the reader to my views of how this might best be done as outlined in Immanuel Wallerstein, *World-Systems Analysis: An Introduction,* Durham, NC: Duke University Press, 2004.

ORLANDO PATTERSON

About Public Sociology

Michael Burawoy's account of public sociology exhibits some of the virtues, and many of the worst intellectual vices, of contemporary sociology. The piece is well informed, intellectually lively, and dashed with a few useful insights, such as the distinction between sociology and the career trajectories of sociologists (Thesis V) and the different styles of sociology around the world and the questionable international role of American sociology (Thesis IX). Contrary to his repeated misrepresentation of me as an "elitist" in his frequent talks around the country and the world on this subject—a fabrication that verges on the slanderous in light of my long engagement with radical political change and social programs aimed at the alleviation of poverty in the postcolonial Caribbean—I firmly believe that the public use of sociology, properly executed, is part of a communicative process in the public sphere that is necessarily democratic in both intent and consequence.

At the same time, the essay illustrates some of the worst habits of contemporary sociological thinking, the most important here being its excessive overschematization and overtheorizing of subjects, the construction of falsely crisp sets and categories, and the failure to take seriously the role of agency in social outcomes, even while theoretically applauding it, or to acknowledge the profoundly moral or valorized nature of the sociocultural universe we study and the distinctive intellectual challenges this valorized reality poses.

Let's take a closer look at one of the most glaring of these: the over-schematization and theoretic pretensions of the essay. Burawoy's task is simple: What is public sociology? What are its problems and where is it headed? He begins by imposing a fourfold schema (that Ouija board of the discipline), which is plausible enough. Not content with this, how-ever, Burawoy proceeds to square the grid, proposing that the content of each cell become a new dimension, generating a sixteen-celled array of sociological types! I am not exaggerating—see Thesis IV.

If this enterprise we all care about is to be taken seriously by nonso-ciologists, we have to begin by being less promiscuous in our use of cat-egories. But there is an even more serious requirement: sociologists have got to learn that the universe they study is imprecise, and for this reason most of the sets we work with are at best fuzzy.

In what follows I will draw on over four decades of personal expe-rience in public sociology, and on the lives of other sociologists in America and other parts of the world, in an attempt to describe the main types of public sociology and the reasons why there is so little of it in America *relative to* the large number of professional sociol-ogists in this country. What do past and present members of the profession who are generally acknowledged to be public sociologists do, qua public sociology? At the narrowest, they are engaged in one way or another with various publics beyond the strictly professional community. Engagement entails the attempt to communicate with, and influence, the particular public they are involved with. If the com-munication is democratic, as it should be, the influence is mutual, or at least has the potential to be so. The public in question may be transna-tional, or the nation at large, or it may be more specialized and local—one's city or state or local farm community, an interest group or ethnic community.

PUBLIC AND POLICY SOCIOLOGY: A FALSE DISTINCTION

Burawoy and several others writing on this subject, including Pierre Bourdieu, have argued that those who work for a client—political or business—are not to be considered public sociologists. Indeed, Bour-dieu went so far as to call such sociologists "scabs" (Carles 2001). Burawoy and those he echoes offer no good reason for this distinction, and I strongly disagree with them. Working for a client may or may not be public sociology, depending on the nature of the task, the principles and intention of the social scientist, and the involvement of an audience beyond the expert and the client.

Let's take the case of the Council of Economic Advisers to the American president. Sitting on this council offers any scholar an extraordinary opportunity to practice public social science, and it is absurd to suggest that the terms of employment rule out such work from the domain of public sociology. It depends entirely on what the expert does with the job, as the following cases demonstrate. A year before he took up the chairmanship in 2003, Harvard economist Greg Mankiw was severely critical of President Bush's enormous deficits and had nothing but contempt for supply-side economic theories as well as policies based on this view, going so far as to use it as a case study in bad economic thinking in his popular economics textbook. Nonetheless, within weeks of taking up the chairmanship, Mankiw did a complete about-turn and was fully supporting the president's profligate deficit spending and massively regressive tax policies on supply-side grounds. Here we have a scholar serving his employer in an intellectually dishonest way that completely disregards the national public, or any public for that matter. What makes his actions all the more deplorable is that there were several precedents of economists who chose to abide by their principles and placed the public interest (as they saw it) over the wishes of their boss. In 1983–84, for example, Markiw's senior colleague at Harvard, Marty Feldstein, who chaired the council under Reagan, publicly disagreed with his boss's fiscal policies and warned the public in speeches and op-eds that the price it would pay would be years of trade and budget deficits (Frankel 2003). Feldstein's behavior in the chairmanship was a classic instance of honorable public social science behavior. The main difference seems to be the degree to which social scientists remain true to their principles and what they have learned from their discipline and their willingness to speak truth to power in defending the public interest as they understand it.

This remains true even in cases where the political and policy views of the professional are greatly at variance with those of the client. An example from my own experience can illustrate this. Not long after Gerald Ford took over the presidency upon the resignation of the disgraced Richard Nixon, it became apparent that his very sheltered political life as a congressman from an upper-middle-class suburb in Michigan had left him painfully ignorant of important areas of public life in the country that he now led. To correct this problem, an in-house educator at the White House arranged a series of crash-course tutorials for the president on important economic and social issues of the day. A small group of experts on the subject in question were invited to spend the better part of a working day at the White House, where they had lunch with the president and put on a lively debate for him, making sure that all points of view were represented. One topic on which the president needed education was ethnicity; apparently he hardly knew what the word meant when he took over, even though the country was then going through the so-called ethnic revival, a movement with political implications in view of the fact that the revival was really mainly a backlash by so-called white ethnics against the newly emerged black solidarity movement. I was invited to join a group of five scholars on this occasion, my role being to argue the case against any promotion of ethnicity by the government, which I then considered, and still do, a development with neofascist dangers. I accepted the assignment, in spite of my radically different political orientation from the rather conservative president (indeed, at the time I was actually a special advisor to Prime Minister Michael Manley of Jamaica, then the second-most-radical head of state in the hemisphere). Did this mean that my engagement at the White House did not count as public sociology? Absolutely not. I consider it a public duty to help in the education of the leaders of any country regardless of my ideological differences with them. I was giving expert advice, as I interpreted it, about a vitally important development in the country to someone in a position to do something about it. Of equal importance, however, is the manner in which I gave my expert advice. I told the president outright that the ethnic revival was a right-wing reaction against the civil rights movement and the growth of African American political consciousness and that the state should stay out of it. This ran against the advice being given by his own political aides, as I discovered two weeks later when the president announced a new White House initiative to aid the preservation of ethnic communities. It was another battle lost, but an honorable defeat in my career as a public sociologist.

An expert who offers a range of viewpoints and leaves the decision to the client is indeed behaving like a hired hand and is not in my view a public sociologist. Boldly presenting one's point of view is a sine qua non of public intellectual activity. A second requirement is that what one does be of public interest.

The fact that one works for a client is an irrelevance, as is the question of whether one is paid or not. Two further cases from my own experience with the private sector will further clarify the issue. I was once asked by *Forbes* magazine to debate the issue of affirmative action before a large audience of personnel executives from America's top five hundred companies. I was handsomely paid and lavishly quartered. My work for *Forbes* was public sociology in every possible sense of the term. I was attempting to educate the five hundred most influential employers in the nation, and whatever they took away from our meeting was likely to influence in some way the employment prospect of a good number of minority and women executives.

Contrast this with a lecture and discussion session I had with the marketing staff of one of the nation's largest pharmaceutical companies several months ago. Neither I nor my audience was in any doubt about the objective of our engagement—they were there to pick my brains about how they could use America's central civic value—freedom—to sell their products. This was, to be sure, perfectly respectable work—no Pierre, this is not "scab" work. We live in the world's most successful capitalist society (with incomes to prove it), and however much sociology may choose to forget and deny it, marketing is one of the discipline's stupidly abandoned orphans, jointly parented by two of the preeminent founders of modern American sociology, Robert Merton and Paul Lazersfeld. Nonetheless, this was not public sociology.

Why? Simply that, unlike the *Forbes* case, there was no public involved. This was a wholly private affair between employer and expert. In the work for *Forbes* there were large and important publics—minority and women aspirants to executive jobs. And there was a major public issue—the glass ceiling that these groups encounter at certain points in their careers. What's more, to the degree that the emergence of a solidly grounded middle- and upper-class minority is considered important for the long-term solution of one of America's most chronic social problems—the historic ethnic exclusion of minorities—our debate addressed a national issue. The same holds for women's equality. The only consequence of my work for the pharmaceutical company, if any, pertained to its private gain, which, to repeat, is a perfectly honorable thing in this ultracapitalist America that so generously endows me and the likes of Michael Burawoy.

Any action by a sociologist beyond the academy, then, that entails and engages a public is public sociology. The engagement may be for any kind of client and may be more indirect than direct; it really does not matter. Indeed, the insistence by people who write about public sociology that the sociologist must be directly engaged is not only romantic nonsense but dangerous, for it implies that the sociologist need not be as alert to the publics he or she is likely to be engaging, however indirectly or unwittingly, when doing private work. Sociologists ought to take seriously what radical women sociologists and intellectual activists were the first to make clear—that the distinction between private and public is itself at best fuzzy, although still very useful, and in the wrong heads can be turned against women and other excluded groups.

How many kinds of public sociologies are there? It depends very much on who is doing the classification and the objectives of the analyst. I suggested above that Burawoy's schematization is overdone. Instead of sixteen or even four, I suggest three broad sets of public sociologies: the professionally engaged; the discursively engaged; and the actively or civically engaged. The sets overlap. A single sociologist may engage in all three, as I do.

PROFESSIONALLY ENGAGED PUBLIC SOCIOLOGY

By professional engagement I mean the kind of public sociology in which the scholar remains largely committed to the work but becomes involved with publics and important public issues as an expert. Usually the public comes to the social scientist for advice, rather than the latter seeking out and engaging the public, although this sometimes happens. Now it is the case that a fair number of sociologists do just this, but what is truly remarkable about the current state of American sociology, and the saddest reflection of the state of the discipline, is how few sociologists get publicly involved with issues that they have spent their entire professional lives studying. Most sociological specialists prefer to spend their time talking to other specialists.

In their long-term study of the effects of sociology on public policy, Carol H. Weiss (1993) and her collaborators found such effects "only occasionally evident." The best that could be hoped for is a kind of "knowledge creep" in which there is an "amorphous percolation of sociological ideas into the policy arena." It is revealing that whenever Weiss gives actual examples, she shifts from talking about sociology to "social science," and as often as not the social scientists she has in mind are economists.

A major reason for this state of affairs is the perverse tendency of the discipline to shed or marginalize most applied and descriptive areas of social research, precisely those fields that are of direct interest to policy makers and the nonsociological public in general. This strange proclivity for practical irrelevance began with the professionalization of the discipline in the early part of the century, when social work was shunned by all the emerging departments, along with scholars who were devoted to it. A major early intellectual casualty of this development was Jane Addams, a brilliant founding mother of the discipline in America who suffered from the blatant sexism of her times and continues to do so in the near complete neglect of her important contributions. Unlike all the other social sciences, including economics, sociology has rejected any kind of applied branch, and no major department will today consider hiring anyone, however distinguished in her own right, who works in applied areas such as social work.

But later developments were even more perverse. Several fields that naturally belong to sociology and are, in some cases, technically even more advanced than that found in typical mainstream sociological work have been held at arm's length by the discipline. Demography is the most extreme case in point. What is true of demography is even more the case with criminology, another field that is as natural a subfield of the discipline as the study of the family or organizations. The same holds for fields such as marketing and communications.

By systematically shedding all those areas of the study of society that the public is most interested in and would naturally turn to sociology for expert answers, sociology has committed a slow kind of disciplinary hari-kari. Who in America, except fellow sociologists, wants to learn about the micro-macro problem, the processes of structuration, or the quarrels between rational choice theorists and comparative macrosociologists about the best theoretical and methodological approaches to the study of revolutions? Don't get me wrong. These are worthy issues, and I should be the last person to complain about exotic problems. For heaven's sake, one of my most recent academic papers was on the problem of the relation of slavery to Spartan helotage in Messinia some five centuries before Christ! My complaint, rather, is with the fact that these are primarily the issues that sociology finds legitimate. All the other social sciences, including economics, have made sure that however much they may soar in the theoretical or exotic academic realms they have one applied foot firmly planted in the real world where their expertise is needed.

The main reason for the unwise dissociation of the discipline from fields such as demography and criminology with their rich traditions of professional engagement is the decision by gatekeepers of the discipline, especially after the 1960s, to adopt a normal science approach modeled on physics and its experimental methodology rather than on biology.

Stanley Lieberson and Freda Lynn (2002) have written eloquently on this fateful turn and its implications.

Another major reason why the expert advice of sociologists is often neglected is the structural bias of the discipline and its tendency to neglect—and often abominate—personal choices and responsibility as important components of any explanation of social problems. Let me illustrate with one striking example. Today a major debate rages in America about the state and future of marriage and the family. While there are a few notable exceptions—David Popenoe, Sara McLanahan, Pepper Schwartz, Arlie Hochschild, Linda Waite, and Norval Glenn immediately come to mind—what strikes me as unusual is the absence of a vigorous sociological presence in this heated public debate. Imagine a national debate on the crisis of stagflation, as we had in the 1970s, that was not dominated by economists, and one has some idea of what I am getting at.

This was not always the case. Before sociology shifted toward value-free scientism in the 1960s, almost all sociologists spent some of their time as experts informing and advising appropriate audiences. Typical of the pre-1960s era was Ernest Burgess, the twenty-fourth president of the American Sociological Association (in 1934). Although the model scholar who was thoroughly rigorous in his research and always up on the latest methods of quantitative and qualitative research, Burgess was always concerned with the ways in which his research could benefit the broader public. The big difference between today and the earlier era is that the typical sociologist then was professionally engaged, whereas today only a small minority are. Because there are thousands of professional sociologists in America, possibly more than all sociologists in the rest of the world put together, Burawoy is able to cite several prominent names as examples of expert engagement, but what is striking is how minuscule a *proportion* of the total are professionally engaged.

DISCURSIVE PUBLIC SOCIOLOGY

The situation is not much better in the second of my fuzzy sets of public sociology, what may be called discursive engagement. Jürgen Habermas immediately comes to mind as the great contemporary exemplar of this tradition. However, although he does practice what he preaches, Habermas is more a theorist of this kind of social practice. It existed long before him and continues to be practiced today by publicly engaged sociologists who may never have read him and in ways that differ from many of his own specific prescriptions. Habermas's ideas and practice, however, are useful as a prototype in a preliminary account of what this kind of public sociology is about (I draw here on Habermas 1970 and 1991).

Discursive public sociology is a form of communicative action in which claims about an aspect of our social world, or about a given society, or about society in general, are validated by means of a public conversation between the sociologist, who initiates the discourse with his or her work, and the particular public the sociologist engages. It is a requirement of this communicative process that the audience to whom, and often about whom, the sociologist speaks—and not just other sociologists—is free and able to participate, to talk back or qualify the claims made. Another way of putting it—drawing on Jürgen Habermas and J. L. Austin—is to say that the sociological communication becomes a complex speech act performed in the public sphere aimed at a particular audience. As such, it is more than merely a locutionary statement—an objective account of social reality which is either true or false, although it also strives to be—since its pronouncement is in itself a performative act in which the intention, motive, mode of expression, attitude, beliefs, and feelings of the author are meant to have persuasive force and are thus partly validated by the audience on the basis of its perception of the author's authenticity and eloquence. And, in all cases, such works are perlocutionary acts: they are meant to have an effect upon the audience they engage; they invite responses which may change the author's later communications, for example, in later editions.

Discursive public sociology thrives in Europe, where it is still possible for scholars such as Robin Blackburn to move from decades of editing *New Left Review* and being consulting editor for Verso Press to a professorship of sociology at Essex, which has one of Britain's leading departments of sociology. Scholars such as Clause Offe and Hans Jonas in Germany, Pierre Bourdieu and Raymond Aron in France, and Perry Anderson and Michael Young in Britain are only a few of the many that immediately come to mind. There is also a lively tradition of discursive public sociology in many developing societies, especially India, where the works of scholars such as Veena Das and T. K. Oommen are exemplary.

In discursive public sociology at its best, the sociologist is both rigorous social analyst and critic of society at all levels. The fact that validation comes through what Habermas calls a circular process of interaction helps to keep the analyst honest. But there is another way: constant self-scrutiny of one's own communicative acts and the methods by which one's claims are arrived at. Excellent recent examples of this are found in the works of several Indian sociologists, such as Veena Das (1990), T. K. Oommen (1990), and Yogendra Singh (1984).

Discursive public sociology is distinctive, too, in the kinds of issues chosen for communication. Its practitioners are sometimes, a bit pejoratively, called big-think sociologists, which can easily be misunderstood. The term *big-think* is misleading if taken to mean macrothink. Many discursive sociologists think big about middle-range and small-scale issues; typically, they shift levels as the occasion demands. Herbert Gans's discourse on *Middle American Individualism* (1988) spoke at the macrocultural level; his discourse on symbolic ethnicity, a gem of rigorous social analysis that is also highly critical, paints on a medium-sized canvas, as did his classic work on working-class family life in the North End of Boston.

Whatever the level on which they think, all discursive sociologists were or are deeply engaged with a broader nonsociological audience. As such, they try hard to make their works accessible. An important way in which they did, and continue to do so, is by means of journalistic articles and editorial columns in newspapers and magazines. Journalism has had, of course, a close relationship with sociology. Many of the early founders of the discipline came to it from journalism. In Europe today, nearly all prominent sociologists write for the press.

However, with the rise of scientism in the mid-1960s, the gatekeepers of the discipline began to frown upon this and other modes of discursive communication, creating in people like David Riesman and C. Wright Mills what David Paul Haney calls "a pronounced professional ambivalence, one which they shared with sympathetic colleagues" (Haney, n.d. [1998]). When I referred to David Riesman as the "last sociologist," I was thinking mainly of the deliberate evisceration of this great tradition of discursive sociology that went back to the founding fathers of the discipline. Burawoy is completely inaccurate in his claim that the writers I cited earlier were an exceptional minority, as Haney makes clear in his valuable dissertation on the era. The price sociology paid for its scientist turn was the abandonment of its distinctive role as the discipline primarily dedicated to the critical exploration and discourse on modernity. Haney puts it well:

> The challenge of retaining professional respectability became acute as professional sociologists launched aggressive attacks against both professionals and non-professionals who refined or simply appropriated sociological

research and communicated it to a non-professional readership. These professional condemnations of popularization, in turn, constituted a rearguard action in the name of preserving the autonomy of social scientific expertise from the oversimplifications and misinterpretation of sociological work in the public sphere [by people such as Vance Packard, A. C. Spectorsky, and even William H. Whyte]. The net effect of these tensions among sociologists and between sociologists and wider communities of discourse was to exacerbate the rift between the professional and non-professional discourses on modernity. (1998, 28)

The rift widened between the 1960s and the late 1980s, the era of professional scientism. Happily, the tide began to turn after that, as a younger generation of scholars began to challenge the self-destructive withdrawal of the discipline from the public sphere. A small minority of respected scholars such as Ann Swidler, Robert Bellah and his associates, Amartai Etzioni, Richard Sennett, William Julius Wilson, Alan Wolfe, Theda Skocpol, Christopher Jencks, Paul Starr, and Todd Gitlin are reviving the great tradition of sociology as critical discourse in the public sphere through their writings and editorial work in major newspapers and journals. One of the most promising recent developments in this direction has been the launching of the journal *Contexts,* under the auspices of the American Sociological Association. (Burawoy praises *Contexts* as an exemplary case of sociology's democratic discourse. However, in labeling, and libeling, me an elitist, he failed to note that I was a founding member of the editorial board of *Contexts* and played an active role in launching and helping to nurture it through its first critical years.)

In this renewal the op-ed—invented by the *New York Times* in 1974—is a natural medium for the discursive sociologist. When successfully executed, the op-ed is an exquisite exemplar of Habermasian communicative discourse, a speech act directed at sometimes a million informed citizens, the most articulate of whom fire back with hundreds of lengthy responses, made easier by the Internet. Their comments and criticisms often raise questions that sometimes go to the heart of the scholar's work. While some sociologists have made use of this medium, it is still surprising how relatively few of them have done so, compared with economists and other social scientists.

A final point to note about discursive public sociology is that the typical scholar is not necessarily actively involved with movements within the public sphere. At one extreme she or he may even shun direct personal involvement with activist or even established civic groups. Discursive public sociologists—like their nonprofessional counterparts in public intellectual life—have often been criticized for this lack of active engagement. Habermas has been unfairly criticized on these grounds. Within sociology perhaps the most extreme case in modern times is C. Wright Mills, who adamantly refused to become engaged in any kind of civic organization, to the occasional annoyance of good friends and strong supporters such as David Riesman.

David Riesman, as I have suggested elsewhere (Patterson 2002), was the prototypical discursive sociologist. His classic, *The Lonely Crowd* (1950), is still one of the greatest acts of national self-scrutiny by a sociologist to have animated the American public sphere. The tradition continues in American sociology, but it only limps along. What is striking about the present scene in American sociology is how few leading sociologists take on this role. The tradition is actually alive and well, but it is now largely practiced by nonacademic analysts such as Michael Lind, by academics in other fields such as history and cultural studies, and by journalists such as Andrew Sullivan, Alex Kotlowitz, Scott Malcomson, and Barbara Ehrenreich.

ACTIVELY ENGAGED (OR CIVIC) PUBLIC SOCIOLOGY

The third and final set of public sociologists I wish to distinguish is that marked primarily by the degree of active, civic, especially political, engagement of the scholar. Max Weber has often been mischaracterized on this subject. He is, in fact, a prototype of the actively engaged public sociologist. Weber's views on value neutrality in social science are often cited. I frankly find his many statements on the subject insightful in their particulars but contradictory to the point of incomprehensibility when considered in toto. What is clear is that few sociologists have ever been more passionately involved with public life. He was adamant that political engagement should be strongly informed by one's values.

The tradition of political and other civic engagement by sociologists initiated by Weber persists in Germany, as it does in most countries where the discipline thrives, America being the major exception to this pattern. It cannot be an accident that it is precisely in those countries where prominent sociologists have established a tradition of active engagement in political and civic life that sociology is held in most esteem. In contemporary Germany, Habermas is a revered national figure. More in keeping with the activism of Weber is the highly esteemed sociologist, politician, and statesman Ralf Dahrendorf, who is a former member of the German parliament, a secretary of state in its Foreign

Office, and a commissioner in the European Commission. Dahrendorf is unusual in the fact that he is equally prominent in Britain as both an academic and a public sociologist. In 1993 he was made a life peer of the realm by Queen Elizabeth. While Brazil holds the distinction of being the first state to elect a sociologist as its head, Germany may technically stake its claim to that title since Theodor Heuss, the first president of the Federal Republic, considered one of the nation's most prominent statesmen of the postwar era, was a noted member of the German Sociological Association.

In France sociology is also held in high esteem, thanks to the combined academic repute and civic engagement of scholars such as Alain Touraine, Pierre Rosanvallon, Raymond Boudon, and, of course, Pierre Bourdieu. They work in a tradition of active engagement that goes back to the main founder of the discipline in France, Émile Durkheim. In Britain, although nonsociologists and journalists like to carp at sociologists, the long tradition of active engagement by sociologists there has earned grudging respect for the discipline. In America, it is the rare sociologist who becomes politically involved with national politics.

Can sociologists ever escape their sociological training and imagination in public sociological work? Should they even try to? The two most famous politically engaged sociologists of the second half of the century seem, at first sight, to offer contradictory responses to this question. Pierre Bourdieu, who at his death in 2002 was arguably the world's most famous and influential sociologist, insisted in both his words and his deeds—especially during the last, politically militant decade of his life—that the sociologist necessarily brings his or her specialized training to social and political work in the public sphere. Loïc Wacquant, Bourdieu's collaborator and a leading interpreter, tells us that "Bourdieu continually fused scientific inquiry and political activism. Doing social science was always for him an indirect way of doing politics: what changed over time is the dosage of those two elements and the degree of *scientific sublimation* of his political pulsions" (Wacquant 2004). Further, sociologists have a moral obligation to bring their training to work in the public sphere, because it is precisely when sociology moves from the abstract to the publicly engaged, the "nitty gritty," as Bourdieu calls it, that it becomes a powerful means of personal liberation from the external and internalized forces of domination in modern capitalist society. As he himself wrote:

> I believe that when sociology remains at a highly abstract and formal level, it contributes nothing. When it gets down to the nitty gritty of real life,

however, it is an instrument that people can apply to themselves for quasi-clinical purposes. The true freedom that sociology offers is to give us a small chance of knowing what game we play and of minimizing the ways in which we are manipulated by the forces of the field in which we evolve, as well as by the embodied social forces that operate from within us. I am not suggesting that sociology solves all the problems in the world, far from it, but that it allows us to discern the sites where we do indeed enjoy a degree of freedom and those where we do not. (Bourdieu and Wacquant 1992)

But consider, now, the second-most-famous sociologist of the second half of the twentieth century and, as the only member of the profession to ever lead a country, the most powerful: Fernando Henrique Cardoso, who became president of Brazil after a landslide victory in 1994. (On Cardoso's sociology and its relation to his politics, see Kane 2004.) Cardoso was for most of his adult life a leading neo-Marxian academic sociologist, one of the founders of the dependency school of Third World development studies, and a former president of the International Sociological Association (Cardoso 1978).

So what happened when a neo-Marxian sociologist became president of one of the world's largest countries? He became a leading advocate of neoliberal, market-driven reconstruction of his economy. I have no record of what Bourdieu thought of this transformation, but I suspect that his views, if available, would be unprintable. Using the policy prescriptions of free-market economics, Cardoso was enormously successful at reducing inflation and restoring fiscal stability to Brazil, and he became the darling of his nation's entrepreneurial elite and the International Monetary Fund. In fairness, he also consolidated Brazil's transition to full democracy, a major achievement in its own right. However, assessed in terms of neo-Marxian sociology, or even mainstream American liberal sociology, which focuses on inequality and improvements in the provision of basic needs to the mass of the population, Cardoso's regime was a failure. Brazil remained at the end of his presidency one of the most unequal economies in the world, its bourgeoning *favellas* vast and hellish urban jungles of unimaginable misery, its African-descent population—by most measures, the majority—mired in poverty and utterly excluded from a racist elite whose only counterpart is apartheid South Africa, a condition made worse, until recently, by the country's bizarre dominant national narrative of racial democracy.

How could this have happened? What does it convey about the limits of politically engaged sociology? According to a now-famous report in the Brazilian daily *Folha de S. Paulo*, which has acquired the status of a

Brazilian urban myth and Third World intellectual legend, Cardoso, while serving as finance minister prior to winning the presidency, told a group of businessmen deeply curious about his sociological writings that they could safely "forget what I wrote." Cardoso has denied ever making such a statement, but what remains undeniable is that he ditched every tenet of the dependency theory he had so ardently advocated for most of his academic career as a sociologist (see Goertzel 1995).

Cardoso's experience made painfully clear the political and policy irrelevance of most macrosociological thought on the sociology of development. The problem of dependency theory was not so much that it was erroneous—although many have their doubts—but that it explained the realities of Third World underdevelopment at such a high level of systemic abstraction that there was nothing one could do with it when placed in a position of power, or of advising those in power. Cardoso also learned quickly where his theory was most deficient—that it made no room for human agency.

I learned this from my own experiences as special advisor to the late prime minister Michael Manley, whose democratic socialist government attempted the radical transformation of postcolonial Jamaica during the 1970s. I knew Manley long before he became prime minister of Jamaica in 1972, and in our dinners and many conversations with each other he was especially interested in the Caribbean version of dependency theory that social scientists belonging to the Caribbean New World group, myself included, had developed while teaching at the University of the West Indies. Unlike Cardoso, Manley continued to take dependency theory seriously after becoming prime minister and even wrote several books on the subject while still in office. It didn't work. In fact, the consequences were disastrous. His call for a new world economic order—which is the only logical policy implication of dependency theory—was grandiose and engendered enormous tensions both externally, especially with the United States, and internally. Castigating the local managerial elite as a comprador class is not a good idea when you are introducing a vast number of new programs requiring managerial talent, especially when that managerial class has easy exit to North America. Maligning the International Monetary Fund with rhetoric taken from unequal exchange theory has unfortunate consequences if your foreign earnings are exhausted and the exchange rate of your currency is plummeting. Dependency theory, in short, worked wonderfully in graduate seminars. As the foundation of real policies in the real world, it was a nonstarter.

Unfortunately, much the same holds for the policy implications of most contemporary sociological theories. The problem with sociology is that it does not take personal agency seriously, even though it has become fashionable to note the need to take account of it in recent scholarship. However, the subject is treated at an almost metaphysical level in discussions of the so-called duality of structure and agency. In theoretical terms, scholars who talk about agency nonetheless proceed to develop theories of revolution and social movements devoid of ideology or human leadership. In practical terms, sociology remains highly suspicious of all notions of personal initiative and responsibility. Indeed, it is routine to castigate anyone foolish enough to take agency seriously as a reactionary bent on blaming the victim, as I have discovered in my attempts to do so in my studies and academic talks on the problems of gender and familial relations among African Americans.

I suggest that this is the real reason why sociology finds itself marginalized today in the United States and not, as Burawoy argues, the fact that the country is moving to the right while sociology is moving leftward. Of course, if, as I suspect, Burawoy holds that taking personal responsibility seriously is a right-wing move, then he is correct. And that, I fear, is the problem. Sociology has condemned itself to a version of public action that is out of this world. It does not even apply to communist China anymore.

But sociology's version of public action is a dogma that the discipline seems suicidally committed to, and it explains why the vast majority of leading sociologists largely shun political and other active engagement, even in areas where they have devoted a considerable amount of academic energy. Nowhere was this more evident than in the marginalization of the discipline during the major shift in welfare policy in the mid-1990s. It will be recalled that for decades prior to the 1996 welfare reform act (known officially as the Personal Responsibility and Work Opportunity Reconciliation Act), sociologists had insisted with extraordinary unanimity that the poor, especially the black poor, could never learn to fend for themselves without major government subsidy, that poverty was wholly the result of structural factors, that talk of welfare dependency and personal responsibility was reactionary, and that the only decent policy for the poor was to give them more of what they lacked, money, until such time as the radical restructuring of the economy allowed for their final transition from poverty. Even scholars who argued for a more interactive approach, in which historically inherited and institutional structures had to be interpreted in light of their internalized effects on the poor by means of which the poor became the agents of their own victimization, were dismissed as callous reactionaries. No matter that in Europe nearly all radical sociologists took such a view as given, Bourdieu's notion of *habitus* being only one way of phrasing this commonplace.

It was because of this disciplinary dogma that sociologists ended up condemning the welfare reform act and predicting catastrophic consequences as a result of its implementation. As the world now knows, nothing of the sort took place. For all its transitional problems, the welfare reform act has been a major policy success. Millions of poor people were tugged into assuming responsibility for their own lives and found, to their great personal satisfaction and relief, that they could make it on their own. Most ex–welfare recipients now insist that the act was the best thing that ever happened to them. This entire episode has been an acute embarrassment for the discipline, something that it has yet to come to terms with. Amazingly, instead of engaging in serious disciplinary self-scrutiny, many sociologists are still carping and sniping at the "failures" of the act. Most, however, have quietly retreated to their offices and classrooms, where their *one-sided* structural explanations can go unchallenged by reality.

CONCLUSION

In this essay I have argued that there are three broad and overlapping classes of public sociology: the professional, the discursive, and the active, or civic. I have suggested that the discipline emerged in Europe as a publicly engaged endeavor and has remained so outside of America. Unfortunately, in America, where most sociologists work, a different course has been followed. Up to the middle of the last century, American sociologists were very engaged, especially in professional and discursive ways. This tradition, however, was deliberately discouraged and even maligned after midcentury with the development of scientistic sociology and the expansion and professionalization of the discipline. It is the passing of that earlier tradition that I mourned in my article "The Last Sociologist" (Patterson 2002), on David Riesman. Whatever Burawoy may say, however much he may huff and puff to the contrary, the fact remains that there is no place in contemporary sociology for the modern equivalent of a Weber or a Mills or a Riesman. There are still people who work in that great tradition, but they go by other professional names and earn their keep by other means.

I have, additionally, taken issue with Burawoy's contention that the reason sociologists are not more publicly involved is that the country has moved to the right while sociology has moved leftward. This is a romantic conceit. I have proposed, instead, that the real reason the discipline is so conspicuously absent from major public engagements (always allowing for the relatively few overworked exceptions), especially in active policy and practice, is to be found in certain deep-seated professional assumptions and ideological dogmas. Chief among these are the overwhelming structural bias of sociological thought; the high level of abstraction on which most explanations of the world are offered; the fatal decision by gatekeepers, in the turn to scientism, to model the discipline on experimental physics rather than on biology; the subsequent insistence by professional journals that every account of reality be subsumed under covering theories; the perverse reluctance to incorporate rigorous inductive disciplines such as demography and criminology; the stupidly arrogant denigration and rejection of applied work by the leading departments of the discipline; and the refusal to acknowledge the vital *interactive* role of real human agency—real choices, real personal responsibility, real individual freedom, real preferences, real values—in the people they study and write about, even as they hypocritically exercise precisely such agency in their own competitive lives and expect it, indeed demand it, from their own loved ones and others close to them.

REFERENCES

Bourdieu, Pierre, and Loïc Wacquant. 1992. *Invitation to Reflexive Sociology.* Chicago: University of Chicago Press.

Burawoy, Michael. 2005. "2004 Presidential Address: For Public Sociology." *American Sociological Review* 70: 4–28.

Cardoso, Fernando Henrique. 1978. *Dependency and Development in Latin America.* Berkeley: University of California Press.

Carles, Pierre (director). 2001. *Sociology Is a Combat Sport.* Bio-documentary on Pierre Bourdieu.

Collins, Patricia Hill. 1986. "Learning from the Outsider Within: The Sociological Significance of Black Feminist Thought." *Social Problems* 33 (6): 14–32.

———. 2000. *Black Feminist Thought: Knowledge, Consciousness, and the Politics of Empowerment.* New York: Routledge.

Das, Veena, ed. 1990. *Mirrors of Violence: Communities, Riots, and Survivors in South Asia.* Delhi: Oxford University Press.

Frankel, Jeffrey. 2003. "Advice to a Fledgling Economic Adviser." *Financial Times,* 30 March.

Gans, Herbert. 1988. *Middle American Individualism: The Future of Liberal Democracy.* New York: The Free Press.

Goertzel, Ted. 1995. "President Cardoso Reflects on Brazil and Sociology." *Footnotes,* November.

Habermas, Jurgen. 1970. "The Scientization of Politics and Public Opinion." In *Toward a Rational Society: Student Protest, Science, and Politics,* J. Habermas, chap. 5. Boston: Beacon Press.

———. 1991. *The Structural Transformation of the Public Sphere.* Cambridge, MA: MIT Press.

Haney, David Paul. N.d. (1998). "Democratic Ideals, Scientific Identities, and the Struggle for a Public Sociology in the United States, 1945–1962." PhD diss., University of Texas, Austin.

Kane, Richard F. 2004. "The Sociology and Politics of Fernando Henrique Cardoso." Master's thesis, Illinois State University.

Kelley, Robin D. G. 2002. *Freedom Dreams: The Black Radical Imagination.* Boston: Beacon.

Lieberson, Stanley, and Freda Lynn. 2002. "Barking Up the Wrong Branch: Scientific Alternatives to the Current Model of Sociological Science." *Annual Review of Sociology* 28: 1–19.

Mills, C. Wright. 1959. *The Sociological Imagination.* New York: Oxford.

Oommen, T. K. 1990. *State and Society in India: Studies in Nation-Building.* Newbury Park, CA: Sage.

Patterson, Orlando. 2002. "The Last Sociologist." *New York Times,* 19 May.

Riesman, David. 1950. *The Lonely Crowd: A Study of the Changing American Character.* With N. Glazer and R. Denny. New Haven, CT: Yale University Press.

Singh, Yogendra. 1984. *Image of Man: Ideology and Theory in Indian Sociology.* Delhi: Chanakya Publications.

Wacquant, Loïc. 2004. "Pointers on Pierre Bourdieu and Democratic Politics," *Constellations* 11(1).

Weiss, Carol H. 1993. "The Interaction of the Sociological Agenda and Public Policy." In *Sociology and the Public Agenda,* ed. W. J. Wilson, 23–39. Newbury Park, CA: Sage.

ANDREW ABBOTT

For Humanist Sociology

Michael Burawoy's presidential address to the American Sociological Association takes us beyond the fulminations of the past, bringing open-mindedness and magnanimity to conversations long shrill and angry. One could quarrel about details. But Burawoy's breadth and statesmanship call us away from minor things, directing us to his major conceptual argument: the crossing of a means/ends distinction with an inside/outside distinction to produce the fourfold classification of professional, policy, public, and critical sociology. This fourfold classification—extended by a dynamic interpretation of the four as mutually reconcilable and even mutually reinforcing enterprises—seems to me to be Burawoy's major intellectual contribution.

With this analysis, however, I have some serious problems. To be sure, none of my problems qualifies my admiration for Burawoy's intervention, both as a fresh analysis and as an act of statesmanship. All the same, my problems ultimately add up to a deep disagreement.

From the outset, I worry about Burawoy's implicit association between critique/reflexivity and left politics. Nearly all the examples he invokes to illustrate critical and public sociology are on the left, and nearly all of what he deems professional and policy sociology is politically quietist or on the right. A dutiful magnanimity papers this over at times, for example in the citation of Linda Waite's conservative book on marriage (this volume, 41). But in the end the argument pretty much assumes that all critical and reflexive thought in sociology is and will be on the left.

This assumption seems problematic on several counts. First, the roles could be reversed. Does Burawoy want to argue that in a strong and successful socialist state—there have been some, and we can hope there will be some more—critical sociology would take the form of being even further to the left (in standard terms) than that state itself? Would not the core of critical sociology in such a place rather be an attack on the dangers of excessive and imposed equality—its lack of aspiration and motivation; its quelling of passions intellectual, artistic, and spiritual; its inability to imagine great new meanings for the future? This was the critique of democracy in Tocqueville's *Democracy in America* (1835–40), as it was the critique of mass society in Ortega y Gasset's *The Revolt of the Masses* (1932), and the core of Schumpeter's case against socialism in *Capitalism, Socialism, and Democracy* (1942). It seems to me that Burawoy has to accept these kinds of writings as critical sociology and hence to abandon his strongly implicit (even if explicitly denied) claim that all critique is on the left.

Not only is it possible to envision societies in which critique is not on the left; it is also clearly possible for sociology in this society to be highly reflexive without being right or left at all, a possibility Burawoy's four types do not admit. The easiest example for me here is my own experience in developing a critique of the temporality of variables-based sociology and in producing an alternative methodology in the guise of "narrative positivism" (Abbott 1992). On the one hand, this project does not fit Burawoy's Lakatosian model of "professional sociology." It was not only profoundly critical of mainstream professional knowledge but also highly reflexive, looking carefully at the assumptions behind our practices and what those assumptions imply about our ways of conceiving of the social world. Yet on the other hand, it was not politically critical; as far as I was concerned it was founded on the purely intellectual question of how it is that we think about value over time, rather than on my moral or social values about temporality or anything else. Thus this line of work was not critical sociology in Burawoy's sense, but at the same time it wasn't professional sociology either. It was neither. Or perhaps it was both.

To be sure, the popularity of my critique of the positivist mainstream arose from its political utility to others—those who wanted to attack standard methods for political reasons. This explains why my turning from pure critique to creating new methods put me out of favor with (at least some of) the left. "Narrative positivism" was roundly criticized by my erstwhile admirers because it was not founded on the belief (theirs) that what made narrative important as methodology was that it gave voice to the subaltern. In their eyes I was wrong to see narrative as "merely" an alternative way of conceiving the social process.[1]

Now to be sure, subsequent reflection has persuaded me that one could make the case that there was a values critique implicit in this strand of my work; recoding human individuals as the mere intersections of reified variables did turn out to be an important—perhaps the most important—way that social scientists contributed to the formation of mass society. Therefore, to take a stand against variables-based methods was in its own way a rebellion against the massification and dehumanization of people. But that certainly wasn't my original intent.

So not only is reflexive work not necessarily left; it can also be to all intents and purposes apolitical. These facts raise problems for Burawoy because in the course of his analysis he more or less conflates the normative, the moral, and the political under the one head of the critical. By identifying critique with leftness, he equates (as we have seen already) a particular politics with all of reflexivity. And since he attributes the legitimacy of critical sociology to its moral vision, he in effect also asserts that only opposition (i.e., critique) is morally justified. It follows from this argument (and from Burawoy's assignment of scientific norms as the legitimacy basis of professional sociology) that one cannot be in the professional mainstream and have moral vision or justification. Yet it is obviously possible to choose—morally, reflexively, and critically—to be in the dominant mainstream. One can be a heedless mainstream sociologist and even a cowardly one. But one can also be in the mainstream for moral reasons as profound as those that put others in opposition.

These worrisome problems about the conflation of reflexive, critical, and moral work in sociology set the stage for my more fundamental difference with Burawoy, which concerns our diagnoses of sociology's problem. He thinks sociology's problem is in the nonacademic sphere. I think it is in the academic one. He is willing to separate instrumental and reflexive knowledge. I am not. These differences have profound consequences for our views of the state of the discipline.

Burawoy takes sociology's great problem to be its underachievement in and indeed its undervaluing of a reflexive engagement with general public issues on their own terms. He feels we have lost our presence in the public sphere. In my view, by contrast, sociology's problem is not with the inside/outside dimension of Burawoy's fourfold table but with the means/ends one. In my view, the problem is that sociology's academic leaders have adopted the distinction between instrumental and reflexive work that Burawoy adopts here. (Indeed, I think he makes this distinction because the people he is discussing make it.) I believe this distinction to be a disastrous error. Not only do conspicuous empirical exceptions to it exist. More important, the division itself is both a cognitive mistake and a normative delict, because sociology is simultaneously a cognitive and a moral enterprise. It is precisely by ignoring this fact and letting critical and instrumental production separate themselves in the academy—in terms of who does them, in terms of what kinds of projects involve them, in terms of the intellectual relations of production themselves—that sociologists have opened themselves to the pathologies that Burawoy sees: self-referentiality and servility on the "instrumental" side and dogmatism and faddishness on the "reflexive" one. These happen not because "good" versions of instrumental and reflexive work have somehow degenerated into something less than themselves but because the two should not be separated in the first place. There are no "good" versions of purely instrumental or reflexive work.

I leave aside the task of demonstrating at length that sociology is a cognitive or intellectual enterprise, in large part because Burawoy himself does not problematize this assertion. When he says at one point that "few would . . . defend pursuing knowledge simply for knowledge's sake" (this volume, 33), he is assuming that sociology is at least a cognitive enterprise and that the main issue is whether we are cognitive alone or cognitive and something else besides. Thus, we both take the cognitive strand of sociology for granted. Now, for Burawoy the reason this cognitive strand is not the only one is that he thinks sociology must serve a greater end or further purpose than mere knowledge. (That is, he wants to move to a different position on his inside/outside dimension.) But for me, the reason sociology cannot be an internalist, purely cognitive enterprise involves Burawoy's means/ends dimension. It has to do with the fact that sociology is inevitably value-laden.

The standard proof of the value-ladenness of sociology begins with the insight that an individual's (e.g., a social scientist's) ideas are situationally determined. We all analyze from a particular social location, and imagining that we can escape that location and its values is a delusion. This is true enough. Indeed, the degree to which it is true often escapes us. Even such abstract and apparently neutral decisions as choosing what to explain are essentially value choices. Equality is the most common example. We try to explain inequality because we think equality is a natural state of affairs. But thinking equality is a natural state of affairs is obviously a value judgment on our part, not something that suggests itself "naturally" in the lifeworld. There is no particular cognitive reason to expect equality—or inequality, for that matter—in the lifeworld.

Such a value choice need not be left/right, as is the equality/inequality one. Thus, we may think that the important thing in life is to end up well. In that case, we will appraise an interval of time by looking at the level of welfare at the end of it. Or we may by contrast think that what matters is to maximize our enjoyment (or that of others) starting from now. In that case we will appraise a future by looking at the full curve of potential enjoyment through it and pulling future rewards back into the present via discounting. This is a thoroughly value-laden choice—the choice between now and later—but it is not a right/left choice. Indeed, the supposedly conservative discipline of economics favors the dynamic "now," while the liberal discipline of sociology favors the bourgeois "later."[2]

Yet however powerful it is, the situational determination of knowledge is not the heart of sociology's value-laden character. There is a much deeper—and much simpler—reason for it, one that guarantees that any sociological output is "positioned," even if those who produce it are somehow capable of the famous view from nowhere. This reason is the value-laden quality of the social process itself.

The aim of social science is to explain or understand social life. But the social process is constituted—among other things—of values; human life as an activity consists of assigning values to social things and then pursuing them. This means that even an arbitrary choice of explanandum will involve taking something as natural, as not needing explanation; the act of explanation categorizes social phenomena into things needing explanation and things not. Since the things so categorized themselves involve values (because values permeate the social process), the act of explanation entails implicit value-choices even if investigators are magically universalist. Indeed, even if explananda were selected arbitrarily, that selection would still impose values. The value-ladenness of sociology thus lies not so much in the imposed values of the sociologists as in the fact that the social process is itself a process of values: not so much in the knower as in the known. There is, therefore, literally no such thing as "professional sociology"—a sociology without any values in it. Even the most apparently objective categories of analysis are just so many congealed social values. One cannot even perceive the social process as it actually is without engaging it morally (whether one intends to do so or not), because it is itself in large part a process of moral values.

Now, this does not prevent sociologists from acting as if this were not true. And when Burawoy's "professionals" act as if they can do a purely abstract sociology that involves no values, what happens is exactly what happens to anyone who misspecifies a regression equation. The value-ladenness of the underlying enterprise finds its way out into their results under the guise of something else. This is obviously what is involved in the marriage debate mentioned above. But it is involved also in the argument mentioned earlier against positivism; by coding people into reified categories, positivism contributes in turn to the reification of those categories—racial, ethnic, socioeconomic, occupational, and so on. By ignoring values, that is, it hides them, transforms them, presents ideology as fact, and so on. The step to what Burawoy calls "servility"—to the simple service of power—is then a very short one; to do research on delinquency is to accept the funders' definition of delinquency, and so on. This is why profound inquiry does not long survive in heavily funded areas; you have to sell part of your intellectual birthright to get the mess of pottage from the National Institutes of Health or the National Institute of Justice or whomever.

The same problem obtains in reverse for those on the critical side who ignore the reality of sociology's cognitive strand and the intellectual power of the standards the "professionals" set. The major schools of critique have, in general, lacked the technical skills to attack mainstream positivism on its own turf. As a result they have resorted to simply announcing the crisis and dissolution of positivism, a crisis and dissolution completely in the eyes of the beholders. By conducting their attack on positivistic service of power at such a general level, the critics did not hit their opponents in a way that hurt them. By contrast, the mainstream was much more worried by reflexively generated forays into radically new types of formal methods: by Harrison White and his many students into structural network analysis; by David Heise, Peter Abell, and myself into narrative positivism; by Charles Ragin into Boolean logics; and now by the hosts of young people flooding into agent-based modeling.

In short, I argue that sociology is at one and the same time a cognitive and a normative enterprise. When we pretend that it is not, our work becomes arbitrarily deformed. Note that this means that I simply do not accept Burawoy's distinction—footnoted by him to Weber and the Frankfurt School, but as easily footnoted to the Parsons of *The*

Structure of Social Action (1937)—between means and ends in social life. While this is sometimes a useful distinction to deploy ad hoc, to reify it into a general model for knowledge seems wrong. What are means for one person or society or time are ends for another. For example, pace Burawoy's casual remark earlier noted, history is littered with people and societies and institutions for whom knowledge was an end in itself. (Good thing, too, if you think any of the heritage of Western antiquity is worth having today; the Muslim savants and Irish monks who preserved the Western tradition were not "public scholars" in Burawoy's sense.) And history is equally littered with people and societies and institutions for whom Burawoian critique and morality were a means to something else they thought more important—salvation, health, domination, and so on. To accept a means/ends distinction as anything other than a local analytical tool buys into a reified functionalism that many of us have spent our careers trying to dismantle.

Now, one might argue that we can justify Burawoy's separation of instrumental and reflexive knowledge by some practical strategy. Division of labor is his own candidate. For him, the cognitive and the value strands of the sociological enterprise can be carried on by largely different groups of people—a "mainstream" of professional sociology and a "loyal opposition" of critical sociologists—as long as they are in a continuous dialogue. I disagree. This cannot work, for exactly the reasons Burawoy has himself argued. To become purely one kind of sociologist, instrumental or reflexive, is to face at once the overwhelming pressures that conduce automatically to the pathologies Burawoy outlines: self-referentiality and servility on the instrumental side, dogmatism and faddishness on the reflexive one. To assume that these will be overcome by dialogue is a kind of pluralist wishful thinking. It may be what is rhetorically required of leaders of the field—presidents of associations and editors of major journals—but do we really believe it?

If division of labor is not an option, could we then think that one could articulate these different activities with the professional life cycle? Perhaps we might do professional sociology as young people, then reflect (and perhaps regret) as we grow older. But there are those who start with critique (as to some extent did Burawoy), then move on to more Lakatosian, professional work. Similarly, one could save public sociology for late in life on the model that one might then actually know something useful. But it is quite clear that many young people find that public sociology—indeed what we might call advocacy sociology—provides an essential role for them. Indeed, I don't think either of these life course models is practicable; any sociologist must be at all times both instrumental and reflexive (let's call these "cognitive" and "normative"). The damage that is done to the cognitive enterprise of sociology by ignoring the value-laden character of the thing we study is done immediately. It's not something we gradually think our way out of over a lifetime. It is something toward which we must be continually vigilant. The same is true in reverse for the comparable damage done by being purely critical.

If we recognize, then, that academic sociological research must inevitably be both instrumental and reflexive, we must ask what is the right way to enact this duality in practice. The simplest answer seems to be that cognitive and normative thinking must be perpetually succeeding phases in the research process. Any project and any scholarly life must see a continual succession of the one, then the other, then the one, and so on. We have to alternate between reflection—questioning our assumptions and in particular our value assumptions—and routine cognitive analysis.

But as my earlier discussion showed, this constant questioning of ourselves and our "biases" can deal with only that portion of the value-ladenness of sociology that arises from the position of the knower. It does not deal with the portion that arises from the intrinsically value-laden character of the thing known—of the social process itself as a process of values. To do that, it seems to me, we need to imagine a nonpolitical basis for moral perception. We must envision political commitment as something that can be added to the underlying moral stance required by all sociology, something added when scholars wish to take positions on behalf of particular publics. That is, I want to insist on the separation between morality and politics that Burawoy denies. And although I argued earlier that reflexivity can occur within purely instrumental (Burawoy's sense) sociology, my current logic implies that such sociology must nonetheless fail if it does not include a moral dimension, because the very social process that we analyze is constituted of value-materials and so we cannot actually know it without perceiving these in moral terms. Yet we do not wish to simply adopt particular versions of those values in the process of analysis, for that will politicize our work ex ante, and as Burawoy correctly notes, that politicization in turn undercuts its "expert" legitimacy in public forums.

One resolves this dilemma by taking what I shall call the humanist position. On this argument, the social process is made up of human beings, and our analysis of them must aim at being humane. This doesn't mean, for example, that we can't code variables trying to describe these people. (That is, positivism could be humane in my sense.) But it does mean that we have to ask ourselves about the ways in which our doing such coding does violence to the nature of these people as moral beings in the value and meaning space that is inevitably theirs by virtue of their humanity. And we have to modify our practice continuously, not in the direction of making it more and more "scientific" or "clean," but in the direction of making it more and more humane. This does not necessarily mean vaguer, fuzzier, more ethnographic, and so on as is customarily assumed (e.g., as it was by my left critics mentioned earlier). It does mean "giving voice to the subject"—not necessarily by the quaint but absurd procedure of quoting him or her at length out of context, but by figuring out how to translate the moral activity of that subject into our own ways of imagining what is happening to him or her in the social process.

This project of humane translation can, I think, avoid the Scylla of self-referential disengagement and the Charybdis of dogmatic politicization. Any subject I study is a human being, deserving of the same dignity and care I would take in understanding myself. Yet all are other to me in various ways and at various levels and can be reached only by a continuing effort at translation. As a humanist, however, I have to accept whatever it is that I am trying to translate into my world in order to understand it. Here, it seems to me, is where I part company with the "political" position on reflexivity. If I set myself Terence's rule that nothing human will be alien to me, I am going to be translating into my own universe of meaning not only some wonderful and comprehensible and excellent things whose acquaintance will broaden and develop me, but also some horrible and strange and frightening things. These last will include not only things I am politically opposed to but also immoral and evil things that are nonetheless the products of the social process and that must, at the least, be humanely understood in order to be permanently eradicated (by, say, imagining a social process that has guarantees against producing them. It may well be that the defining mark of what is evil is that it cannot be translated by a humane effort, although if I admit that, we are perhaps almost back to the identity of politics and morals that I am trying to escape.).

In summary, I am making a case for sociology as a humanistic, inherently moral enterprise. I do not think that this obliges us to some particular methodology. There is no reason why we should not conceive of a positivism that is humanistic by relaxing some of the stricter assumptions of classical positivism. Indeed, this was my aim in "narrative positivism" in the first place—to make a space in positivist methods for the sequential framework through which we actually experience our lives. The belief that humanism as a moral stance obliges us methodologically is another one of these unnecessary conflations that have so damaged the sociological understanding in the last forty years. (For an extended analysis, see Abbott 2001, chap. 1.)

But I should also underscore the difference between taking a political position as a sociologist and adopting a humanistic (moral) stance as a sociologist. In the former, which I take to be the core of Burawoy's public sociology, the sociologist brings his or her skills to the aid of some particular project of action that he or she judges to be a worthy end of human life. But there is extensive disagreement in the lifeworld about what exactly are the worthy ends of human life. So this "sociology in aid of a particular project" takes what we may call a political position. By contrast, the humanist sociologist is interested in understanding the social world (as a value enterprise) rather than in changing it. (I have discussed this position at some length in Abbott 2001, chap. 7.) The humanist thinks it presumptuous of the sociologist to judge the rights and wrongs of others. He or she starts from the presumption that the other is a version of humanity, to be granted the dignity of being taken seriously on his or her own terms, to be understood or translated by whatever methodology into something recognizable both in his or her original world and in that of the analysis. A humanist sociologist is hesitant to judge that others "have false consciousness," that is, that we the sociologists know their own needs better than they themselves do. It is in this latter sense—understanding the other in terms of (definitionally imperfect) translation into our own world—that sociology does indeed constitute, in my view, the pursuit of knowledge for knowledge's sake. Burawoy's mistake in dismissing this position flows from his belief that the only form of moral behavior is political behavior in the broadest sense. That is, he thinks that a moral person who understands the moral nature of the social process must of necessity want to change it. I think he is wrong about that. The project of understanding the social process—which is in itself a moral process and cannot be otherwise analyzed—is inherently a moral project, whether we go on to exercise our undoubted political right to urge change or not.

This is the core of my disagreement with Burawoy's argument. But beyond it lie some more vague concerns, not so much disagreements as disquiets. One of these involves the differing rhythms of academic and political life. General political life moves with a rhythm that differs from both the steady aging that governs individual academic careers and the equally steady twenty-five-year cycle that governs most subdisciplines in sociology. Today's senior generation entered sociology in the heyday of American liberalism and has watched the society move ineluctably to the right for almost their entire careers. Once to the left of our faculty, we are now to the left of our students. But we should not be trying (as Burawoy seems to be trying) to permanently define public sociology in terms of that particular (and particularly awful) experience. Consider the role of Anthony Giddens in the halcyon days after the avalanche victory of New Labour in 1997. Here was a public sociologist indeed, but one in power—closely connected with the prime minister, theorist of the "third way," and eventual recipient of a life peerage. We have to realize that the temporal disjunctures between academic and political life will inevitably make the relation of public and professional sociology a complex and erratic one.

Second, Burawoy to a large extent ignores (as I do, following him) that we are in the middle of a large and largely imponderable change in the nature, distribution, ownership, and structure of knowledge and expertise. The visible surface of this is, of course, the ever-growing Internet, the digitization of huge amounts of text, and the increase of licensing, patenting, and other types of capitalist control of knowledge. Deeper underneath is the transformation of our production processes—research, writing, and even thinking—occasioned first by the personal computer and canned statistics, and later by Google and PowerPoint. Deeper still is the steady and quite rapid drift of the entire culture toward visual rather than printed media and toward oral rather than written communication.

It is quite impossible to predict even the intermediate outcome of this process. But its impact on academic life and practice is already immense. It has brought us students without the reading and writing skills we brought to college, just as we lack their visual and to some extent even their oral skills. It has enabled us to publish two or three times the amount that our teachers published in their professional lifetimes, whether or not we have two or three times as much to say. It has changed our writing process from painful, linear creation into the more facile editing of recorded speech. It has seduced us into performing analyses of whose mathematical or conceptual foundations we have only the haziest idea. It has led us to use information of a quality that would have horrified our own advisors. It has so overwhelmed us with material to read that we seldom read anything very carefully.

Now there are lots of reasons for all these things, and there are differing degrees and extents to differing parts of this process. But the fact is that academic production of all four of Burawoy's kinds has over the last thirty or so years been turned—with the help of magnificent new tools and with the eager assistance of academics themselves—into a game of making out such as Burawoy himself so well described in *Manufacturing Consent* (1979): a giant speedup combined with massive overproduction and loss of quality control. Because of this, the very shape and nature of knowledge are changing. We should not be thinking about the future of any part of sociology without recognizing this development.

A third issue concerns our intellectual capital. The reorganization of library and information resources means that more and more of the previously common body of knowledge is subject to copyright and ownership. Resources that used to be dispersed and uncontrollable are concentrated and subject to controls ranging from licensure to simple closure. This concentration presents extraordinary opportunities for manipulation; if all copies of a book are online, it is not particularly difficult to make the book say something different in 2025 than it said in 2023. It is similarly easy to make all the old books disappear. Of course, focal search will always find things, but we all know that what our students look at is what is most easily found on the Internet. And who is going to decide what is easily found?

One of the great safeguards of scholarly freedom of thought has been the distributed, uncentralized, and often random nature of academic knowledge. This is quickly disappearing. The rapid turning of classroom instruction into a simulacrum of television via PowerPoint and similar software will bring with it an extraordinary concentration and narrowing of presented viewpoints, far beyond the mild-mannered textbook system, whose books written by marketing committees now seem almost emancipatory. In such a world the discipline really has to think about its intellectual capital, its ideas. Where are they going to be stored, propagated, recreated? How do we defend variety and difference in a world where powerful actors control more and more of our knowledge resources? It's all very well to talk about freeware and the democracy of the Internet. But most of us can remember when there were several operating systems, numerous database systems, dozens of word-processing systems, and so on. Now there's Microsoft and a bunch of pygmies. If Google has its way, the same could be true of libraries. I'm not sure that's a good idea.

In this context it is worth remembering—and Burawoy clearly has remembered—that one of the discipline's most important structural resources is the collection of tenured positions in major universities. I quite agree with him that these positions should not be wasted on the corrupt policy sociology into which all too much professional sociology degenerates. On the other hand, I think the discipline's own internal intellectual continuity is enough under threat that it is not wise to greatly increase the level of public sociology in these departments. To hold itself together over time, the discipline needs these departments to do one thing: to train people of ability and commitment in the skills and the moral character that are necessary to sociology. It is much more important that these people get trained than that public sociology be strongly represented in elite departments. For if the training of a core group is weakened, sociology's prospects for the long run are nonexistent. And the great departments have one immense advantage in teaching: not so much their particular faculties as the simple fact that they attract groups of committed students who stimulate, challenge, support, and train each other. What matters most in these departments is the commitment to teaching, to research, and to the moral intensity of the sociological enterprise. We should think of that first, not whether these departments are public enough.

Finally, I wish to underline a crucial failure in the critical oeuvre that Burawoy so clearly admires. The deepest moral obligation of the sociological imagination is not critique, but vision. The great failure of the left in the last thirty years has been to define itself—at least within sociology—largely in terms of the amelioration of problems: the elimination of inequality, oppression, bias, degradation, and so on. Where the left imagination has failed (and of course the right has never tried, since at this point in its history it lacks imagination altogether) has been in imagining what a truly humane society could look like or, if that is impossible, what a humane social process would look like. We do not advance into the future merely by getting rid of this or that social problem, important as that may be. We advance by imagining what the future can be. Other than sporadic books here and there, the critical sociologists have not produced such visions. By contrast, Marx fired the imaginations of his time, not only because he had a painstaking (and highly "professional") instrumental analysis, and not only because he made a reflexive critique of the social science of his time, but chiefly because he had a vision of what a new society might look like. We should live up to his example.

For sociology, at least, Michael Burawoy has taken a step in that direction. He has actually proposed a new vision for our discipline. I disagree with major parts of it. But I'm very thankful that somebody, at last, has made an attempt to imagine the future. A discipline with such leadership must surely flourish.

NOTES

1. My new methods were also thought to fall away from my auspicious beginnings as a contingency theorist (i.e., my thinking in *The System of Professions* [1988]—apparently theorizing in terms of contingencies is left). This debate can be found in Hanagan and Tilly 1996 and Abbott 1996. The present piece is too short to take up the issue of what "left" and "right" really mean. I accept here the more or less vernacular usage that Burawoy seems to employ. Note that we should not allow ourselves the kind of sliding redefinition in which *left* is automatically redefined to contain everything that is democratic, humane, and emancipatory in political thinking.

2. The marriage debate that Burawoy (this volume, 41) mentions involved a "case for marriage" based on the surprisingly uncontested assumption that the purpose of erotic/family life is to end up well rather than—for example—to live intensely and die early. From the latter point of view—which would emerge under any economic model with serious discounting—there is very little "case for marriage" at all. For a detailed analysis of the temporality of outcome conceptions, see Abbott 2005.

REFERENCES

Abbott, Andrew. 1988. *The System of Professions: An Essay on the Division of Expert Labor.* Chicago: University of Chicago Press.

———. 1992. "From Causes to Events: Notes on Narrative Positivism." *Sociological Methods and Research* 20: 428–55.

———. 1996. "La Síntesis de Otros Tiempos y La Del Futuro" ("The Once and Future Synthesis," tr. E. A. Scholz). *Historia, Antropología y Fuentes Orales* 1: 31–39.

———. 2001. *Chaos of Disciplines.* Chicago: University of Chicago Press.

———. 2005. "The Idea of Outcome." In *The Politics of Method in the Human Sciences,* ed. G. Steinmetz, 393–426. Durham, NC: Duke University Press.

Burawoy, Michael. 1979. *Manufacturing Consent: Changes in the Labor Process under Monopoly Capitalism.* Chicago: University of Chicago Press.

———. 2005. "2004 Presidential Address: For Public Sociology." *American Sociological Review* 70: 4–28.

Hanagan, M., and L. A. Tilly. 1996. "Síntesis Perdida, Síntesis Reencontrada?" ("Synthesis Lost, Synthesis Regained?," tr. E. A. Scholz). *Historia, Antropología y Fuentes Orales* 1: 11–29.

Ortega y Gasset, José. 1932. *The Revolt of the Masses.* New York: Norton.

Parsons, Talcott. 1937. *The Structure of Social Action: A Study in Social Theory with Special Reference to a Group of Recent European Writers.* New York: The Free Press.

Schumpeter, Joseph A. 1942. *Capitalism, Socialism, and Democracy.* New York: Harper.

INTERDISCIPLINARITY

Whose Public Sociology?
The Subaltern Speaks, but Who Is Listening?

> This volume [W. E. B. DuBois's *Black Reconstruction in America, 1860–1880*] is announced as a "brilliantly new version" of United States history from 1860 to 1880. It is, however, in large part, only the expression of a Negro's bitterness against the injustice of slavery and racial prejudice. Source materials, so essential to any rewriting of history, have been completely ignored, and the work is based on abolition propaganda and the biased statements of partisan politicians.
>
> And the temper is as bad as the sources. . . . The result is not history but only a half-baked Marxian interpretation of the labor side of Reconstruction and a badly distorted picture of the Negroes' part in Southern life.
>
> Avery Craven (1936, 535)[1]

In his essay "For Public Sociology," Michael Burawoy has created a vision of "big-tent" sociology—a sociology that has room for everyone and in which everyone's contribution is indispensable to the success of the collective enterprise. He makes a detailed and convincing case for inclusivity and diversity as essential to the vitality of sociology. While he sees professional sociology as the bedrock, he argues that policy, critical, and public sociology inject vitality through their connection to "real life" and to alternative viewpoints and communities. The essay calls forth feelings of pride about our chosen field. It encourages us to see sociology as a community of interdependent scholars, practitioners, critics, and activists. "For Public Sociology" is also an accessible and engaging piece: it invites each of us to think about where we fit in the larger landscape of sociology. I am sure many sociologists are playing the game of classifying themselves and their colleagues within his fourfold typology of professional, policy, public, and critical sociology.

THE MAN WHO LOVED SOCIOLOGY

As a woman of color doing sociology outside of a mainstream sociology department, what struck me most immediately was how confidently Burawoy lays out a grand mapping of the field of sociology. Why does he feel qualified/entitled to define the boundaries of sociology and how it relates to the "neighboring disciplines" of economics and political science and to expound upon the "divisions of labor" within the field? Is it an accident that this grand scheme has been created by an American-based white male full professor teaching in one of the leading sociology departments in the country?

To embark on such a project requires a sense of ownership and belonging. Burawoy clearly has such a sense. Here is a man who, more than anyone I know, loves sociology and sociologists and who invests tremendous energy in training the next generation of scholars in the field. In contrast, many of us who are not in a privileged position, whether by reason of race, ethnicity, gender, institutional positioning, or status, in the academic prestige hierarchy more often lack an unalloyed sense of ownership and belonging.

Can one imagine a woman of color or a community college teacher, for example, being in a position of and having an interest in constructing a grand map of sociology? Would she be seen as someone with the broad perspective and "objectivity" needed to present a plausible mapping? Would she find a ready audience for such an effort? Or would it be assumed that her special position as a subaltern would color her views and cloud her judgment?[2] Would she be allowed to speak as a disembodied voice from nowhere in particular as Burawoy, at least in this essay, tends to do? Or would she be expected to begin by acknowledging that she is speaking from her own necessarily limited standpoint as a woman of color?

As sociologists we are aware that knowledge is always developed from a particular subject position and is therefore always partial and perspectival. Indeed, Burawoy himself acknowledges the significance of standpoint when he praises the contributions of feminist theorist Dorothy Smith and black feminist theorist Patricia Hill Collins, who have developed standpoint theory within sociology. However, historically, in sociology as in other disciplines, the standpoint of hegemonic groups tends to be acknowledged not as partial but as perspectiveless and as representing the whole—in this case "sociology"—while the standpoint of historically subordinated groups is viewed as limited and distorted, even regarding their own situation.

Thus, I cannot help but point out that the author's social position is all-important not only to the specific mapping he has produced but also to having undertaken the task at all. In particular, I would argue that his location and experience in a highly ranked sociology department in a major research university, where he has spent his entire career and also served as chair, are fundamental in shaping his concerns.

In the first place, there is the carving up of the social world into three fields—economics, political science, and sociology—each with its own sphere of intellectual focus, that is, the market, the state, and civil society. This concern for claiming a specific turf for sociology and parity with the other fields reflects not only the process of male-dominated professionalization but also the reification of boundaries through the organization of the university, which divides knowledge into discipline-based departments, relegating newer, interdisciplinary fields like ethnic studies and women's studies to the devalued margins. Within Burawoy's framework, sociology departments compete for resources and recognition on the basis of their standing in relation to other sociology departments at top-tier institutions and by advocating for the rigorousness of sociological methods and the uniqueness of sociological knowledge in relation to methods and knowledge in other social sciences.

Yet, for those working on specific topics, such as women and work, not only are these disciplinary boundaries artificial; they post obstacles to understanding. It was feminists who pointed out the way in which the conceptual separation of markets as ruled by economic factors and family/household as ruled by emotion/feeling obscured the nature and importance of unpaid labor to the economy. They pointed to the need to take into account the role of state policy in defining what constituted "real work" and the way in which the market relied on women's unpaid reproductive labor, as well as the organization of family life, to unravel gender inequality with respect to work.

A second characteristic of Burawoy's analysis is a marked bias toward looking sideways at peers and upward at superiors, that is, to elaborate on sociology's relation to the "peer" disciplines of economics and political science. These fields are rivals or even superiors in size and esteem within the university. Burawoy makes only glancing mention of anthropology and geography, which are viewed as lesser fields. He makes no mention at all of marginalized fields/departments such as ethnic studies, African American studies, or women's studies, even though these are fields in which many sociologists do their scholarship and teaching and in which some have appointments. This tendency follows the usual pattern in which the higher-status people and groups do not pay attention to and thus are unaware of the presence of those of lower status, while those of lower status usually have to pay some attention to those of higher status. In a somewhat analogous circumstance, the master can ignore the presence of the servant and remain unaware of her situation or feelings, while the servant has to be highly attuned to the master's situation and feelings.

A third feature of Burawoy's framework is the centering and elaboration of "professional sociology," which is defined as what professors with PhDs in sociology do (i.e., research and writing and teaching) in a doctoral-granting sociology department in a prestigious American university. This is the core on which all other "dependent" wings—critical, policy, and public sociology—rely for their "tools" (methods, theory, empirical findings). Burawoy is at the center of professional sociology, so naturally he would see it as the center of the world, much as American sociology sees itself as "sociology" and judges non-U.S.-based sociologies by its parochial standards.

THE WOMAN WHO WENT OUT INTO THE COLD

Since I've raised the issue of subject position, here is mine. I am an Asian American woman. During graduate school at Harvard, I studied with such éminences grises as Talcott Parsons and George Homans, but I did not find my real sociological passion until after graduate school, when I became involved in feminism and began doing studies of women and work. I spent the first half of my academic career in sociology departments at Boston University, Florida State, and SUNY-Binghamton. For the past fifteen years I have taught doctoral and undergraduate students in the Ethnic Studies and Women's Studies Departments at the University of California, Berkeley. I am not associated with the Berkeley sociology department in any way. I have, however, remained active within the discipline, as a deputy editor of *American Sociological Review* and in various appointed and elected positions in the American Sociological Association and the Society for the Study of Social Problems, but because of my location outside a sociology department, I feel distant from academic sociology. I am primarily motivated and animated by a desire to understand the deep and entangled roots of race and gender inequality in American society, and I seek to trace these roots by whatever approach seems suitable and effective. Because of my interests and my work with students from various disciplinary backgrounds, my work is increasingly historical and interdisciplinary. Finally, I am very much involved in kin relations and ethnic community activities in the San Francisco Bay Area, where my family roots were planted more than a century ago.

Writing from this perspective, I offer some observations on sociology generally and on public sociology in particular. In what follows, I use the term *public sociology* to refer to what Burawoy calls "organic public sociology." I find Burawoy's explication of two varieties of public sociology, traditional and organic, useful, but it also strikes me that using the same term, *public sociology*, to refer to both traditional and organic varieties renders the term incoherent. Traditional public sociology is what professional sociology does as part of professionalization, namely, gaining recognition as a legitimate "science" and improving its standing vis-à-vis other disciplines. The aim is to have sociologists be viewed as experts with special knowledge. Thus it is oriented primarily toward audiences that have some power to make decisions, whether as franchised citizens or as political or cultural leaders. Organic public sociology, on the other hand, is aimed at empowering subaltern groups, giving them voice, illuminating and validating their reality, and offering tools that can be used for mobilizing to make change. Importantly, organic public sociology is based not on claims of superior knowledge but on situated knowledge based on lived experiences of specific publics and on deep and thick ties between sociologists and their publics.

1. *The process of defining and mapping a discipline parallels the process of defining and mapping citizenship. Both involve matters of recognition and membership, that is, who belongs. What makes someone entitled to call herself a sociologist? Both involve boundary drawing and exclusion, that is, what is and what is not included in sociology.*

A discipline/nation defines itself relationally, that is, in relation to specific "others," who are simultaneously defined/created. Generally this is done through *contrast schema*: that is, what "is" is defined by what it is *not*. The particular contrast that Burawoy has chosen, namely political science and economics, is logical given his location in a doctoral-granting institution, where political science and economics are large, well-endowed, and predominately male departments, and sociology would like to play with the big boys in those fields. In nondoctoral institutions, other contrasts and kinships may be more salient. For example, in smaller colleges, the relevant comparison might be between sociology and psychology or anthropology, and the unique territory of sociology would be defined in terms of its focus on groups rather than the individual or on social structure rather than culture/lifeways.

The particular choice of contrasting fields is important, not least because of its gendered and racial implications. Political science and economics are both overwhelmingly male fields and are often viewed as "hard" social sciences. Setting up political science and economics as the "neighboring" (and competing) disciplines has the effect of reinforcing the relation between maleness and prestige and feeding the fear that having too many women will lower a department's standing. In comparison, psychology and anthropology have greater proportions of women, and anthropology in particular is viewed as a "soft" social science. Thus viewing anthropology as a "neighboring" and competing discipline would be less likely to reinforce maleness as a condition for prestige or to fuel a fear of having too many women.

Defining what is included in sociology simultaneously involves exclusion of what is not "real" sociology. Historically, academic sociology "professionalized" as did other fields, such as medicine, by redefining itself as rigorously "scientific" and nonpolitical, by ejecting members of marginalized groups who might lower the prestige of the field, and by setting up barriers to new entrants from marginalized groups. Several major historical studies have documented the central role played by women sociologists such as Marian Talbot, Jane Addams, Sophonisba Breckinridge, and Florence Kelley in the establishment of the Chicago school of sociology in the early twentieth century. Many of the early University of Chicago male sociologists, including the founding chair, Albion Small, were committed to social reform and participated actively in the activities of Addams's Hull House. However, the process of professionalization, particularly under the chairship of Robert Park, involved excluding "applied" sociology, social reform, and political involvement. These concerns were separated out and assigned to two new departments, home economics and social administration, headed and staffed by women sociologists (Deegan 1987; Delamont 1992). This gendered history of creating separate male and female spheres and a division of labor along gender lines is critical to understanding the roots and continued orientation of professional sociology.[3] In a sense, the early women sociologists were pioneers and champions of organic public sociology, which languished in academic sociology departments. Unfortunately, these concerns eventually also declined in the new women's fields. Home economics lost its critical edge, and social work became increasingly psychologically oriented and connected with social welfare bureaucracies.

In our own times, a similar process of excluding activist, reform, and political concerns has taken place in the wake of Third World and women's movements, which challenged the omission of people of color and women from academic canons in all academic fields, including sociology. These movements pressured universities and colleges to "diversify" faculty so that these omissions might be addressed. But, rather than leading to fundamental changes in the structure of traditional departments, pressures to diversify were diverted onto new ground, and to the formation of new departments or programs in ethnic studies, African American studies, Chicano-Latino studies, Asian American studies, women's studies, and gay, lesbian, and bisexual studies.

Predictably, there has been resistance to fully institutionalizing the new interdisciplinary programs. Initially they were not allotted their own faculty lines, so appointments to teach in these programs had to be made through traditional departments. In our own field, departments of sociology were often unwilling to hire faculty for these positions, claiming that there were no candidates who met the department's standards. For example, over the course of the 1980s, I was recruited for ethnic studies/Asian American positions at three different University of California campuses. The likely outcomes were telegraphed to me during the interview process. The chair of the San Diego sociology department told me that he firmly believed that his department "did not need to study race." A white male sociology faculty member at Santa Barbara lamented during my interview that "X" (a non-PhD historian) had not applied for the position, as he was the "only qualified" Asian American scholar. During this same period, I was offered "straight" sociology positions at various East Coast institutions, including a highly-ranked Ivy League school, so it seemed evident to me that different standards were being applied to candidates being recruited for joint ethnic studies/sociology positions than to 100 percent sociology appointments.

Requiring new interdisciplinary programs to obtain approval from established sociology departments was doomed, since important elements of traditional sociology viewed studies of race and ethnicity as intellectually inferior. Difficulties in getting faculty appointed and general foot-dragging and resistance by established departments sparked moves to departmentalize the subaltern fields, so that they could make their own appointments without being at the mercy of traditional departments. At present, there is a tension in many interdisciplinary subaltern fields between, on the one hand, desire for autonomy and, on the other, fear that "ghettoizing" race and gender concerns and activism within subaltern studies relieves sociology and other "mainstream" departments of responsibility for addressing race and gender in theory and research or diversifying their faculty.[4]

2. *Race and gender (as well as other axes of power and difference) are central organizing principles in the institutional structuring of sociology and in ordering relations among sociologists and among types and subfields of sociology.*

Organization along lines of race and gender involves both material/concrete aspects and rhetorical/ideological aspects. Burawoy adopts the term *division of labor* as a neutral term to describe how sociologists are allocated or allocate themselves among the four types of sociology. This term is very commonly used in sociology to refer to a social pattern that characterizes all societies and institutions. Within the functionalist framework, division of labor occurs because it is more efficient to have people specialize rather than having everyone do every necessary task, and it also creates social cohesion based on interdependence among members of a group or society.[5]

Division of labor, however, is a freighted term for women sociologists and sociologists of color. Whenever I see or hear the term, it conjures up images of inequality and exploitation. To state the obvious: positions in the divisions of labor are not freely chosen (individual taste/preference) or randomly assigned (luck of the draw); nor are they always assigned according to capability or merit (human capital). Rather, divisions occur systematically along lines of power and difference: male/female, black/white, middle class/working class, native/immigrant. In turn, divisions of labor help to constitute and reify categories and categorical differences. For example, work that is done mostly by women becomes "feminine" and helps to define femininity; work that is done mostly by Latino immigrants comes to epitomize "menial" and helps to define "Latino-ness." The concept of division of labor raises questions like, who gets to do the intellectual or managerial work and who has to do physical labor and follow orders? In the case of sociology, who gets to do grand theory, perform large-scale funded research, and nurture PhD students, and who gets to do work on "narrow," "less important" topics (e.g., the family,

"Asian Americans"), do community outreach, and teach large numbers of undergraduates?

Clearly, gender and race are central in defining the "who" in these questions. Here I am thinking about Burawoy's statement about the entry of women and people of color into sociology and the bringing of their concerns into the field and therefore expanding the view of sociology. He also notes that today 51 percent of PhDs are granted to women and 20 percent to racial minorities. Yet, what he doesn't say is that this level of representation of women and minorities among those with sociology doctorates is not reflected in the faculty ranks, especially in those very doctoral-granting departments. Moreover, the higher the prestige of the institution, the lower the percentage of women and minorities is likely to be. Thus, those who most closely meet the definition of doing "professional sociology" are disproportionately white and male. Moreover, to the extent that professional sociologists also have their "public sociology" moments, they are likely to do it in relation to a literate elite audience, via op-ed pieces in the *New York Times* or being interviewed on National Public Radio, while "other" sociologists are left to work with more modest outlets such as speaking at meetings of worker organizations or minority communities.

3. *Power and hierarchy are embedded in the project of mapping sociology and differentiating it into professional, policy, critical, and public wings and contribute to the cementing of inequality within sociology.*

Mapping the subtypes of sociology can be seen as an act of inclusion in that it recognizes various "wings" of sociology. However, from a subaltern perspective, it can also be seen as a way of containing and controlling them. By spelling out what kinds of knowledge each specializes in and what its audiences are, Burawoy's scheme defines the "proper" aims and activities of each wing. Thus, for example, in Burawoy's scheme, theory and primary research are the purview of professional sociology, while public sociology merely translates sociological concepts and research findings so that the public can understand them or use them to address public issues. This mapping leaves out the possibility that groundbreaking theorizing and research can be and are produced by organic public sociologists. They are the ones who confront the discrepancy between dominant knowledges and their experiences in the community or shop floor and develop alternative knowledges to account for their lived experience.

The "uncanny" resemblance between Talcott Parsons's fourfold table of functions that any system has to fulfill to survive and Burawoy's fourfold mapping of sociology deserves to be highlighted as significant, rather than being relegated to an acknowledgment in a footnote. Oddly, for a Marxist sociologist, Burawoy seems to have adopted a structural functionalist model of sociology, one that generates stasis rather than dynamism. Burawoy differs from Parsons in that he recognizes "fields of power" within sociology. He argues that instrumental knowledge holds sway over reflexive knowledge, and thus professional and policy sociology dominate over critical and public sociology. He hopes that professional sociology's domination takes the form of hegemony rather than despotism. He notes that alternative knowledges generated by some critical and public sociologists "should be allowed breathing space to develop their own capacities and to inject dynamism back into dominant knowledges." In other words, the dynamism of sociology will depend on the restraint and generosity of professional sociologists rather than on the agency and activism of subaltern sociologists. I am afraid Burawoy's model uncomfortably resembles the pre–civil rights era sociological understanding of race relations, which focused on white attitudes instead of black agency as the key to ending legal segregation.

4. *A disproportionate share of university-based critical and organic public sociology is done by sociologists who are located in interdisciplinary fields, such as ethnic studies, women's studies, justice studies, education, environmental studies, and labor institutes.*

One might expect that sociologists in subaltern fields would be more likely to be or become organic public sociologists than their counterparts in traditional sociology departments, first because of their own personal histories and current experiences and second because they have natural publics to which they feel accountable, namely, subaltern students and local subaltern communities. They cannot help but be aware—though perhaps this memory will fade over time—that student and community activists were critical in convincing universities to establish their programs and departments in the first place.

Professional sociology—this seems to be a core feature of "professionalism," which involves the policing of boundaries—has historically lagged in grasping the dynamics of social change and appreciating new critical perspectives. In the 1930s and 1940s, sociologists did not fully appreciate the significance of W. E. B. DuBois's reinterpretation of Reconstruction and black agency in the Civil War and Reconstruction.

(See the excerpt from the *American Journal of Sociology*'s review of *Black Reconstruction* at the beginning of this essay.) Later, in the 1960s, as James McKee pointed out in *Sociology and the Race Problem* (1993), sociologists of race were completely taken by surprise by the civil rights revolution. They were locked into an assimilationist framework (derived from the experience of European immigrants) that posited a generally linear process of incorporation into the dominant society. Blacks faced a long road to assimilation, both because their culture differed from that of the mainstream—they were essentially a "folk people"—and because of white racial prejudice. According to established sociological wisdom, blacks would undergo a slow process of modernization, but ultimately their integration into mainstream society would depend on transforming the hearts and minds of whites. Both sets of changes would take several generations to accomplish. Sociologists of race did not recognize black discontent and agency and the possibility that massive political mobilization and government intervention could bring about major social transformation even without changing white attitudes.

In contrast, subalterns tend to be skeptical of dominant paradigms. Aware that these paradigms often "invisibilize" their experiences or distort or contradict them, they are moved to develop alternative frameworks that make sense of their experience and that make it possible to envision change. In the heat of struggle over black rights and empowerment, activists and scholars of color developed the *internal colonialism* model. First adopted by Stokely Carmichael (Carmichael and Hamilton 1967), it was elaborated in particular by Chicano scholars such as Guillermo Flores (1973) and Mario Barrera (1979). In sociology the courageous white sociologist Bob Blauner (1972) systematized internal colonialism as a counter to the writings of Milton Gordon, Nathan Glazer, Daniel Moynihan, Irving Kristol, Michael Novak, and other neoconservatives who repudiated the group-oriented aims of the black power movement. The *racial formation* framework that has become the major alternative to the internal colonialism and assimilation models looks at race as a social-political construction that evolves out of political struggle (Omi and Winant 1986, 1994). This framework was formulated by sociologist Michael Omi while he was a student activist and further developed as a faculty member in the Ethnic Studies Department at Berkeley, and by Howard Winant, who had been a labor organizer before starting his doctoral work.[6]

Critical race theory (CRT) emerged from the writings of legal scholar activists who were frustrated by the stalling of progress toward equality and disillusioned by the liberal color-blind approach within the law. The acknowledged founder of CRT is Derrick Bell, who wrote from his experiences as a black man and a civil rights lawyer. Other influential critical race theorists are legal scholars Mari Matsuda, Richard Delgado, and Kimberlie Crenshaw, educational theorist William Tate, and African American scholar Molefi Kete Asante. Although they vary in their focus, all share certain orientations, namely, that racism is ordinary rather than aberrant within American institutions; that both elite and working-class whites gain materially and/or psychically from racism and therefore have little incentive to support change; that race, including whiteness, is a social construction; that race must be studied in intersection with gender and other axes of inequality; and that subalterns have a unique angle of vision based on their experience which, far from being biased and subjective, may be more complete than that of dominants (Delgado and Stefancic 2001).

Within sociology, Patricia Hill Collins is the most widely cited and eminent critical race theorist. Her *Black Feminist Thought* (1990) was a pioneering work in elaborating intersectionality and standpoint theory. She noted that elite white men have controlled traditional scholarship, which has therefore excluded or distorted the experience of black women. At a more fundamental level, elite white men also controlled the knowledge validation process, which worked to invalidate or suppress black women's thought. Thus, black women have developed an alternative epistemology for deriving and assessing knowledge. It is noteworthy that she was primarily located in an African American studies department when she wrote *Black Feminist Thought* and drew on the insights of African American feminists and Afrocentric scholars.

Despite these new conceptual models, the assimilationist framework persists, and indeed reigns, in professional sociology. The concept of segmented assimilation has been added to account for the differential "success" of immigrant groups in climbing the American socioeconomic ladder. Although it adds important nuances to the traditional assimilation model, it still takes for granted the existing socioeconomic hierarchy and examines how different groups fit into it rather than how these groups may challenge the hierarchy and seek collective empowerment through organizing and activism rather than individual advancement by acquiring human capital to achieve individual mobility.

A similar analysis could be done of the slow and reluctant pace at which the field of sociology has moved to adopt critical perspectives on women and gender. With the development of interdisciplinary feminist scholarship in the 1970s, the term *gender* was introduced into sociology, history, anthropology, literature, and other fields to refer to socially constructed and historically specific meanings and relations organized around reproductive differences. As with racial inequality and racism, gender inequality and sexism were made central questions by activist scholars who found that existing theory, even critical theory, did not provide terms and concepts that adequately accounted for women's experience and for the pervasiveness of women's subordination. Theories of the origins and maintenance of women's oppression were formulated by scholars involved in feminist movements. They drew on Marxist, psychoanalytic, and other critical theory, but "reread" them in light of women's experiences and perspectives. These theories were introduced into sociology by feminist sociologists who interacted with other scholars working in women's studies programs and departments.

Yet, more than a decade after feminists had introduced fresh thinking into traditional disciplines, Judith Stacey and Barrie Thorne wrote "Missing Feminist Revolution in Sociology" (1985). They noted that feminist insights had failed to transform the basic conceptual frameworks of the field. While history, literature, and anthropology had undergone major paradigm shifts as a result of integrating issues of women and gender into their subject matter, sociology had not experienced a major transformation in its basic conceptual frameworks. Sociology remained locked into functionalist approaches to gender that emphasized stasis rather than change. The language of "sex roles," intended to distinguish between the social and biological, nonetheless neglected the possibility of fluidity in masculinity and femininity and in relations between men and women and elided issues of power and inequality.

5. *Professional sociology has a colonial relationship with subaltern fields and with critical and public wings of sociology: that is, professional sociology gains by being able to place women and minority PhDs in subaltern fields rather than incorporating them as faculty in their own departments and by selectively extracting knowledge and theory from subaltern fields and from critical and public wings without disturbing the existing hierarchy of prestige and privilege.*

Because of the concentration of professional sociology in traditional sociology departments and of critical and public sociology in subaltern departments (as well as at state and community colleges), the relation between professional sociology and public sociology (as practiced by feminist sociologists, sociologists of color, Third World scholars, and others) is akin to neocolonial relations. As mentioned above, the growth of interdisciplinary studies has made the new programs and departments alternative places where sociology departments can place significant numbers of PhDs in tenure-track jobs—particularly minority and women graduates. However, the flow of positions is asymmetrical. Sociology departments, particularly at top-tier institutions, do not hire PhDs from subaltern fields. The exception is when the prestige of the institution compensates the lack of prestige of the department; thus an applicant with a comparative ethnic studies degree from Berkeley might be hired by a sociology department in a second-tier state institution or a four-year liberal arts college.

Yet, as I also mentioned above, these interdisciplinary fields are often where innovative theorizing takes place. Once the ideas prove fruitful, traditional sociology adopts them, selectively incorporating them without, however, changing "business as usual." It restricts the reach of innovations by ghettoizing them within specialties such as sociology of race and ethnicity, sociology of gender, or sociology of the family. It continues to neglect race and gender in other subfields, such as political sociology or organizational sociology. Alternatively, they trivialize race and gender by simply adding them to the list of variables that need to be correlated with other variables in order to "explain" variation, rather than problematizing and historicizing race and gender categories and their meanings.

6. *Organic public sociology may enjoy more fruitful (and egalitarian) collaborative relations with organic public wings of other disciplines such as history, economics, geography, and legal studies than with professional sociology.*

Contentious social issues are often most fruitfully addressed by research and activism that bring multidisciplinary perspectives into dialogue. Because of my grounding in feminist and women-of-color scholarship, the examples that spring to mind most readily involve feminist collaborations across disciplines. One example is the coalition among scholars, activists, and welfare rights organizations that was forged in the wake of President Clinton's call for "an end to welfare as we know it." One of the groups involved in this coalition was the Women's Committee of 100, initially created by feminist historians of the state but quickly expanded to include scholars in political science, philosophy, sociology, social welfare, and economics, as well as lawyers, welfare recipients, and leaders of feminist and professional organizations. In addition to opposing the destruction of the U.S. welfare system (in the name of "welfare reform"), the members articulated various visions of welfare justice and new understandings of care: work, motherhood, and citizenship (Boris 1998; Kittay 1998; Mink 1998). Another noteworthy effort involving activists and scholars from a variety of disciplines was in addressing the causes and consequences of the escalating growth of prisons and incarceration both domestically and globally. For instance, one national group was formed, with local chapters (Critical Resistance), dedicated to dismantling what social historian Mike Davis first called the prison industrial complex (Critical Resistance Publication Collective 2000). Many of the same scholars have been involved in INCITE: Women of Color Against Violence,[7] which focuses on the relation between violence against women and violence generally (Richie 1996, 2000), and in global movements to address the incarceration of women, many of whom are imprisoned for engaging in economic survival strategies (Sudbury 2004).

It can also be shown that public projects launched by scholars from other disciplines can provide useful models for public sociology. One example is the Labor and Working Class History Association (LAWCHA), which describes itself as "an organization of scholars, teachers, students, labor educators, and activists who seek to promote public and scholarly awareness of labor and working-class history through research, writing, and organizing." LAWCHA supports projects to make labor and working-class history accessible to union members, working-class communities, and public school students by developing materials and curricula and includes scholars from other disciplines, including sociology, economics, political science, and law.[8]

A FINAL WORD

In this essay I have tried to clarify two questions: First, who does the mapping of sociology, and second, how does positionality shape the mapping? From the position of privilege and power (as seen from the vantage point of a top-rated PhD-granting sociology department in a foremost research university), the perspective is one of seeing the great panoply of our discipline and categorizing its elements. But from the position of those who are more marginally positioned, looking not down at the landscape but up at the individuals and institutions with prestige and influence, the view looks quite different. We might say that one map seems to glitter with hope and promise when sociologists and their myriad publics reach "common understandings across multiple boundaries, not least but not only across national boundaries, and in doing so shedding insularities of old" (this volume, 58). From my position as a person of color and as a feminist, it is hard to be so sanguine about the future of our discipline and the role of organic public sociology within it. When I see the resilience of traditional and outmoded theories and points of view, when I see recurring patterns of inequality, and when I see the continual outsourcing of people and progressive ideas to subaltern programs and departments, I believe we have missed and continue to miss an opportunity to truly and meaningfully incorporate public sociology into the center of sociology.

NOTES

1. Craven was a University of Chicago historian, rather than a sociologist. Nonetheless, the *American Journal of Sociology* editors chose him to write the review of DuBois's *Black Reconstruction*, and as the premier journal of sociology, it affected the views of its sociological audience. Even though DuBois was a professor of sociology at Atlanta University for some years, the *Journal of Social Forces*, published by the sociology department at the University of North Carolina, did not review *Black Reconstruction*. During the same period, the *Journal of Social Forces* published book reviews on most books written about the South and many books on European history.

2. As the excerpt from the review of *Black Reconstruction* illustrates, dominants often view blacks and other minorities as too biased or emotional to be able to come to an "accurate" assessment of their own situation. The subtext is that whites are dispassionate and thus able to objectively weigh the evidence on slavery and other issues affecting blacks.

3. See Nichols 1997 about the Social Darwinist and Social Gospel orientation of early Harvard sociology. He notes the close ties between sociology and social work at Harvard prior to 1931, when Pitirim A. Sorokin, a champion of a natural science perspective, shifted from the department of economics to chair a separate department of sociology.

4. When I speak of subaltern fields in this essay, I am primarily referring to programs and departments that focus on gender and women's studies and the various fields of ethnic studies. However, most of the subaltern analysis also applies to sociology as taught and practiced in state colleges, community colleges, and other locations where faculty are often too busy teaching to do much research and where "mapping of the discipline" is an unobtainable luxury.

5. This is not at all Burawoy's intellectual orientation, of course. In his many writings on labor and labor processes, Burawoy offers a Marxist perspective that is critically attuned to power and inequality. Thus it is all the more striking that in speaking/writing in his professional role, he has seemingly adopted a functional analytic framework.

6. The paradigm shift from the internal colonialism model to racial formation in the late 1980s and early 1990s can be seen in Tomás Almaguer's earlier and later work on race in California. Whereas his 1979 PhD dissertation and early articles (e.g., Almaguer 1971) were framed within an internal colonialism framework, his later book, *Racial Fault Lines* (1994), reinterpreted similar materials from a racial formation perspective.

7. www.incite-national.org.

8. www.lawcha.org.

REFERENCES

Almaguer, Tomás. 1971. "Toward the Study of Chicano Colonialism." *Aztlan* II: 7–21.

———. 1994. *Racial Fault Lines: The Historical Origins of White Supremacy in California.* Berkeley: University of California Press.

Barrera, Mario. 1979. *Race and Class in the Southwest: A Theory of Racial Inequality.* Notre Dame, IN: University of Notre Dame Press.

Blauner, Robert. 1972. *Racial Oppression in America.* Berkeley: University of California Press.

Boris, Eileen. 1998. "Scholarship and Activism: The Case of Welfare Justice." *Feminist Studies* 24 (Spring): 27–31.

Carmichael, Stokely, and Charles V. Hamilton. 1967. *Black Power: The Politics of Liberation in America.* New York: Knopf.

Collins, Patricia Hill. 1990. *Black Feminist Thought: Knowledge, Consciousness, and the Politics of Empowerment.* New York: Routledge. Second ed. published 2000, Boca Raton, FL: Taylor and Francis.

Craven, Avery. 1936. Untitled review of *Black Reconstruction* by W. E. B. DuBois. *American Journal of Sociology* 41: 535–36.

Critical Resistance Publication Collective. 2000. "Critical Resistance to the Prison Industrial Complex." *Social Justice* 27 (special issue).

Deegan, Mary Jo. 1987. *Jane Addams and the Men of the Chicago School, 1892–1918.* New Brunswick, NJ: Transaction Books.

Delamont, Sara. 1992. "Old Fogies and Intellectual History: An Episode in Academic History." *Women's History Review* 1: 39–61.

Delgado, Richard, and Jean Stefancic. 2001. *Critical Race Theory: An Introduction.* New York: New York University Press.

Flores, Guillermo. 1973. "Race and Culture in the Internal Colony: Keeping the Chicano in His Place." In *Structures of Dependency,* ed. F. Bonilla and R. Girling, pp. 189–223. Palo Alto, CA: Nairobi Press.

Kittay, Eva Feder. 1998. "Dependency, Equality, and Welfare." *Feminist Studies* 24 (Spring): 32–43.

McKee, James B. 1993. *Sociology and the Race Problem: The Failure of a Perspective.* Champaign-Urbana: University of Illinois Press.

Mink, Gwendolyn. 1998. "The Lady and the Tramp (II): Feminist Welfare Politics, Poor Single Mothers, and the Challenge of Welfare Justice." *Feminist Studies* 24 (Spring): 44–78.

Nichols, Lawrence T. 1997. "Sociology in the Women's Annex: Inequality and Integration at Harvard and Radcliffe, 1879–1947." *American Sociologist* 28: 5–28.

Omi, Michael, and Howard Winant. 1986. *Racial Formation in the United States from the 1960s to the 1980s.* New York: Routledge.

———. 1994. *Racial Formation in the United States from the 1960s to the 1980s,* 2nd ed. New York: Routledge.

Richie, Beth E. 1996. *Compelled to Crime: The Gender Entrapment of Black Battered Women.* New York: Routledge.

———. 2000. "A Black Feminist Reflection on the Antiviolence Movement." *Signs: Journal of Women in Culture and Society* 25: 1133–37.

Stacey, Judith, and Barrie Thorne. 1985. "The Missing Feminist Revolution in Sociology." *Social Problems* 32: 302–16.

Sudbury, Julia. 2004. "A World without Prisons: Resisting Militarism, Globalized Punishment, and Empire." *Social Justice* 31: 9–30.

BARBARA EHRENREICH

A Journalist's Plea

I take it as a great honor to be included in this volume as a "public soci-ologist" and as a sign of the progress of public sociology that I *can* be included. Was it only five or ten years ago that the word *journalist* was a term of invective among social scientists—used to rein in academics who strayed beyond their academic audiences? So the inclusion of an intellectual misfit like myself—someone whose formal education was entirely in the natural sciences, who works as both a journalist and an amateur social scientist—signals a new openness and generosity of spirit within the profession. I welcome this chance to join the ongoing conversation called "sociology."

But my inclusion here does not abolish my outsider status. In my everyday work, I face sociology with a combination of neediness, impa-tience, and frustration. And this is true whether that work is "merely" journalistic or is concerned with broader, more enduring questions.

To speak first as a journalist: there are, of course, vast differences between journalism and sociology, even when they address the same issues. Sociologists possess methods and standards particular to their line of work; journalists have their own repertory of approaches and, in the responses of other journalists, even a kind of "peer review." If there is a single crucial difference, it is in the two professions' relationship to time. A sociologist can burrow in her office for years with a single project; a journalist usually has hours, days, or at best a few weeks in which to absorb a body of material and fashion it into a sharply pointed, communicable form. To pick up on the Walter Benjamin quote cited by Michael Burawoy in his opening essay here: A journalist can never step out of the "storm." From the 8:00 A.M. CNN news, through the morning *New York Times* and a dozen blogs or Listservs absorbed during the day, the journalist—especially the "opinion" journalist or commentator—is being hit by scores of stories inviting immediate response. There is never enough time for reflection; today's arresting story will be next week's old news.

Hence the neediness journalists bring to their encounters with social scientists. You, we figure, have had the time to comb through the data and reflect on the results. In my normal work, I call or otherwise contact a social scientist at least once a week for information, confirmation, or just a quote to add a touch of legitimacy to an otherwise highly opinionated piece. Sometimes I know exactly whom to call; it may even be a friend or acquaintance whose work I am aware of. Otherwise it may take a frustrating series of calls before I can locate a helpful source. The dependency is real; without you, it may be impossible to sort fact from lie or ephemera from deep, long-standing trends.

Here's an example of my dealings, as a journalist, with the world of sociology—one that highlights the satisfactions as well as the frustrations. In the spring of 2004, entertainer Bill Cosby issued a series of tirades against the poor of his race, and especially the youthful poor, for a wide range of sins. They use bad words, fail to give their children normal names like "Bill," and in rising numbers, engage in petty theft, drop out of school, or bear their children too young and out of wedlock. Addressing black progress in general from his billionaire status, Cosby declared that "the lower economic people are not holding up their end in this deal."

I was disgusted by this latest assault on the poor by the rich and, more importantly, convinced that Cosby had his facts wrong. As far as I could recall, he was wrong about black dropout rates and wrong about the alleged increases in black youth crime and out-of-wedlock births. But how to verify this? It would have taken me weeks to assemble the necessary data, and I had at best a couple of days. Fortunately, I remembered reading (in the weekly *In These Times*) a sociologist named Michael Males, who specializes in studying youth-bashing. A few minutes of Googling produced his contact data, and I had Males on the phone. He confirmed my impression that Cosby's accusations were erroneous (the crime rate and out-of-wedlock birthrate among black youth have both been falling, not rising) and provided me with a succinct "expert" quote.

But I was frustrated too. Why wasn't Males himself leading the charge against Cosby? When I urged him to write an op-ed piece—and even gave him the contact information for a newspaper opinion editor who might be disposed to use it—Males demurred. He was too busy, maybe in a few weeks. Well, in a few weeks it might be too late. Cosby's accusations would have blown through the collective consciousness without refutation. Luckily, another social scientist—religious studies scholar Michael Eric Dyson—stepped up to the plate with an entire book, *Is Bill Cosby Right? Or Has the Black Middle Class Lost Its Mind?* (2005), which not only refutes Cosby on the facts but explores the growing class divide among African Americans. Unfortunately, though, this feisty book came out a year after Cosby's remarks and their embrace by noted black intellectuals, including Henry Louis Gates Jr., who, as a scholar of literature, can perhaps be forgiven for not checking Cosby's "facts."

Maybe I'm asking too much of sociologists. I want you to be there when I call with my next question, and it would certainly help me make that call if the Web site of the American Sociological Association would list sociologists by their areas of interest, so I don't spend hours trying to find the right sociologist to talk to. I also want you to not just wait around for a journalist to call but to step into the fray yourselves. Write op-eds, for example, and if you're not sure how to go about doing that, consult the nearest school of journalism. And at the same time, I want you to continue to generate insightful new academic work that potentially bears on pressing current issues.

In fact, I have a long agenda for you, some of which may already be under way. To give a few examples of areas where sociology, of the "public" sort, might make a useful contribution to our understanding of the world today:

> *The warfare state versus the welfare state:* Historically, the welfare state has grown along with the military, if only as a way to guarantee a continued source of human material for mass armies. Think of Prussia's Bismarck, England's Bevan, or the widows' pensions that were established in the wake of the American Civil War. But, as political sociologist Frances Fox Piven has pointed out, today we are presented with a historical anomaly: rising militarism and an ever-shrinking welfare state, including veterans' benefits. This would seem to lead to a dangerously unstable situation, with more well-trained mass murderers like Gulf War I veterans Timothy McVeigh and John Muhammad. But how are

shrinking benefits—and declining hourly wages—perceived and absorbed by military personnel and their families? What accommodations do these families make and how lasting are these accommodations likely to be? What informs the apparent complacency of the policy makers who are busily undermining the life chances of the class that risks its young in faraway wars?

The corporation as a site for internal predation: In the 1950s, American sociologists produced towering works of scholarship on the corporation, exploring the corporate culture and its demands on the white-collar worker. Corporations have changed dramatically since the days of C. Wright Mills and William H. Whyte. Most strikingly, in an age of downsizing, "right-sizing," and outsourcing, they no longer offer stable employment even to well-educated, high-achieving people. In fact, the better one does and the more one is paid, the more likely one's salary is to be seen as a tempting cost cut by the people who occupy the "C-suites"—the CEOs, CFOs, and so forth. Yet I can think of only two recent books exploring the new, predatory corporate culture—sociologist Richard Sennett's *The Corrosion of Character* (1998) and business journalist Jill Andresky Fraser's *White-Collar Sweatshop* (2001). Like it or not, corporations are the basic units of our economy, and we need much more insight into their internal functioning. What are the psychic demands on the individual white-collar functionary, who is now likely to hold ten jobs in the course of a career rather than two or three? What happens to the corporate discards? What are the consequences of all this churning for long-term corporate profitability and stability?

Religious substitutes for the welfare state: America is in the grip of a religious revival, although, compared to the Great Awakening of the early nineteenth century, it is a curiously unemotional one. Few of the evangelical churches that anchor the current revival feature ecstatic religious experiences; rather, they offer a blend of fellowship and concrete services, including, for example, child care, after-school care, support groups for battered women, and networking events for the unemployed. They are becoming an alternative welfare state, whose support rests not only on "faith" but also on the loyalty of the grateful recipients, much like Hamas, which draws in poverty-stricken Palestinians through its own miniature welfare state. To what extent does the rise of evangelical Christianity reflect the decline of the secular, public, welfare state? And to what extent does it actively promote that decline, for example, through the tacit endorsement of illiberal candidates?

So those are some of the things I want from sociology when I approach it as a journalist. But I come to sociology not only as a journalist-slash-consumer seeking quick answers, an expert imprimatur, or thoughtful analyses of current trends. I also approach sociology as a kind of social thinker myself—even a kind of sociologist, as Burawoy has been kind enough to label me. When I approach sociology from this vantage point, I am looking for something I can only call companionship: other people who are, like me, trying to understand what the hell is going on here, in the society or societies we find ourselves embedded in.

Sociology is the obvious place to seek such companionship, since it takes as its subject matter society itself, or the full range of our collective existence as humans. Furthermore, it has had a couple of centuries to develop and refine sophisticated methods of inquiry and interpretation. I respect these methods and feel a certain awe for the breadth of the sociological undertaking, but here too I bring a certain impatience to the enterprise. You have the tools, you have, in "society," an endless supply of material. But *what is the question?*

To an extent, large questions went out of style in the social sciences sometime in the 1980s, when postmodernists began to challenge the local biases—masculine, white, Western, and so forth—that tend to contaminate vast theoretical syntheses or generalizations of any kind. In the face of this critique, many in the social sciences hunkered down into the pursuit of microprojects about, for example, employment discrimination, voting behavior, and gun ownership, and much useful work has come out of this modest, craftsperson-like approach. But without an underlying and animating question, a discipline—sociology, for example—is little more than turf, a way of marking departmental boundaries and shaping individual careers. Research projects come to be defined by the methods at hand, rather than by burning questions. A similar decadence pervades the natural sciences, where research agendas are often determined by a group's capital equipment—a cyclotron or amino acid–sequencing devices.

At one point in sociology's past, there was such an underlying question, or at least we can discern one running through the concerns of such patriarchs of the discipline as Émile Durkheim, Karl Marx, and

Max Weber. They looked at the society defined by urban, industrial capitalism with a deep sense of loss (and, in Marx's case, opportunity).
They bemoaned the lost solidarity and emotional spontaneity of prein-
dustrial society and asked, in their very different ways: How do we
maintain our humanity, our sustaining mutual bonds, in the face of an
economic system that demands so much psychic repression and isolation? What is tearing us apart and how might we find ways to resist it
and restore the cohesion, the *communitas,* that makes us human?

Twentieth-century sociology was forced to revise that question. In the
wake of fascism, the Frankfurt School faced the fact that cohesion is not
necessarily a social good, that it can become the connective tissue of the
state-as-killing-machine. Later social psychologists, like Stanley Milgram,
demonstrated experimentally that human sociality—or at least the inclination to accommodate and get along—can lead to Auschwitz or, in our
own time, Abu Ghraib. The sociality that anchored Durkheim and, to an
extent, Marx lost its intrinsic moral valence. It is not only atomization
and anomie we have to worry about, but the pull of immoral collectivi-
ties—the totalitarian state, the military subgroup, the viciously intolerant
religious community. And if we cannot trust our own solidaristic impulses to lead in kindly and inclusive directions, the question becomes
—well, I leave it to you to frame that question of how we are to live
together in large numbers, different as we are, and with each of us full of
conflicting needs.

My point here is that once you acknowledge that there is, or should be,
a unifying underlying question, then you have to admit that sociology
cannot handle it alone. To put it another way, a question-driven discipline, as opposed to a mere chunk of academic turf, must reach out to
other disciplines, even at the risk of disrupting boundaries and ceding
turf. When the question drives the research, it may propel the researchers
in surprising directions. I am not talking about being merely "interdisciplinary"; I am talking about a complete disregard for the disciplinary
boundaries laid out in the early twentieth century, much as a journalist
brings his or her research into a topic in the news.

First, there should be no controversy about sociology's need for history. The dependency goes both ways; history without sociology is a
story of personalities, of "kings and battles." But sociology without history may be even more misleading. In the mid-twentieth-century sociology textbooks I sampled for my book *Fear of Falling: The Inner Life of
the Middle Class,* people were assigned to "roles" and aggregated into
"institutions," which all miraculously interacted to reproduce the same

arrangements from one generation to the next. Even today's far more sophisticated texts seem to leave many students with a fairly static notion of social divisions—in which, for example, class is seen as just another colorful form of "diversity," along with race and gender. Sociology without history is always in danger of becoming an endorsement of the status quo, of presenting society as a fait accompli, when it should be approached, in most instances, as a crime scene.

Nor should there be much controversy about sociology's need for psychology, particularly in the area of emotion. Sociologists Erving Goffman, Arlie Hochschild, and many others have pioneered a "sociology of emotions" that dares to trespass into the question of how it feels, for example, when a service worker is forced to manufacture smiles. Yet if you read through the scores of sociological articles on the important subject of crowd behavior published since the 1960s, you will find, as anthropologist Charles Lindholm observed, an almost exclusive focus on such relatively dry matters as "the structure of the group . . . its pattern of recruitment, its ideology and its contradictions, [and] the mechanisms used to gain commitment," with no sense of "the excitement of participation in an ecstatic group" (Lindholm 1990, 81, 83). Similarly, the sociology of sports fandom remains stuck in a purely sociological paradigm centered on the fans' identification with sports teams as a source of affiliation and imagined status. The raw excitement of the game and its relation, for example, to the patriotic fervor that accompanies the outbreak of war remain seriously understudied, perhaps because such studies cannot go forward without assistance from the alien discipline of psychology.

More controversially, I would suggest that sociologists let their questions carry them, when necessary, into the realm of biology. Yes, "sociobiology" has a sorry record of endorsing gender inequality, and the current reckless anticipation of a gene determining every facet of human behavior—despite the fact that humans possess only twice as many genes as a roundworm—stands as a warning against facile social applications of biology. But there have been fascinating recent breakthroughs in neurophysiology that sociologists would do well to attend to. For example, the identification of a set of neurons that seem to be the seat of both empathetic and imitative responses may shed light on many aspects of collective behavior. Neuronal firing patterns do not "determine" behavior, but such patterns, laid down over millennia of evolution, no doubt shape the human propensities for altruism or, for that matter, violence. When sociologists say "we don't go there," which seems to be the current stance, they rob themselves of potentially paradigm-rocking insights into the human condition.

Perhaps what I want is a sociology, or at least a public sociology, that is more like journalism—willing to go anywhere in pursuit of answers, even to go boldly, when the questions carry them there, where no social scientist has gone before. The difference, of course, is that journalism is content-free and fixated on the ephemera of "the news." Sociology, in contrast, should always remain true to its one big underlying question, which, however you exactly phrase it, is ultimately a moral question: How can we organize ourselves to live together in dignity and peace?

There is a scary paradox here. If a question-driven sociology has no boundaries, how can it be a discipline at all? Can sociology, or any discipline, survive as a conversational community when any (ethical) methodology or any source of insight is permitted? These are questions for real sociologists to work out—people who do the daily work of preparing lectures, mentoring graduate students, and judging their colleagues' work. I can only say: Welcome to the storm.

REFERENCES

Dyson, Michael Eric. 2005. *Is Bill Cosby Right? Or Has the Black Middle Class Lost Its Mind?* New York: Basic Civitas Books.

Ehrenreich, Barbara. 1989. *Fear of Falling: The Inner Life of the Middle Class.* New York: Pantheon Books.

Fraser, Jill Andresky. 2001. *White-Collar Sweatshop: The Deterioration of Work and Its Rewards in Corporate America.* New York: W. W. Norton.

Lindholm, Charles. 1990. *Charisma.* Cambridge, MA: Blackwell.

Sennett, Richard. 1998. *The Corrosion of Character: The Personal Consequences of Work in the New Capitalism.* New York: W. W. Norton.

REJOINDER

MICHAEL BURAWOY

The Field of Sociology
Its Power and Its Promise

Sociology in the United States has spanned three waves over the past 150 years. It was born as a utopian project during the nineteenth century; it was disciplined into a science during the course of the twentieth century; and now, in its third wave, it harnesses that science to its earlier moral concerns in order to give vitality to public sociology. This is the thesis of my rejoinder, which situates my critics in the field of sociology, navigating its successive waves.

The three waves of sociology reflect and refract broad societal responses to three waves of market expansion. The first wave of marketization led to a spontaneous reaction from an emergent civil society that not only softened the blow of labor commodification but also sought to transcend capitalism with socialist, communitarian, and cooperative experiments. In sociology's first wave, which in the United States stretched from the Civil War to World War I, the field was closely associated with this burgeoning civil society. It was married to moral reform and, therefore, in its origins possessed a strong public character.

The second wave of marketization took off after World War I with renewed global intensity, leading to equally profound reactions, but this time from nation-states—in such varied forms as fascism, communism, and social democracy. In the United States the state-regulated capitalism of the New Deal found its reflection in a professional sociology, concerned with social control, social order, and social problems. A latecomer to the social sciences, this second-wave sociology began to shed its association with moral reform, aiming to establish a codified body of knowledge that could be deployed in the policy world. Although there were powerful strands of public sociology throughout this period—from Edward Ross to David Riesman, from W. E. B. DuBois to Erving Goffman—the hallmark of the second wave was the rise of a professional sociology whose outward orientation, to the extent it had one, focused on power and money. At its apex professional sociology built relations with major foundations, with market research, and with federal agencies.

Professional sociology not only supplied technical tools for policy sociology but also supplied its own rationale—the theory of mass society that gained currency in the United States after World War II. It was a theory that denied the very existence of articulate publics and thereby justified either ignoring them or speaking for them. Ties to states and corporations led professional sociology to emphasize its expert rather than its public role. However, this did not last for long. Under attack from critical sociology—invigorated by the civil rights, antiwar, Third World, and feminist movements of the 1960s and early 1970s—professional sociology underwent a veritable revolution. A new generation of sociologists, with ties (real and imaginary) to effervescent publics, now rewrote the sociology of politics, of culture, of work, of development, of the economy, of the family, of urbanization, of race and ethnicity, of gender and sexuality, and, more generally, of inequality. Casting aside models of irrational mass behavior, social movement theory epitomized the transformation of sociology, successively incorporating the centrality of social conflict, resource mobilization, political process, and framing. From the perspective of sociology, "publics" had now thrust themselves onto the political stage as rational and articulate actors. The theoretical conditions for the renaissance of public sociology were born as sociologists rediscovered civil society and its public sphere.

The political impetus for the renaissance of public sociology emerged later, in the 1980s, with the resurrection of market fundamentalism. This third wave of marketization was actively promoted by the U.S. state—a state that had reversed itself and begun to deny the very existence of society. Policy makers by now had less use for sociology, and sociology had less leverage with state and business. Deregulating the economy, cutting welfare, starving education, and privatizing public services (not to mention imperial adventures abroad) recreated the specter of the nineteenth century, when sociology had first sprung up to aid "the self-defense of society." With third-wave marketization, or neoliberalism as it is more popularly known, public sociology was reborn.

Today, in its third wave, sociology's external focus turns from the policy world to the world of publics. But second-wave professional-policy sociology has not simply disappeared. Indeed, it is mounting a struggle against resurgent critical-public sociology, claiming that the latter threatens the unity of our discipline, endangering its legitimacy, devaluing its professional credentials, and contaminating its scientific neutrality. Nonetheless, second-wave sociology, with its decaying linkages to the state, is giving way to third-wave sociology that shifts the balance away from policy to public sociology, reshaping professional and critical sociology along the way. As the state forsakes its progressive face, losing any semblance of universality, it compels sociology to seek allies in the realm of publics. Third-wave sociology joins first-wave moral reform to second-wave professional science to produce a renewal of public sociology, recasting our discipline.

STRUCTURING THE FIELD, MAKING SENSE OF THE CHAOS

Successive waves of sociology cannot be reduced to a succession of different types of knowledge, for example, from public to professional to policy to critical and back to public sociology. Rather, successive waves reconfigure the content of and the relations among all four knowledges. The coexistence of professional, policy, public, and critical sociologies, albeit in continually changing constellations, has been an ever-present and necessary feature of our discipline. That these four knowledges crystallize into a dynamic division of labor that defines our field is not an accident of history but springs from their origins in two fundamental questions: "Knowledge for whom?" and "Knowledge for what?" In other words, are we addressing fellow sociologists (or other academics), or audiences beyond the academy? Are we interested in matters that take for granted a specific set of values and societal goals, or are we interested in the interrogation of those values and goals? These are not arbitrary questions—they have a genealogy that stretches back to ancient philosophy and forward to the most contemporary of theorists.

Here I am less concerned with ancient lineage and more with how these two questions—knowledge for whom and knowledge for what— define the components of our disciplinary field. Instrumental knowledge answers the question "Knowledge for what?" by focusing on means rather than ends. It divides into professional sociology, aimed at puzzles (external anomalies and internal contradictions) defined by our research programs, and policy sociology, aimed at solving problems defined by clients. Reflexive knowledge, on the other hand, is concerned with ends rather than means. It divides into critical sociology, which interrogates the normative assumptions and constructs the value foundations of professional sociology, and public sociology, which engages in public dialogues about major issues that affect public life. Here, then, is the fourfold division of sociological labor—each type of knowledge interdependent on but also at odds with the others.

The fourteen commentaries in this volume, which seem to be a bewildering cascade of claims and counterclaims, make sense when located within the division of sociological labor. Each protagonist adopts a perspective tied to his or her place in the (di)vision of sociology and defends that position-taking through antagonism and alliance with other position-takings. Even those—indeed, especially those—who make no mention of the division of labor or who seek to abolish it nevertheless reproduce its elements. Thus, Immanuel Wallerstein's triumvirate of functions—analytical, moral, and political—broadly corresponds to professional, critical, and a conflation of policy and public sociology. Leaving aside this conflation, to which I will return later, Wallerstein would have us carry out all three functions simultaneously, repudiating any notion of specialization. His own Olympian trajectory notwithstanding, such a vision of the Renaissance man is not an option for the vast majority of academics today.

Rather, we have here not four dimensions of a single sociology but four distinct knowledges—cultures with their own repertoires and practices—that form a dynamic set of oppositions and interdependences. In place of Wallerstein's ahistorical, decontextualized fusion of functions, I propose a historically emergent and geographically variable division of labor that portrays our discipline (and other disciplines) as a field of power. The four knowledges are knitted together in a configuration of domination that varies over space and time. The domination of professional sociology in the United States, for example, emerged through its successive dialogues with public, policy, and critical sociologies. If professional sociology still dominates U.S. sociology today (even as it makes a greater space for public sociology), public sociology is relatively stronger in South Africa and Brazil, and policy sociology is prominent in Scandinavian societies, just as a subterranean critical sociology has often been strong in authoritarian societies. In considering the global division of sociological labor, we need to recognize not only how certain knowledge configurations concentrate in certain nations and regions but also how these in turn interconnect with and dominate each other.

We can think of sociology as a field of power because the field leads sociologists to place themselves within and among the four quadrants that define the division of labor.[1] Riveted to our engagement with one another, denigrating the positioning of others in order to normalize and elevate our own, we miss the structure of the field as a whole that sets limits on our maneuvering. This is the first face of the power of the field—what one can call disciplinary power or disciplinarity—that creates the playing field, made up of the four interconnected positions and corresponding practices, acknowledged if not legitimated by all. In what follows I shall try to show that beneath the chaos of our discipline, represented in the preceding essays, there is indeed a patterning that reflects the power of the disciplinary field over its participants. Each displays an intuitive sense of the possible positions in the field and of the actual or putative positions held by others. Each defends his or her own position by reference to other positions, often by stereotyping and pathologizing them. Thus, professional sociologists often disparage public sociology as "pop" sociology, servile to its audiences, while casting themselves as paragons of disinterestedness. Public sociologists, on the other hand, may respond by appropriating disinterestedness for themselves while viewing professional sociology as trivial and irrelevant, as servile to academic careerism. Such oppositions are produced by the field's division of labor and its disciplinarity.

Such antagonisms are complicated by the second face of the power of the field—its power over other fields. Disciplinary power is directed outward as well as inward. Commentaries on public sociology, here and elsewhere, develop position-taking within the field in order to be effective (or not) outside the field, that is, to be effective on other disciplines but also on other spheres of life. Beyond the academy, there are parallel fields—policy fields and public fields, themselves structured into dominant and subordinate positions—that are more or less accessible, depending on one's location within the division of sociological labor. Moreover, building connections to other fields can be part of a strategy to protect or accumulate internal power within sociology. Yet external alliances can also lead to the erosion of fortress mentalities within the discipline, taking us beyond sectional oppositions to embrace the underlying interdependencies that give integrity to our field and contribute to its effectivity beyond.

Disciplinary fields are not static. The division of sociological labor changes over time, and indeed also over space, as do its effects on other fields. This reconfiguration is shaped by broad changes in state, economy, and civil society, which thereby affect the discipline's effects both within and beyond the academy. If we are interested in public sociology, then we need to understand not only how broader forces are changing the structure of our field but also how those broader forces set limits on field effects beyond sociology. Thus, with the eclipse of welfare capitalism, sociology enters its third wave, marked by its ever-more-hostile reception from nation-states as they turn from market regulation to market fundamentalism. Sociology is an unwelcome visitor to the corridors of power, and so, if it seeks a presence beyond the academy, it has no alternative but to forge alliances with publics—many of them also threatened and weakened by markets and/or states.

In this rejoinder I will show how my critics position themselves within the division of sociological labor, and how compiling these positionings enriches our understanding of the field as a whole, both its internal functioning and its potentialities for bringing about social change. We shall see that the sociological field is held in tension by forces pulling in different directions—alliances defending the past tangling with those calling forth the future. I will explore three such alliances. The first is between professional and policy sociology, defending second-wave sociology, still battling the ghosts of sociology's first wave, mistaking it for the third wave. The second alliance, between critical and public sociology, challenges second-wave sociology in the name of its third wave. The third alliance is rather tenuous and still fraught with contradictory impulses. It brings together policy and public sociology, seeking to liberate sociology's insurgent third wave from the insularity of the second. I close by considering the relation of third-wave sociology to other disciplines and to publics beyond the academy.

DEFENDING THE SECOND WAVE: THE PROFESSIONAL-POLICY NEXUS

We begin with professional sociology because it is still the heart of the disciplinary field. The position-takings even here, however, are multiple, reflecting responses to the successive waves of sociology. Lynn Smith-Lovin's desire to expunge values is a legacy of the reaction to first-wave moral reform, and Arthur Stinchcombe's cautiousness is a response to the limitations of second-wave policy interventions, while Andrew Abbott's humanist sociology makes a concession to third-wave public sociology by recognizing the centrality of values. But they all defend not just the autonomy but the unchallenged supremacy of professional knowledge to the point of denying the division of sociological labor.

Recognizing that we do have different values, Smith-Lovin argues that institutionalizing them as public sociologies would endanger the consensus necessary for advancing cumulative knowledge. It would, she claims, divide our community where we need unity. We should, therefore, keep our values to ourselves and try, as best we can, to pursue a value-free science. But, if values are so central to our sociological being, to hide them under the pretense of value neutrality will all too easily result in the tyranny of the majority, making minority claims illegitimate. For example, by giving legitimacy to the values behind gay studies, one allows the development of novel theoretical perspectives and corresponding innovative methods that spill over into and invigorate other areas. This is, indeed, Abbott's position: a humanist sociology that insists on the inseparability of science and values, of instrumental and reflexive knowledge. For him there's no question of hiding values, but neither is there a question of politicization from without. Values yes, politics no. He is as opposed to specialists of reflexive knowledge—whether critical or public sociology—as he is to specialists of instrumental knowledge.

This is more easily said than done. Our field is not simply a field of force, akin to a magnetic field, but it is also a playing field in which the practice of professional sociology has a gamelike character. In order to advance our research programs, we have to suspend doubt in the values and rules that uphold them and concentrate on doing science. We can't simultaneously play the game and question its foundations. I agree with Abbott that values are central to our practice as sociologists, but in order to interrogate those values we have to step outside science and devote ourselves to a different knowledge-practice, what Max Weber called value discussion. Critical sociology can perform its critical function only if it can maintain some distance from the science it problematizes. Specializing in critique is sufficiently disruptive but, because of its separation, not too disruptive. It allows progressive research programs to advance and helps degenerate programs wither away. That, for example, was the function of critical theory with respect to structural functionalism.

If Smith-Lovin and Abbott see professional sociology as threatened from without, whether from public sociology's values or its politics, Arthur Stinchcombe sees professional sociology as limited from within. Ours is an immature science, he says, with underdeveloped research programs. We don't have enough truth (nor the capacity to transmit what truths we do have), so we need to spend more time locked up in the ivory tower accumulating more truth. When we are ready we can venture forth to sell our wares. It's a particular truth Stinchcombe is after—reliable prediction. But that's just the sort of truth that cannot be conjured up within the academy but calls for an intense engagement with the world beyond. Thus, one of Stinchcombe's favorites—Leon Trotsky—turned out to be so prophetic in his analyses of the fate of the Soviet Union precisely because of his deep involvement in its molecular movements. Even economists, practitioners of the paradigmatic social science, are notoriously bad predictors of macrophenomena. There are, of course, notable exceptions, such as John Maynard Keynes, but he is the exception that proves the rule. He too was deeply engaged with the society around him, giving him the broader vision to diagnose the dilemmas of capitalism. In short, to have a chance in the business of prediction, one must venture beyond the academy.

Stinchcombe, an exemplar of the very best of second-wave sociology, is interested not in talking to publics but rather in developing a predictive science for policy makers. Douglas Massey, too, is interested in an instrumental knowledge for policy makers, but unlike Stinchcombe, he is extremely confident, almost euphoric, about sociology's potential contribution. He cites his own contribution to the congressional bill to end housing segregation and his attempt to influence immigration legislation. He expresses no doubts about sociology's technical capacity. For him, our effectiveness in the policy world depends on sociology's persuasive power, its scientific authority, and here he believes the politicization of our discipline is only a liability. The American Sociological Association should not be discrediting sociology's standing by passing ineffectual resolutions. Instead we should be promoting serious research, cultivating a reputation for impartiality and objectivity, building professional respect and scientific prestige. His model of nonpartisanship is the Population Association of America. His criterion of success is "clout in Washington." In effect, Massey would like to see our profession as a disciplined political organization for influencing the state. Impartiality and objectivity, thereby, become a tool and a weapon—a tool for disciplining sociologists and a weapon for persuading others. He is trying to redeem second-wave sociology in a period of its decline.[2]

Massey's "weak politics" ultimately aspires to a "strong politics" of disciplinary control that we can find, for example, in the field of economics. Unlike economics, however, we don't have the sine qua non of centralism—a singular doctrine to go along with our scientific methods, putting us at a disadvantage when dealing with political entities that demand coherent policy recommendations. What marks our profession is its multiplicity of research programs, mutually enriching each other, destined to speak to a plurality of publics rather than agencies of the state. Moreover, we live in an age of market idolatry and possessive individualism, when higher circles have diminishing tolerance for notions of social justice, social welfare, and social equality—when the very notion of the social is held in disrepute. Perhaps government and legislative agencies at the regional or local level are more receptive to sociology, if only because they have to bear the costs of federal laissez-faire, but sociology's comparative advantage today still lies in cultivating relations to publics.

CHALLENGING THE SECOND WAVE: THE CRITICAL-PUBLIC NEXUS

Like professional and policy sociologies, critical and public sociologies are natural allies. If public sociology involves dialogue between sociologists and publics, critical sociology creates the space and the foundations for such a dialogue, by challenging the professional-policy alliance of second-wave sociology. This was the thrust of critical sociology from Robert Lynd to Pitirim Sorokin, C. Wright Mills, and Alvin Gouldner. Critical sociology is our field's internal engine for public sociology.

Among our commentaries, we can distinguish the critique of the content of sociology from the critique of its institutional form. Orlando Patterson points to professional sociology as inimical to the development of a public sociology, especially since its scientization in the 1950s with its supposed bias toward structuralism and abstraction. Perhaps he is talking about Harvard sociology, because if the intellectual center of gravity of sociology has moved in any direction over the last forty years, it is toward social process, historical change, and collective action. Indeed, it is this transformation of professional sociology that created the foundation of sociology's third wave.

Alain Touraine, speaking from a pinnacle of French sociology, has been the strongest and most original proponent of the still-incomplete revolution toward a sociology of the actor. Classical sociology, with its laws of societal development and its systems analysis, is no longer relevant in an era of neoliberal capitalism that has destroyed society and replaced it with disparate processes of domination—deinstitutionalization and desocialization on the one side and the ascent of groups defined by their culture (not their function) on the other. In this new world, public sociology takes the helm in recovering the subject through the defense of human rights and the search for actors. If before the initiative came from professional sociology, now public sociology in alliance with social actors, so he claims, is driving critical, policy, and professional sociology. Touraine is the prophet of third-wave sociology!

From within the United States, sociology looks less rosy, especially from its more critical margins. Although a lifelong practitioner of public sociology, Patricia Hill Collins is far more skeptical than Touraine about its possibilities and promise. The reed of public sociology is a thin one indeed, so much so that she fears that it might wilt in the heat of naming. Labeling public sociology makes it an easier target for those dominant professional forces hostile to its expression, leading to ghettoization, marginalization, and stigmatization. Alternatively, and just as problematic, institutionalizing it—if that were ever possible—could routinize it, sapping it of its imagination and critical powers. Finally, at a time when the very idea of "public" is denigrated, it is asking for trouble to call something public sociology! Perhaps. But I think this is where we make a stand. Now is precisely the time to defend the idea of public before it disappears, injecting it with new meaning and vitality. Without a public, real and virtual, practical and discursive, sociology may as well be dead.

To be sure, Collins is right to be wary of naming. The issue, however, is less the fact than the act of naming—who does the naming, who controls the naming and determines its meaning. There are two types of naming: "labeling," which dominant groups foist on subordinate groups, and "consciousness raising," through which subordinate groups develop insights into and contest their subordination. The first challenge to domination, as feminists long ago made clear, is the capacity to recognize and name it. Indeed, Collins herself concludes that "the name is less important than to know she is not alone," but the name is what allows her to find common cause with others and thus to carve out a place for public sociology within our discipline.

If the first step is naming, that is, reclassifying the categories we use to perceive and judge the world, the second step is to seek institutional change that will create more freedom for the subjugated. Judy Stacey offers seemingly modest proposals to lessen the domination of instrumental over reflexive knowledge and thereby promote public sociology. She would have a moratorium on publishing one year in three to free up time for public sociology, introduce guidelines for promoting faculty on the basis of public sociology, make sociological writing more accessible to wider audiences, have public intellectuals regularly visit departments, and promote interdisciplinary exchange to erode disciplinary boundaries and intercontinental exchange to make U.S. sociology more cosmopolitan. Sociology should take the lead in transforming academic culture. The danger, of course, in piecemeal reform is that it could intensify subordination. But reform is not the heart of the matter. In putting forward these proposals Stacey is effectively underlining just how deeply entrenched are the hierarchies within our field and how difficult they would be to dislodge. But imagining possibilities is the first step to realizing them!

Institutional reform may be off the map for now, but there is nonetheless plenty of space for public sociology within the interstices of professionalism. To be sure, the official rewards are few and far between —although they are becoming more numerous as the idea gains currency—but we don't practice public sociology for professional recognition. Just as a sense of vocation commits us to teaching, whether or not it is formally rewarded, the same is true of public sociology. Doing public sociology is its own reward. It is why so many of us became sociologists. How often do I hear senior sociologists—William Julius Wilson in his response is a case in point—advising graduate students and junior faculty to postpone their public sociology until they have tenure? From my observations, many graduate students would never survive the ordeals of graduate school were it not for their ventures into public sociology— sometimes open, sometimes secretive. That is what gives their commitment to professional sociology its meaning. If graduate students were to defer public sociology until they were mature and secure, our profession would be not only more boring but depleted of some of its best talent.

In the United States, for the foreseeable future, professional sociology will dominate the discipline, but there is an ongoing battle for its soul—a battle that has ramifications beyond the United States. Here critical sociology plays a pivotal role, directed against professional sociology's faltering alliance with policy makers and propelling it into a new alliance with public sociology.

RIDING THE THIRD WAVE: SUBJUGATING POLICY TO PUBLIC SOCIOLOGY

The rise of third-wave sociology is marked by sociology shifting its outward orientation from policy to public sociology. Here our leading spokesperson is Frances Fox Piven, architect and veteran of the welfare rights movement of the 1970s. Taking a position diametrically opposed to Massey's messianic defense of second-wave sociology, Piven calls for a dissident public sociology accountable to popular classes rather than elites, using participatory techniques of research. The state is so tainted—its democracy corroded, its legitimacy lost—that it cannot be the audience for our research endeavors. As the political climate moves ever rightward, so we in the university have a special responsibility, she argues, to defend the interest of the poor and downtrodden. We must propagate our critical values quite openly, conduct the best research in their name, and not be concerned about our prestige and standing among power elites whose interests too easily distort our endeavors. Our impact on policy must be indirect through the organization of publics.

Sharon Hays extends Piven's outspoken critique of policy sociology to professional sociology. Far from being divisive—and here she takes a position directly opposed to that of Smith-Lovin—public sociology should become the unifying foundation of our discipline. For Hays the division of sociological labor is, thus, the enemy of public sociology, not because it fragments our discipline but because it reproduces the very hierarchy that thwarts public sociology. Like Abbott and Smith-Lovin, firmly placed within the division of labor, nonetheless Hays too wants to get rid of it.

Undoubtedly subjugation to professional sociology can be seen as an impediment to public sociology, but scientific knowledge is different from—even at odds with—public knowledge. Scientific knowledge is accountable to peers rather than publics, its truth lies in correspondence with the world rather than in consensus, and its legitimacy lies in building research programs rather than being immediately relevant to the issues of the day. To be sure, professional sociology suffers from pathologies of self-referentiality and irrelevance, often driven by a narrow careerism, but public sociology has its own dangers of distortion, vanguardism, and pandering. These are two different knowledges, requiring different conditions of production, each necessary for the flourishing of the other. Professional sociology cannot be simply harnessed for public projects; it has a logic and autonomy of its own, just as public sociology has to be given space to develop its communicative action.[3]

If William Julius Wilson, public sociologist par excellence, sees this intimate connection between professional sociology and public sociology, he misses what Hays sees all too clearly, the hegemony of professional sociology. From his vantage point, professional, public, policy, and critical knowledges form a single seamless whole. Wilson cannot comprehend what all the fuss is about—why all the opposition to public sociology, and why sociologists don't make greater efforts to get their ideas out. Sociology will survive only if it has a public profile. There's no danger that public sociology will discredit the profession, because good public sociology is and has to be good professional sociology. This view reflects Wilson's own path into public sociology. *The Declining Significance of Race* (1978), intended for his professional peers, caught fire in the public sphere. It was a case of spontaneous combustion. The book began as the public face of professional sociology; it was only when Wilson had to defend it on radio and television, in the press, and in a host of public forums that he truly entered the world of public sociology. After that he never looked back—the public, the professional, the critical, and the policy appeared to melt into one.

Of all the figures in this symposium, Orlando Patterson is the most enigmatic. Surfing between second and third waves, he dissolves the distinction between public and policy sociology. For him it's all a matter of maintaining independence—whether he is writing an op-ed for the *New York Times*, discussing dependency with the prime minister of Jamaica, advising the president of the United States on matters of ethnicity, addressing personnel executives from the top five hundred corporations, or helping pharmaceutical companies deploy the concept of freedom to make more money. We are living in a capitalist society, he says, so we should serve it to the best of our ability. The brunt of his attack is aimed not at the world beyond but at the world within our discipline. Thus, paradoxically, with one hand he seeks to rehabilitate the lost science of market research, while with the other he condemns the narrowness of professional sociology upon which it is based. Fortunately, history has moved on. Professional sociology has directed its methodological advances onto the big issues of the day, and now the values that inform its research are increasingly at odds with those propagated by power elites, so that few sociologists are willing and even fewer are able to become consultants of the capitalist class.

But Patterson and I agree completely on one point: the public face of professional sociology must be distinguished from traditional and organic public sociologies. I have already referred to the first, so let me elaborate on the second and third. Traditional public sociology is addressed to publics that are broad and national, that are largely anonymous and passive, that are relatively thin inasmuch as they involve limited internal interaction, and that are often mainstream in their orientation. Traditional public sociology, whether it be one of Patterson's or Wilson's op-eds in the *New York Times* or a best-selling book, emanates from the protected sphere of the university and engages publics at a distance. In this context the media are indeed mediators, becoming a public unto themselves, whose structure we need to understand if we are to get through to the lay publics beyond. After all, engaging with the media is quite different from our customary academic communication with our peers. Sociologists have not been laggards here, with such notable scholars as Herb Gans, Todd Gitlin, Bill Gamson, or Bob McChesney showing just why our access to the media is limited and how we may expand it. Perhaps, as Barbara Ehrenreich suggests, part of the problem is that we simply don't try hard enough or don't try at all. Still, we need to understand this enterprise and the conditions of its possibility.

The second type of public sociology—organic public sociology—is much less visible but no less important. It circumvents the media in favor of a direct unmediated relation to publics, which might include neighborhood associations, communities of faith, labor movements, environmental groups, in other words, publics that are local, thick (with intensive interaction among their members), active, and often counterpublics that make demands on municipalities or state governments. As nation-states become ever more attuned to the demands of markets in a global context, so local states and local communities have to bear the human costs and are thus more attuned to the perspective of sociology. Here organic public sociologies can flourish, but not without dilemmas, since the publics themselves can become more demanding, calling on sociologists to service their immediate needs, subverting their autonomy, and pushing them in a policy direction.

Third-wave sociology will also valorize teaching as a form of organic public sociology in which there is a mutual adjustment between the vision of the sociologist and the lived experience of the student. Through this lens teaching becomes a triple dialogue: first, between student and teacher, in which each learns from the other; second, among the students themselves as they learn to discuss their lived experience with one another; and third, between students and various secondary publics with whom they interact. There are models of teaching, including service learning, that quite deliberately invoke these forms of dialogue as principles of pedagogy—models quite different from those associated with professional and policy sociologies.

Indeed, the classroom can be seen as a laboratory for public sociology, a source of techniques of dialogue that can be transported beyond the academy in the manner that Paulo Freire celebrated in his *Pedagogy of the Oppressed* (1970). To be sure, the conditions in the classroom are quite unique in that students are a captive audience, thereby potentially distorting dialogue. By contrast, to engage publics beyond the academy, the sociologist has to compete with many other messages from more powerful sources. Nonetheless we should think about and experiment with various strategies in the more protected environment of the university. Students should be seen not as a drag on our professional careers but as our first public—first in the sense that we meet them early on in our careers, first in the sense of their being inescapable, first in the sense that they are our most immediate public, first in the sense that they are our largest public (roughly a million students take introductory sociology every year), and first in the sense that we do have a chance of persuading them!

THIRD-WAVE SOCIOLOGY AND THE SOCIAL SCIENCES

So far I have examined sociology from the inside out, highlighting the ways in which each commentator takes as reference point opposing positions within a field of power and the implication this has for the way each sees the external power of the field. How does sociology look from the outside looking in? Writing as a consumer of sociology, Barbara Ehrenreich complains that we simply don't do enough to meet the demands of journalists. Either we don't address public issues or we don't make the effort to publicize our work. There is a sense of frustration and incomprehension with the gap between sociology's public potential and our professional parochialism. In particular, she has limited tolerance for disciplinary boundaries that might impede our coming to terms with public issues.

Ehrenreich is correct. Public sociology calls for multidisciplinary collaboration. Whether organ trafficking or labor organization, incarceration in prisons or tracking in schools, the degradation of the environment or community medicine, these questions are, indeed, ones in which disciplines can pool their knowledge, their expertise. Of course, professional sociology also borrows ideas from neighboring disciplines. But such interdisciplinary borrowings are absorbed into and governed by the logic of our own research programs, with little concern for their integrity in their originating discipline. Just as we are aghast at the way economists appropriate sociology, so they in turn are no less aghast, if they notice at all, at the way we appropriate economics. This distinction between multidisciplinary collaboration in the realm of public sociology and interdisciplinary borrowing in the realm of professional sociology only serves to underline once again the separation—but also the interdependence—of these two knowledges.

If Ehrenreich complains about the limited influence of our field, Evelyn Nakano Glenn complains about the opposite. Speaking from a place in an interdisciplinary program, she resents our overbearing presence. The public sociology I propose is an outpost of professional sociology, designed to keep the discipline alive, not one that organically connects to subaltern publics—the specialty of subaltern disciplines. Glenn asserts that I too easily endorse disciplinary hierarchies and boundaries which subjugate interdisciplinary departments and programs—ethnic studies, African American studies, women's studies, and others—which in their origin and nature were constituted to speak to and on behalf of specific publics. Indeed, their ideas have affected sociological knowledge through their infusion into critical sociology. Their always-precarious place in the hierarchized world of the academy mirrors the subjugation of their publics in the broader political and economic fields. A dissident public sociology needs to collaborate with them in earnest—they continue to be a source and inspiration for third-wave sociology.

Glenn complains that I take as my point of reference the stronger disciplines of economics and political science and overlook the subaltern disciplines. True, but this is not because I have some fondness for these disciplines, but because they represent sociology's other, particularly in times when state and economy collude in the cooptation, regulation, surveillance, and repression of society. Economics is at the vanguard, closely followed by political science, in constituting the foundations of neoliberal thought, which is bent on the destruction of everything to do with the idea of "public." They are producing ideologies that are threatening all arenas of autonomous politics, not least the university in which they thrive—the university that every day becomes more like a private corporation than a responsive community of scholars and students. To be sure, both political science and economics are fields of power, possessing subaltern tendencies with which we can forge alliances, while the prevailing forces generate ideologies that justify a world ever more productive of and callous toward the weak and the poor. In the endeavor to fight off the tyranny of markets (propagated as freedom) and despotism of states (camouflaged as democracy), public sociology finds its allies in anthropology, in human geography, and in the hybrid disciplines created to defend subaltern publics.

I repeat this point because it is so fashionable to talk of the anachronism of the disciplines—whose pertinence is confined to their genesis in the nineteenth century—and of the need to compound the social sciences into a single discipline. To do so would be to invite the rule of the most powerful discipline, namely, economics, which has already made major inroads into political science. Even sociology, with its long and deep traditions of antiutilitarianism, is not impervious to economism. Propagators of rational actor theory, methodological individualism, often in the guise of social capital theory, have attempted, albeit so far unsuccessfully, to capture sociology.

Yes, the disciplines emerged in the nineteenth century with the rise of global capitalism, but we should not forget that U.S. sociology was born out of a conflict with economics as the latter took its neoclassical turn. It became an independent discipline (formally in 1905 with the creation of the American Sociological Society), splitting from economics because, for the most part, it saw capitalism through a more critical lens. Today third-wave marketization is returning us to the nineteenth century with a vengeance. Sociology is destined to play the same public role it played then, along with other disciplines (and fractions thereof), fighting to protect civil society and its endangered publics. But now the battlefield has expanded beyond the local and the national to a global terrain, where third-wave sociology not only defends labor rights and social rights but incorporates both under the greater universalism of human rights.

With over a century of professional knowledge behind us, and in alliance with other national sociologies, far more experienced and sophisticated in the practice of public sociology, today we are better equipped to thwart market fundamentalism. At the same time, the assault on human life and dignity is more ubiquitous and thus more insidious—because taken for granted—than previous waves of marketization, demanding a concerted response from within the trenches of civil society, a battle conducted on local, national, and global terrains. This, then, is the promise and the challenge of public sociology.

NOTES

Note: Thanks to Dan Clawson, Robert Zussman, and Erik Wright for their comments.

1. We can also create a parallel (homologous) matrix out of two types of academic capital—professional standing (publications, their number and their influence) and prestige of institution (reputational rankings). An individual's position in this matrix combined with career trajectory would go a long way to explain the position he or she occupies in the division of sociological labor. In other words, position in the division of sociological labor determines the exercise of power but also selects the likely characteristics (types of capital) necessary to occupy that position. It would not be difficult to interpret the position-takings of the fourteen commentators in terms of their academic capital and career trajectories, but here I am more concerned with the position-takings themselves and how their interrelations and combinations shape the field of sociology.

2. Massey himself has provided eloquent testimony to the demise of second-wave sociology in a recent account of how his own scholarly work on immigration, far from influencing legislation, was peremptorily "blackballed"—no reasons given—by the Bush administration. See Massey 2006.

3. This is not to say that public sociology should not be held to the highest scientific standards, formally guaranteed by the professional moment within the public sociology quadrant. A case in point is Dalton Conley's op-ed in the *New York Times* (December 1, 2005), proposing that men should have the right to compel women to continue their pregnancy so long as men legally commit themselves to being prepared to raise the child themselves. In her open letter to Conley, Carol Joffe draws on existing bodies of research, with which Conley seemed unfamiliar, to show that his proposal would further subjugate young and poor women in particular, even to the point of endangering their lives. Conley's intervention was a "private sociology," deriving from speculative knowledge and personal experience, Joffe claims, the very antithesis of public sociology.

REFERENCES

Freire, Paulo. 1970. *Pedagogy of the Oppressed*. New York: Seabury Press.

Massey, Douglas S. 2006. "Blackballed by Bush." *Contexts* (Winter): 40–41.

Wilson, William J. 1978. *The Declining Significance of Race: Blacks and Changing American Institutions*. Chicago: University of Chicago Press.

Editors and Contributors

EDITORS

DOUGLAS L. ANDERTON, DAN CLAWSON, NAOMI GERSTEL, JOYA MISRA, RANDALL STOKES, AND ROBERT ZUSSMAN are in the sociology department of the University of Massachusetts at Amherst. From 2000 to 2005 they were editors of the American Sociological Association's Rose Series in Sociology. Michael Burawoy approached them about editing a book on public sociology and worked with them to make that happen.

CONTRIBUTORS

ANDREW ABBOTT: Gustavus F. and Ann M. Swift Distinguished Service Professor in the Department of Sociology and the College at the University of Chicago. Author of *The System of Professions: An Essay on the Division of Expert Labor* (American Sociological Association Distinguished Scholarly Publication Award) and *Time Matters: On Theory and Method*.

MICHAEL BURAWOY: Goldman Distinguished Professor in the Social Sciences, University of California, Berkeley. Author of *Manufacturing Consent: Changes in the Labor Process under Monopoly Capitalism*; *The Politics of Production: Factory Regimes under Capitalism and Socialism*; and *The Radiant Past: Ideology and Reality in Hungary's Road to Capitalism*. Past president of the American Sociological Association.

PATRICIA HILL COLLINS: Distinguished University Professor of Sociology at the University of Maryland, College Park. Author of *Black Feminist Thought: Knowledge, Consciousness, and the Politics of Empowerment* (American Sociological Association Jessie Bernard Award, C. Wright Mills Award of the Society for the Study of Social Problems); *Black Sexual Politics: African Americans, Gender, and the New Racism*; and *From Black Power to Hip Hop: Racism, Nationalism, and Feminism.*

BARBARA EHRENREICH: Journalist. Author of *Fear of Falling: The Inner Life of the Middle Class; Nickel and Dimed: Surviving in Low-Wage America;* and *Bait and Switch: The (Futile) Pursuit of the American Dream.*

EVELYN NAKANO GLENN: Professor of Women's Studies and Ethnic Studies and founding director of the Center for Race and Gender at the University of California, Berkeley. Author of *Unequal Freedom: How Race and Gender Shaped American Citizenship and Labor; Mothering: Ideology, Experience, and Agency;* and *Issei, Nisei, Warbride: Three Generations of Japanese American Women in Domestic Service.* Past president of the Society for the Study of Social Problems; American Sociological Association Jessie Bernard Career Award.

SHARON HAYS: Professor of Sociology and Streisand Professorship in Contemporary Gender Studies at the University of Southern California. Author of *Flat Broke with Children: Women in the Age of Welfare Reform* and *The Cultural Contradictions of Motherhood.*

DOUGLAS S. MASSEY: Henry G. Bryant Professor of Sociology and Public Affairs, Princeton University. Author of *American Apartheid: Segregation and the Making of the Underclass* (American Sociological Association Scholarly Publication Award) and *Return of the L-Word: A Liberal Vision for the New Century.* President of the American Academy of Political and Social Science; past president of the American Sociological Association; past president of the Population Association of America.

ORLANDO PATTERSON: John Cowles Professor of Sociology at Harvard University. Author of *Slavery and Social Death: A Comparative Study* (American Sociological Association Scholarly Publication Award); *Freedom in the Making of Western Culture* (National Book Award for Nonfiction); *Rituals of Blood: Consequences of Slavery in Two American Centuries.* Order of Distinction, government of Jamaica.

FRANCES FOX PIVEN: Distinguished Professor of Political Science and Sociology at the Graduate School and University Center, City University of New York. Author of *Regulating the Poor: The Functions of Public Welfare*

(C. Wright Mills Award of the Society for the Study of Social Problems); *Poor People's Movements: Why They Succeed, How They Fail; Challenging Authority: How Ordinary People Change America*. President of the American Sociological Association; American Sociological Association's Distinguished Career Award for the Practice of Sociology; Annual Award of the National Association of Secretaries of State; Lee/Founders Award of the Society for the Study of Social Problems.

LYNN SMITH-LOVIN: Robert L. Wilson Professor of Sociology, Duke University. Author of *Analyzing Social Interaction: Advances in Affect Control Theory* and over sixty scholarly articles. Past vice president of the American Sociological Association and past president of the Southern Sociological Society. American Sociological Association Section on Social Psychology Cooley-Mead Award; American Sociological Association Section on Emotion Lifetime Achievement Award.

JUDITH STACEY: Professor of Sociology and Professor of Social and Cultural Analysis, New York University. Author of *In the Name of the Family: Rethinking Family Values in a Postmodern Age; Brave New Families: Stories of Domestic Upheaval in Late Twentieth-Century America; Patriarchy and Socialist Revolution in China* (American Sociological Association Jessie Bernard Award).

ARTHUR L. STINCHCOMBE: Professor Emeritus of Sociology, Political Science, and Organizational Behavior, Northwestern University. Author of *Constructing Social Theories* (American Sociological Association Distinguished Scholarly Publication Award); *Economic Sociology;* and *Sugar Island Slavery in the Age of Enlightenment*. American Sociological Association Career of Distinguished Scholarship Award.

ALAIN TOURAINE: Directeur d'études at the Ecole des Hautes Etudes en Sciences Sociales; founder of the Center for Sociological Analysis and Intervention and the Center for the Study of Social Movements. Author of *Post-Industrial Society; Critique of Modernity;* and *The Return of the Actor*. Officer of the Légion d'Honneur and of the Ordre National du Mérite.

IMMANUEL WALLERSTEIN: Senior Research Scholar, Yale University, and Director Emeritus, Fernand Braudel Center for the Study of Economies, Historical Systems, and Civilizations at Binghamton University. Author of *The Modern World-System* (American Sociological Association Distinguished Scholarly Publication Award); *After Liberalism; The End of the World as We Know It: Social Science for the Twenty-first Century;*

Decline of American Power: The U.S. in a Chaotic World. Past president of the International Sociological Association; American Sociological Association Career of Distinguished Scholarship Award.

WILLIAM JULIUS WILSON: Lewis P. and Linda L. Geyser University Professor, Harvard University. Author of *The Declining Significance of Race* (American Sociological Association Sidney Spivack Award); *The Truly Disadvantaged* (C. Wright Mills Award of the Society for the Study of Social Problems); *The Bridge over the Racial Divide: Rising Inequality and Coalition Politics.* Past president of the American Sociological Association; MacArthur Prize Fellow; National Medal of Science.

Index

Abbott, Andrew, 14, 16–17, 36, 195–209, 246–47, 252, 259
Abell, Peter, 200
Abu Ghraib prison, 236
accountability, 41–43, 129–32
achievement scores, gap in, 137–38, 143
activist public sociology, 15, 187–92
Addams, Jane, 19, 24, 182, 218
Adorno, Theodore, 34
affiliation, evolutionary ecological model of, 132
affirmative action, 30, 93, 180
Afghanistan, war in, 135
African Americans, 67, 101–5, 18, 107, 109, 147, 162, 163, 219, 228n2, 256; assimilationist view of, 223; in Civil War and Reconstruction, 213, 222, 228n1; class divide among, 232–33; discrimination against, see racism; educational policy and, 137–40, 143; effects of segregation on, 151–53; feminist, 214, 224; poverty among, 37, 136–37, 153; problems of gender and family relations among, 191; white ethnic backlash against, 179; see also civil rights movement
agency: black, 222; interactive role of, 190, 191, 193

agent-based modeling, 200
Agriculture, U.S. Department of, 79
Almaguer, Tomás, 229n6
American Apartheid (Massey and Denton), 153
American Dilemma, An (Myrdal), 28
American Journal of Sociology, 18, 228n1
American Prospect, 150
American Sociological Association (ASA), 3–5, 20, 35, 50, 79, 82, 91, 104, 111, 122, 126, 183, 195, 216; breakaway faction of, 159; Council, 30, 58n2, 130, 145; criteria of truth advanced by, 13; Distinguished Publication Award, 153; international representation in, 93, 100n1; lack of political clout of, 151; membership of, 45–46, 51–52; newsletter of, see *Footnotes;* outreach and lobbying by, 57; political neutrality advocated for, 146–49, 155, 248; political positions taken by, 26, 30; Population Section, 153, 154; publications of, see *Contexts; Footnotes;* Rose Monograph Series, 4; Section on International Migration, 154; task force for institutionalization of public sociologies of, 57–58, 96–98; Web site of, 233

American Sociological Review, 3, 4, 28, 36, 152, 216, 223
American Sociological Society, 48, 257
American Sociologist, 4
Anarcho-Syndicalism, 54
Anderson, Perry, 184
Anderton, Doug, 4
Annual Review of Sociology, 36
anthropology, 18, 54, 56, 95, 149, 215; interdisciplinarity and, 218, 225, 237, 256
antiwar movement, 129, 158, 242
Arendt, Hannah, 30
Armed Services Qualification Test, 137
Army, U.S., 48, 142
Aron, Raymond, 51, 184
Asante, Molefi Kete, 224
Asian Americans, 152, 216, 219, 221
assimilationist model, 27, 223, 224
astronomy, 127
Atlanta, University of, 38, 228n1
Atlantic Monthly, 140
audiences, academic and extra-academic, 29, 33, 40, 91, 102, 221; discursive engagement with, 184, 185; involvement of, 178; in natural sciences, 53; presenting research findings to, 35; for traditional public sociology, 217; writing for, 5, 11, 19, 25, 28, 96, 101–2, 119–23, 150–55
Auschwitz, 236
Austin, J. L., 184

Barrera, Mario, 223
Becker, Gary, 149
Becker, Howard, 45, 100, 119
Bell, Daniel, 120
Bell, Derrick, 107, 111, 224
Bellah, Robert, 5, 28, 120, 186
Benjamin, Walter, 23, 232
Berger, Peter, 41, 44, 45
Berlin Wall, fall of, 76
Bernstein, Basil, 139–40
Bevan, Aneurin, 233
Beyond Smoke and Mirrors (Massey, Durand, and Malone), 154–55
Biblarz, Timothy, 36–37

Bielby, William, 32
big-think sociologists, 185
Binet, Alfred, 138
biology, 18, 19, 149; interdisciplinarity and, 237–38; methodological model of, 182
Bismarck, Otto von, 233
Blackburn, Robin, 184
Black Feminist Thought (Collins), 101, 224
black power movement, 223
Black Reconstruction in America, 1860–1880 (DuBois), 18, 39, 213, 222–23, 228n1
Black Sexual Politics (Collins), 102
Blau, Peter, 24
Blauner, Bob, 223
Boolean logics, 200
Boston College, 120; Media Research and Action Project, 36
Boston University, 216
Boudon, Raymond, 188
Bourdieu, Pierre, 34, 51, 59n10, 97, 177, 180, 184, 188, 189, 192
Brazil, 188–90, 244
Breckinridge, Sophonisba, 218
British Journal of Sociology, 4
Brown v. Board of Education (1954), 107
Burawoy, Michael, 5–18, 23–64, 67, 68, 70, 71, 74, 77, 102–3, 135, 139, 142–43, 163, 176, 180, 185–86, 192, 204–8, 213, 217, 241–59; ASA presidential address of, 3–4, 13, 79, 80, 82, 91, 124–25, 195; on career trajectories of sociologists, 37–41, 94, 140, 176; on civil society as standpoint of sociology, 55–57, 94–95; disciplinary specialization defended by, 17–18, 52–55, 131, 256–57; distinction between reflexive and instrumental knowledge made by, 196–98, 200–202; on division of sociological labor, 31–34, 81–84, 86, 89, 124, 220, 221, 244–46; and domination of professional sociology, 47–49, 129–32, 244, 246; expert engagement cited by, 183; on fields of power, 44–47, 245; four-cell typology of, 109, 110, 177, 196, 214, 222; internal complexity

elaborated by, 34–37, 177, 181; on internationalization, 9, 49–52, 92–93, 176; journalism and, 96, 232, 235, 255; and knowledge for knowledge's sake, 126, 128; on leftward shift of sociology in rightward shifting world, 125–27, 164–65, 191, 193; on multiplicity of publics, 28–31, 117–23; and naming of public sociology, 107; on pathology of normative model, 41–44; political neutrality advocated by, 10–11, 14, 16; standpoint of, 214–16

bureaucracies, intellectual isolation of, 141–43

Burgess, Ernest, 183

Bush, George W., 75, 164, 178, 258n2

Business Week, 119

Cable News Network (CNN), 232

California, University of, 219; Berkeley, 29, 119, 216, 223, 226; San Diego, 219; Santa Barbara, 100, 102, 219

capitalism, 23, 136, 180, 236, 241, 248, 253, 257; civil society and, 56; control of knowledge under, 205; destruction of social and political controls of, 69; internalized force of domination under, 188–89; international, depredations of, 163 (*see also* globalization); public sphere in, 46; state-regulated, 241; welfare, eclipse of, 246

Capitalism, Socialism, and Democracy (Schumpeter), 196

Cardoso, Fernando Henrique, 3, 98, 189–90

career trajectories, 37–40, 94, 176, 201–2, 257n1; political rhythms and, 205; *see also* tenure

Caribbean New World group, 190

Carmichael, Stokely, 223

Castro, Fidel, 77

Catholic Church, 141, 164

Caucus of Black Sociologists, 26

Caucus of Women Sociologists, 26

Causes of World War Three, The (Mills), 39

Challenger disaster, 32

Chavez, Hugo, 77

Cherlin, Andrew, 120

Chicago, University of, 39, 48, 149, 218, 228n1; News and Information Office, 152

Chicanos, 223, 219

China, 67, 142, 191

Christian fundamentalism, 5, 30, 164, 234–35

Cisneros, Henry G., 153

citizenship: concept of, 70–71; defining and mapping, 217

civic engagement, 187–92

civil rights movement, 41, 129, 151, 158, 223–24, 242

civil society, 6, 17, 47, 50, 51, 55–57, 94, 215, 241

Civil War, 222, 233, 241

Class, Codes, and Control (Bernstein), 140

class conflict, theories of, 118

Clawson, Dan, 4

Clinton, Bill, 32, 153, 226

Clogg, Clifford, 133n6

Club Jean Moulin, 76

Cobb, Jonathan, 120

Cold War, 73, 74, 140

Cole, Stephen, 45

Coleman, James, 32, 38, 45, 118

colleges and universities, 56; career trajectories in, 38; hierarchy of, 49, 214–16, 228n4; internationalization of, 93; market solutions to problems facing, 27; public accountability of, 29; public, declining support for, 27, 128; right-wing inroads into, 164–65; tenured positions in, *see* tenure; valuation of disciplines in, 86, 88–89; *see also* faculty; graduate education; students; teaching

Collins, Patricia Hill, 8, 10, 18, 37, 101–13, 214, 224, 250, 260

Collins, Randall, 45

colonialism, internal, 223

Columbia disaster, 32

Columbia University, 120; Bureau of Applied Social Research, 39, 48

Coming of Post-Industrial Society, The (Bell), 120
communications, 182
communicative action, 31–32
communism, 23, 54, 241; collapse of, 76
communitarian movements, 70, 73
community schools movement, 101, 102
computerization, impact on knowledge of, 205–6
concentration effects, 11, 118
Conférence des Nations Unies pour le Commerce et le Dévelopment (CNUCED), 77
Congress, U.S., 141, 155, 162
Conley, Dalton, 258n3
Contemporary Sociology, 120
Contexts, 5, 35, 57, 133n2, 186
contingency theory, 208n1
contrast schema, 217–18
corporate culture, predatory, 234
Corporation for Public Broadcasting, 164
Corrosion of Character, The (Sennett), 234
Cosby, Bill, 232–33
Coser, Lewis, 3
Council of Economic Advisers, 178
Craven, Avery, 213, 228n1
Crenshaw, Kimberlie, 224
criminal justice, 11, 28, 29, 117–18, 227
criminology, 182, 193
Crisis, 39
critical race theory, 17, 18, 26, 33, 55, 223–24
Critical Resistance, 227
critical sociology, 5–6, 20, 25, 48, 75, 78, 84, 91, 118, 197, 216, 242–44, 247, 249–51; career trajectories in, 38, 39; feminist, 129; in division of sociological labor, 33, 81, 89–90; graduate education in, 104; and institutionalization of public sociology, 107–10; interdisciplinarity and, 17, 55, 222–25; internal complexity of, 35, 37; internationalization of, 20; in Latin America, 77; new approach in, 70, 72; normative model of, 42–43; pathology of, 43, 44; positivism attacked in, 200; power of, 46; professional sociology and, 67–68, 73;

reflexive knowledge in, 14, 46–47, 53, 195–98, 201, 222, 244
Critical Sociology, 4, 25
cross-disciplinary borrowing, 54–55; *see also* interdisciplinarity
crowd behavior, 237
Cuba, 67, 77
cultural studies, 187
culture, sociology of, 32
cumulation of knowledge, 129

Dahrendorf, Ralf, 187–88
Dallas Morning News, 152
Das, Veena, 184, 185
Davis, James, 45
Davis, Mike, 227
decision making, participatory, 118
Declining Significance of Race, The (Wilson), 253
Decomposition of Society, The (Horowitz), 45
Defense Department, U.S., 141
deinstitutionalization, processes of, 69
Delgado, Richard, 224
Democracy in America (Tocqueville), 196
demography, 19, 182, 193
Denton, Nancy, 152–53
dependency theory, 67, 189, 190, 253
desocialization, processes of, 69
determinism, social, 67
development, sociology of, 26, 190
Dewey, John, 30
dialectic of enlightenment, 34
discrimination, racial, *see* racism
discursive public sociology, 14–15, 183–87, 192
dissidence, political, 163–66, 251–52
diversity, 219, 237
division of sociological labor, 11, 25, 31–34, 57, 89–90, 201, 243–46, 252; global, 49–52, 82, 92–93, 244; hierarchies in, 81–84, 257n1; integrated, 45; perspectives on, 35; race and gender in, 218–21; social psychology and, 124; specialization and, 40
domination, system of, 69; resistance to, 71
DuBois, W. E. B., 18, 19, 24, 28, 38–39, 112, 213, 222, 229n1, 242

Duke University, 129
Duncan, Otis Dudley, 24
Durand, Jorge, 153–54
Durkheim, Émile, 24, 26, 30, 40, 59n11, 68, 112, 159, 160, 188, 235–36
Dyson, Michael Eric, 233

ecology: organizational, 32; social, 125, 132
economics, 6, 18, 45, 53–56, 94, 149, 214, 215, 228n3, 248, 256; in contrast schema, 217–18; discursive engagement in, 186; free-market, 189; instrumental knowledge in, 17, 53; interdisciplinarity and, 226, 227; media attention to, 119; neoclassical, 53, 136, 257; Post-Autistic, 56–57; professional engagement in, 181–83; supply-side, 178; truths of, 136, 248
economic sociology, 32, 56
Economist, The, 119
Economy and Society (Weber), 141
education, 222; of political and corporate leaders, 178–80; postsecondry, *see* colleges and universities; graduate education; public, 107, 137–42
Ehrenreich, Barbara, 17–19, 32, 96, 98, 187, 231–38, 254, 255, 260
Eichmann, Adolph, 142
Einstein, Albert, 136
Elizabeth II, Queen of England, 188
emotions, sociology of, 38, 125, 237
enlightenment, 117; dialectic of, 34
environmental studies, 222
Essex University, 184
ethnicity, 179, 253; sociology of, 226; symbolic, 185
ethnic studies, 18, 215, 216, 219, 222, 228n4, 256
Etzioni, Amitai, 59n11, 135, 186
Euclid, 136
European Commission, 188
Evans, Peter, 59n9
evolutionary ecology, 132

faculty: cross-disciplinary exchanges of, 99; diversification of, 219; international, 50; public intellectuals as, 98–99; publishing by, *see* publications;

status-differentiated ranks of, 96–97, 221; tenured, *see* tenure
Fair Housing Act (1968), 151, 152
Fair Housing Amendments Act (1988), 152
faith, communities of, 5, 28, 234–35
family, sociology of, 32, 38, 226
family values, debates about, 29
fascism, 23, 236, 241
Feagin, Joe, 4
Fear of Falling (Ehrenreich), 236
Feldstein, Marty, 178
feminism, 17, 27, 33, 41, 48, 51, 55, 76, 158, 214, 216, 228, 242, 250; African American, 214, 224; in critique of status attainment, 129; economics and, 149; interdisciplinarity and, 215, 225–27
fieldwork, 75
Flores, Guillermo, 223
Florida State University, 216
Folbre, Nancy, 149
Folha de S. Paulo, 189
Footnotes, 4, 19, 25, 35, 57, 132
Forbes magazine, 15, 180
Ford, Gerald, 15, 178–79
Ford Foundation, 92
Foucault, Michel, 69
Foundation Saint-Simon, 76
Fourcade-Gourinchas, Marion, 59n9
fractalization, 36
framing, 36
France, 76, 77, 184, 188, 249
Frankfurt School, 34, 200, 236
Fraser, Jill Andresky, 234
Fraser, Nancy, 30
Freeman, Richard, 119
Freire, Paulo, 254
Friedmann, Georges, 71
fundamentalism, 161, 164
future, vision of, 207–8; political engagement and, 136–43

Gains, Herb, 4
Galbraith, John K., 119
Gallagher, Maggie, 41
Gamson, William, 36, 254
Gans, Herbert, 118, 120–22, 185, 254

Gates, Henry Louis, Jr., 223
gay, lesbian, and bisexual studies, 18, 219
gender, 224–25; inequality based on, 217, 220–21, 225, 237; sociology of, 226; *see also* feminism; gay, lesbian, and bisexual studies; women's studies
genetics, 237
geography, 18, 54, 56, 95, 149, 215; interdisciplinarity and, 226, 256
George Mason University, 120
Germany, 76, 77, 184, 187–88, 233; Nazi, *see* Nazism; Wilhelmine, 170
Gerstel, Naomi, 4
Gerth, Hans, 39
Giddens, Anthony, 51, 205
Gitlin, Todd, 120, 186, 254
Glazer, Nathan, 223
Glenn, Evelyn Nakano, 17, 18, 213–30, 255–56, 260
Glenn, Norval, 183
globalization, 20, 27, 68–70, 73
global sociology, 49–52, 82, 92–93
Global South, 9, 20, 51, 52, 93
Goffman, Erving, 237, 242
Gonzalez, Henry B., 152
Goodwin, Jeff, 33
Gordon, Milton, 223
Gouldner, Alvin, 33, 42, 48, 249
graduate education, 39–40, 103–4, 207, 251; disillusionment in, 79, 94; race and gender in, 221; reform of, 9; second language requirements in, 93; writing and, 122
Gramsci, Antonio, 170
Great Awakening, 234
Great Society, 161
Guadalajara, University of, 153
Guevara, Che, 67
Guggenheim Foundation, 152
Guinier, Lani, 105, 107
Gulbenkian Commission on the Restructuring of the Social Sciences, 52
Gulf War, 233

Habermas, Jürgen, 30–32, 59n5, 183–84, 186, 187

Habits of the Heart (Bellah, Madsen, Sullivan, Swidler, and Tipton), 5, 28, 120
Hamas, 234
Haney, David Paul, 185–86
Haraway, Donna, 90n4
Harvard University, 117, 119, 120, 178, 216, 228n3, 249
Hays, Sharon, 8–10, 13, 20, 79–90, 252, 260
Head Start, 138
health care reforms, 32
Heise, David, 200
Heuss, Theodor, 188
Hewlett Foundation, 152, 154
Heyns, Barbara, 138, 139
Hidden Injuries of Class, The (Sennett and Cobb), 120
history, 18, 19, 45, 56, 95, 149, 225; discursive engagement in, 187; interdisciplinarity and, 226, 227, 236–37; philosophy of, 23
Hitler, Adolf, 56
Hochschild, Arlie, 38, 120, 183, 237
Homans, George, 216
home economics, 218–19
Hoover Institution, 120
Horkheimer, Max, 34, 83
Horowitz, David, 164
Horowitz, Irving Louis, 45
House of Representatives, U.S., Subcommittee on Housing and Community Development, 152
housing, discrimination in, 171–73
Housing and Urban Development (HUD), U.S. Department of, 153
Huber, Joan, 45
Hull House, 218
humanistic sociology, 202–8, 247
humanities, reflexive knowledge in, 17, 52, 53
human rights, 13, 145; advocacy organizations for, 28; universalism of, 257
Huntington, Samuel, 70
Hurricane Katrina, 110
hypersegregation, 153

Ibrahim, Saad, 30

imagination, failure of, 207
immigrant rights groups, 5, 28
immigration, 145, 153–55, 258n2; assimilationist view of, 27, 223, 224; policies on, 13, 154–55
Impossible Science, The (Turner and Turner), 45
INCITE: Women of Color Against Violence, 227
India, 142, 184, 185
industrialization, 158, 236
industrial sociology, 71
inequality, 145, 189, 198–99, 228; gender, 217, 220–21, 225, 237; income, *see* poverty; race, *see* racism; sociology of, 27, 42
Institute for Social and Religious Research, 48
institutionalization, 6–10, 57–58, 96, 159, 160; challenges of, 103–12, 250; of interdisciplinary programs, 219–20; reciprocal interchange in, 44; rights in, 71; threat to disciplinary integrity of, 125, 129–32, 247; of views of future, 141
instrumental knowledge, 7, 14–17, 34, 39, 40, 50, 83, 95, 243, 247, 250; duality of reflexive knowledge and, 197–98, 201–2; in natural sciences, 17, 52, 53; power of, 46–47, 222; teaching focused on, 19, 20
intellectual capital, 206
intellectual function, 171–74
interdisciplinarity, 17–19, 52–55, 95, 217–29, 236–38, 255–56; marginalization and, 215, 256; nonpartisanship and, 149
internal colonialism, 223
internal complexity, elaboration of, 34–37
internationalization, 9, 20–21, 50–52, 176
International Monetary Fund, 189, 190
International Sociological Association, 189
Internet, 205, 206
intersectionality, 224
In These Times, 232
Invitation to Public Sociology, An (American Sociological Association), 25

Iraq, war in, 4, 26, 30, 75, 135; opposition to, 130, 131
Is Anybody Listening? (Whyte), 136
Is Bill Cosby Right? Or Has the Black Middle Class Lost Its Mind? (Dyson), 233
Islam, 40, 201
isolationism, intellectual, 21
Israeli-Palestinian conflict, 130
Italy, 77, 170

Jacoby, Russell, 41, 44
Jamaica, 179, 190, 253
Janowitz, Morris, 117
Japan, 143
Jasper, Jim, 33
Jencks, Christopher, 38, 120, 137, 186
Jensen, Arthur, 147
Joffe, Carol, 258n3
Johns Hopkins University, 120
joint-disciplinary coordination, 55
Jonas, Hans, 184
journalism, 231–38, 255
Journal of Social Forces, 228n1
justice studies, 222

Kanter, Rosabeth Moss, 133n4
Kelley, Forence, 218
Kelley, Robin D. G., 105
Kennedy, Edward M., 155
Keynes, John Maynard, 248
King, Rodney, 108
knowledge: control of, 205, 206, 224; cumulation of, accountability based on, 129, 132; for knowledge's sake, 126–28, 201, 204; oppositional, 105–6; situational determination of, 198–99; types of, 42, 243; *see also* instrumental knowledge; reflexive knowledge
Komarovsky, Mirra, 58n2
Koreans, 109
Kotlowitz, Alex, 187
Kristol, Irving, 223
Krueger, Alan, 119
Krugman, Paul, 3, 98, 119
Kuhn, Thomas, 58n4

labeling, 11, 118, 250
labor institutes, 222
Labor and Working Class History Association (LAWCHA), 227
labor movement, 5, 28, 29, 50, 71, 158
Labour Party, British, 51, 205
Lakatos, Imre, 58n4, 196, 201
Last Intellectuals, The (Jacoby), 41
Latinos, 103, 104, 107, 109, 152, 220
Lazarsfeld, Paul, 39, 48
Lee, Alfred McClung, 4, 33, 91
legal studies, 223–24, 226, 227
legitimacy, 42, 129–32; of exotic versus real world issues, 182
Lenin, V. I., 137
Lewis, Oscar, 147
liberation sociology, 6
Lieberson, Stanley, 182–83
Lindholm, Charles, 237
Lippmann, Walter, 30
Lipset, Seymour Martin, 24, 45, 120, 136
Listen, Yankee! (Mills), 39
London, University of, School of Business, 119
Lonely Crowd, The (Riesman), 5, 28, 120, 187
Los Angeles riots, 108
Los Angeles Times, The, 119, 152
Lynd, Robert, 33, 34, 48, 91, 249
Lynn, Freda, 183

MacArthur, General Douglas, 143
Malcomson, Scott, 187
Males, Michael, 232–33
Mankiw, Greg, 178
Manley, Michael, 15, 179, 190
Manufacturing Consent (Burawoy), 206
Manza, Jeff, 28
marketing, 180, 182
market research, 43, 51, 253
markets, 6, 17, 55, 94, 215; expansion of, inequality and, 27; immigration patterns and, 154; invasion of civil society by, 57; privatization and, 107; right-wing mobilization and, 161; social basis of, 55, 56; tyranny of, 256

marriage, 41–42, 183, 195, 208n2; same-sex, 30, 36–37, 130
Marshall, Thurgood, 107
Marx, Karl, 23–24, 26, 112, 159, 207, 235–36
Marxism, 48, 76, 213, 222, 225, 228n3
Massachusetts, University of, 149
Massey, Douglas, 11–13, 15, 145–57, 248, 251, 258n2, 260
mass society, theory of, 242
Matsuda, Mari, 224
May 1968 movement, 76
McCain, John, 155
McChesney, Bob, 254
McKee, James, 223
McLanahan, Sara, 183
McPherson, Miller, 132, 133n3
McVeigh, Timothy, 233
media, 253–54; attracting attention from, 118, 119, 121, 150–51 (*see also* op-ed pieces); presentation of social issues to, 36; right-wing domination of, 164; visual, 205
medical research, 42
Mellon Foundation, 154
mental health policy, 118
merit, standards of, 87, 95, 97–98
Merton, Robert, 24, 37, 39, 180
Mexico, 77, 153–54
Middle American Individualism (Gans), 185
Middletown studies, 48
Milgram, Stanley, 236
militarism, 233–34
military sociology, 142
Mills, C. Wright, 31, 33, 39, 43, 44, 48, 80, 87, 90, 105, 141, 185, 187, 192, 234, 249
Misra, Joya, 4
mobility, theories of, 118
modernity, discourses on, 185–86
modernization theory, 26
moral function, 171–74
moral reform, 241–43, 246
Moskos, Charles, 142
Moyers, Bill, 164
Moynihan, Daniel Patrick, 147, 223

Muhammad, John, 233
multidisciplinary collaboration, 55
Myrdal, Gunnar, 28

NAFTA, 29
naming, 103–8, 250
narrative positivism, 197, 200, 203–4
Nation, The, 150
National Aeronatuical and Space Admin-
    istration (NASA), 32
National Association for the Advancement
    of Colored People (NAACP), 38–39
National Association of Scholars, 27, 164
National Institute of Child Health and
    Human Development, 152, 154
National Institute of Justice, 200
National Institutes of Health, 200
National Public Radio (NPR), 221
National Science Foundation, 140
natural sciences, 77, 182; instrumental
    knowledge in, 17, 52, 53; research proj-
    ects in, 235
Nazism, 23, 56, 71, 141
neighborhood associations, 5, 28
Nemeth, Charlan, 133n4
neoclassical economics, 53, 136, 257
neurophysiology, 237
New Deal, 160, 241
New Left Review, 184
New Men of Power, The (Mills), 39
Newsweek, 118
New World Economic Order, 190
New York, State University of (SUNY),
    Binghamton, 216
New York Times, The, 119, 152, 186,
    221, 232, 253, 258n3
Nichols, Lawrence T., 228n3
Nickel and Dimed (Ehrenreich), 32
Nicolaus, Martin, 26
Nixon, Richard M., 178
nonpartisanship, 145–49, 248
normative model, 41–44; pathologies of,
    43–44
North Carolina, University of, 48, 134n6,
    228n1
Norway, 51, 52, 136, 137
Novak, Michael, 223

Oakeshott, Michael, 160
Offe, Clause, 184
Ogburn, William, 3, 48
Omi, Michael, 223
Oommen, T. K., 184, 185
op-ed pieces, 5, 11, 19, 25, 28, 119–20,
    150, 154, 178, 186, 221, 233, 253
opinion research, 51
oppositional knowledge, 105–6
organic intellectuals, 170, 171
organic public sociology, 5, 11, 15,
    28–29, 217, 228, 253, 254; history
    of, 18; interdisciplinary, 222–27;
    principles and practices of, 49; theoriz-
    ing and research in, 221; women in,
    218–19
organizational sociology, 226
organization theory, 32
Ortega y Gasset, José, 196

Packard, Vance, 186
Pager, Devah, 28
Palestinians, 130, 234
pan-Africanism, 24
paradigm shifts, 223, 225, 229n6
Park, Robert, 30, 39, 59n6, 218
Parsons, Talcott, 24, 59n5, 67, 68,
    200–201, 216
participatory action research, 55
participatory decision making, 118
Patterson, Orlando, 14–15, 41, 44, 120,
    176–94, 249, 253, 260
Pedagogy of the Oppressed (Freire),
    254
Pennsylvania State University, 134n6
Perestroika, 51, 54, 56
Personal Responsibility and Work
    Opportunity Reconciliation Act (1996),
    191
Philadelphia Inquirer, 152
Philadelphia Negro, The (DuBois), 38
philosophy, 54, 226; of history, 23
physics, methodological model of, 182,
    193
Piven, Frances Fox, 11, 13–14, 20,
    158–66, 233, 251–52, 260–61
Polanyi, Michael, 160

policy sociology, 5–6, 25, 51, 52, 68, 72, 75, 91, 118, 216, 242–44, 247–49; career trajectories in, 38; defense of vested interests by, 78; distinction between public sociology and, 177–81, 251–53, 253; in division of sociological labor, 31–34, 81, 90; funding, 129, 131; graduate education in, 104; institutionalization of, 159–63; and institutionalization of public sociology, 106–11; instrumental knowledge in, 14, 46–47, 222, 243; interdisciplinarity and, 17; internal complexity of, 35–37; internationalization of, 20; in Latin America, 73, 77; normative model of, 42–43; pathology of, 43–44; right politics and, 195; tenured positions in, 207; truths of, 136

political engagement, 10–14, 30, 35, 45, 187–92; dissident, 163–66, 251–52; humanistic stance versus, 204; impact on disciplinary integrity of, 128–34; institutionalization of, 159–63; knowledge for knowledge's sake versus, 126–28; marginalization of, 218; nonpartisanship and, 145–49, 248; research-based, 150–55; rhythm of, 204–5; view of future for, 136–43

political function, 171–74

Political Man (Lipset), 120

political science, 6, 18, 45, 54–56, 94, 214, 215, 256; in contrast schema, 217–18; instrumental knowledge in, 17, 54; interdisciplinarity and, 226, 227

political sociology, 26, 32, 56, 226

politics: involvement in, *see* political engagement; social bases of, 55; types of, 43

Popenoe, David, 183

Popper, Karl, 58n4

Population Association of America (PAA), 13, 148–49, 248

Population Reference Bureau, 149

Population Research Center, 149

positivism, 196–97, 200; humanistic, 203–4

Post-Autistic Economics, 56–57

poststructuralism, 17, 55

poverty, 11, 117, 136–37, 158, 163; alleviation of, 17; culture of, 147, 161, 162; educational policy and, 139; racialized, 32, 153, 232; and welfare reform, 191–92

power: dynamics of, 125; fields of, 44–47, 56, 57, 222, 245

Power Elite, The (Mills), 39

pragmatism, visionary, 105

President's Research Committee on Social Trends, 48

Princeton University, 119

prison industrial complex, 227

privatization, 27, 106–7

professional sociology, 5–6, 18, 25, 83, 84, 91, 124, 135, 196, 242–43, 246–49, 252–53; assimilationist framework in, 224; career trajectories in, 38–40; critical sociology and, 67–68, 73; development of, 24; in division of sociological labor, 32–33, 81, 90, 245, 252; dominant position of, 47–49, 83, 105, 109, 125, 128, 131, 177, 216, 222, 251; engagement in public discourse of, 117–18; in Europe, 77; funding of, 131; global sociology and, 92; graduate education in, 104; and institutionalization of public sociology, 106–11, 250; instrumental knowledge in, 14, 15, 46–47, 83, 201, 222, 243; insulation from public involvement of, 118–19; interdisciplinarity and, 17, 218–19, 222–23, 225–26, 256; internal complexity of, 35–36; international status of, 20, 50–52; irrelevance of, 67–68; normative model of, 41–43; pathology of, 41, 43, 44; politicization as threat to, 11–13, 124–34; publicly engaged, 181–83, 192; quality of writing in, 121–23; race and gender in, 221; reshaping, 8; right politics and, 195; scientific methodology in, 88; tenured positions in, 207; traditional public sociology in, 217; transdisciplinary-infusions into, 55; truths of, 136; value-ladenness of, 199–200 professors, *see* faculty

promotion, standards of, 9, 96, 250

Protestant churches: fundamentalist, *see* Christian fundamentalism; mainline, 164

psychology, 18, 19, 218; interdisciplinarity and, 218, 237; social, *see* social psychology

publications: advocacy of quality over quantity of, 9, 95–98, 250; for extra-academic audience, 5, 11, 19, 25, 28, 96, 101–2; transformation of production process for, 205; *see also* writing

public institutions, devaluation of, 106–7

publics, 117–23, 242; deep and thick ties with, 217; engagement with variety of, 28–30, 177, 180–81, 254

Purser, Gretchen, 29

Putnam, Robert, 29

queer theory, 33

race, sociology of, 226

racism, 13, 145, 151, 189, 217, 220–21, 223–25; poverty and, 32, 153, 232; privatization and, 107; research on effects of, 151–53; social causes and consequences of, 30; *see also* critical race theory

Radical Caucus, 26

radical sociology, 69, 73, 77–78

Ragin, Charles, 200

rational actor theory, 257

rationality, substantive, 171, 175n1

Reagan, Ronald, 109, 162, 178

Reconstruction, 18, 213, 222

reflexive knowledge, 7, 14–17, 34, 40, 50, 54, 244, 247, 250; apolitical, 197; duality of instrumental knowledge and, 197–98, 201–2; humaneness and, 203; in humanities, 17, 52, 53, 95; left politics and, 195, 196; and new formal methods, 200; power of, 45–47, 222; teaching focused on, 19, 20

religion: fundamentalist, 161, 164, 234–35; sociology of, 141

Republican Party, 162

research programs, 32–33, 35, 42, 43, 235, 248–49; funding of, 131, 152, 154, 160, 170, 200; instrumental and reflexive knowledge in, 202; international components of, 93; in natural sciences, 53; participatory, 165; political engagement based on, 150–56

Return to Aztlan (Massey and Durand), 154

Revolt of the Masses, The (Ortega y Gasset), 196

Riesman, David, 5, 28, 41, 120, 142, 185, 187, 192, 242

rights, 72; subjects of, 70–71

Robinson, Mary, 98

Rockefeller Foundation, 48

Rosanvillon, Pierre, 188

Ross, Edward, 242

Roy, Arundhati, 3, 98

Russell Sage Foundation, 154

Russia, 142; communist, *see* Soviet Union

Ryan, Charlotte, 36

same-sex marriage, 30, 36–37, 130

Schalet, Amy, 29

Schumpeter, Joseph A., 196

Schutz, Alfred, 37

Schwartz, Pepper, 183

scientism, 183, 185–86, 192, 193

Seattle-Denver Income Maintenance Experiment (SIME/DIME), 129

Second Shift (Hochschild), 120

segregation, 13, 151–54

Selznick, Philip, 59n11

Sen, Amartya, 59n9

Senate, U.S., Subcommittee on Immigration, 155

Sennett, Richard, 30, 120, 186, 234

service learning, 7, 20

sex roles, language of, 225

Sharone, Ofer, 29

Simmel, Georg, 37, 112

Singh, Yogendra, 185

Skocpol, Theda, 29, 120, 186

Sloan Foundation, 154

Small, Albion, 218

Smelser, Neil, 24, 159–60

Smith, Dorothy, 37, 214

Smith-Lovin, Lynn, 5, 10–15, 20, 124–34, 246–47, 252, 261

social administration, 218–19

Social Darwinism, 228n3

social democracy, 241

Social Democratic Party, German, 76

social ecology, 125

Social Forces, 4, 25, 132

Social Gospel, 228n3

socialism, critique of, 196

social justice, 18, 111, 145

social movements: allegiance of intellectuals to, 169, 170; roots of, 129; theory of, 32–33, 342

Social Order of the Slums, The (Suttle), 120

Social Problems, 4, 25, 132

social psychology, 124, 125, 133n4, 236; knowledge for knowledge's sake in, 127

social theory, 26, 37, 112

Society for the Study of Social Problems, 159, 216

sociobiology, 237

Sociological Imagination, The (Mills), 39

Sociology and the Race Problem (McKee), 223

Solow, Robert, 119

Sorokin, Pitirim A., 228n3, 249

Souls of Black Folk, The (DuBois), 28

South Africa, 52, 56, 244

Southern Sociological Society, 125

Soviet Union, 50–51, 56, 67, 73, 160, 248

Speaking Truth to Power (Wildavsky), 135

specialization, 40

Spectorsky, A. C., 186

sports fandom, sociology of, 237

Stacey, Judith, 8, 9, 17, 18, 36–37, 91–100, 225, 250–51, 261

Stalinism, 23, 50, 56, 141

standpoint theory, 37, 55, 56, 214–15, 224

Starr, Paul, 32, 186

state, 6, 55, 56, 94, 215; allegiance of intellectuals to, 169, 170; coercive, 27; despotism of, 256; invasion of civil society by, 57

State Department, U.S., 31

status attainment, feminist critique of, 129

Stiglitz, Joseph, 119

Stinchcombe, Arthur, 11–15, 19, 20, 45, 135–44, 246–48, 261

Stokes, Randall, 4

Stouffer, Samuel, 48

Strand, Kerry, 49

stratification, 26, 32

structural functionalism, 33, 42, 48, 247

structural network analysis, 200

Structure of Social Action, The (Parsons), 200–201

students: changing skills of, 205; engagement with, 30–31, 255; motivation of, 126; *see also* graduate education; teaching

substantive rationality, 171, 175n1

Sullivan, Andrew, 187

supply-side economics, 178

Supreme Court, U.S., 30, 71

Suttles, Gerald, 120

Sweden, 137

Swidler, Ann, 186

Taiwan, 52

Talbot, Marian, 218

Tate, William, 224

teaching, 5, 8, 20, 30–31, 45, 49, 86–87, 214, 254–55; engaged with moral and political questions, 8–9; good, requirements of, 87; instrumental versus reflexive knowledge in, 19

technical rationality, 34

technological change, impact of, 206–7

tenure, 40, 122, 207; in interdisciplinary programs, 226; standards of, 9, 97–98; status distinctions and, 96–97

Terence, 203

Texas, University of, 39, 119

Thatcher, Margaret, 51

Thorne, Barrie, 225

Tilly, Charles, 138

Tobin, James, 119

Tocqueville, Alexis de, 196

Torres, Gerald, 105, 107

Touraine, Alain, 7, 8, 51, 67–78, 188, 249–50, 261
traditional public sociology, 5, 28, 29, 31, 51, 120–21, 217, 253–54
translation, humane, 203
Trotsky, Leon, 98, 248
truth, notions of, 13, 42, 135–44, 247–48
Turner, Jonathan, 45
Turner, Stephen, 45
Tyson, Laura, 119

Uggen, Chris, 28
underdevelopment theory, 26
unequal exchange theory, 190
United Kingdom, 51, 184, 188, 205, 233
United Nations, 77
universities, *see* colleges and universities
urbanization, 158, 236
urban planning, 11, 117
Urban Villagers, The (Gans), 120
USA Today, 152
utopian tradition, 7, 241

value-ladenness, 198–200, 202
value neutrality, 169–72, 247
value rationality, 34
variables-based sociology, 196–97
Vaughan, Diane, 32
Verso Press, 184
Vietnam War, 26, 67, 135; opposition to, 129, 158, 242
visionary pragmatism, 105

Wacquant, Loïc, 188–89
Waite, Linda, 41, 183, 195
Wallerstein, Immanuel, 14–17, 52, 169–75, 244, 261–62
Wall Street Journal, The, 119
Wal-Mart, 32
Warner, Michael, 30
Washington, Booker T., 39

Washington Post, The, 119, 152
Weber, Max, 24, 26, 34, 109, 112, 141, 159, 161, 170, 175n1, 187, 192, 200, 236
Weiss, Carol H., 117, 118, 181
welfare reform, 147–48, 191–92, 226–27
welfare state: religious substitutes for, 234–35; warfare state versus, 233–34
West Indies, University of the, 190
What's Wrong with Sociology? (Cole), 45
White, Harrison, 200
White Collar (Mills), 39
White-Collar Sweatshop (Fraser), 234
Whyte, William H., 136, 186, 234
Wildavsky, Aaron, 135
Wilson, William Julius, 11–12, 32, 117–23, 186, 251–53, 262
Winant, Howard, 223
Wisconsin, University of, 39
Wolfe, Alan, 29, 120, 186
Women's Committee of 100, 226–27
women's studies, 18, 72, 215, 216, 219, 222, 225, 228n4, 256
work, sociology of, 26, 38
world systems, 20
World War I, 241
World War II, 48, 71, 137
writing, 11, 250; accessibility of, 84, 99–100, 120–23; digitization and transformation of, 205; political engagement based on, 150–56; rhetoric and culture of, 9
Writing for Social Scientists (Becker), 100

Young, Michael, 184

Zald, Mayer, 45
Zaslavskaya, Tayana, 51
Zussman, Robert, 4

Text:	10/13 Sabon
Display:	Akzidenz Grotesk
Compositor:	BookComp Inc.
Indexer:	Ruth Elwell
Printer and binder:	Maple-Vail Manufacturing Group

ried mothers and their children. They will show that in the past, especially the recent past, more of the chronically poor end up in prison or jail or are killed by their lover. This gives human interest to inequality of income and of life chances of children. But it does not tell us whether the poor in Norway or Sweden (where they are a lot better off than the American chronically poor) will be enough happier in the future to be worth the price. And, even if it is worth the price, it does not show us that social democratic governments will become more prevalent. When Christopher Jencks et al. (1972) suggested that giving poor families more money rather than more education would increase total happiness, we do not know enough about the future to say whether they were right.

As far as we can tell, the increase in the average income over the last few decades has not increased people's reports of happiness in surveys. But this fact does not tell us anything either, because we do not have a theory of the relationship between reports and some measure of "true happiness." Lenin of course had a different answer than Swedish social democrats about "What is to be done?" In the cross-section, richer people report they are happier, but over time greater riches do not seem to work. So how can we know enough about the future to contribute to controlling it through discourse relevant to individuals or policy relevant to public discourse about the government? And the few participants in public discourse who do not talk about the future will not be glad to know about our confusion on as elementary a subject as what makes people happy.

TRUTH ABOUT THE FUTURE

One fact about the past is that the gap in achievement test scores between African Americans and whites has been about a standard deviation since World War II. Another fact is that, on the Armed Forces Qualification Test, used in World War II, the achievement test score of African Americans has increased about a standard deviation when re-administered recently, so that they are now equal to the whites of about six decades ago. So whatever we did over the last half century was enough to close the gap. It did not close it because whatever it was we did that increased test scores was apparently done to whites as well as blacks.

The most obvious thing we did to both races was to increase average years in school by about four years, or about half again as many as the eight that was common then. So one policy bet would be to give African Americans the time equivalent of six more years in school (or other environments that expose the children to reading, writing, history, and mathematics). We know that achievement scores for African Americans can be increased, because we have done it. The crude data suggest that education as measured in years may contain the cause of that increase and that it apparently takes a lot (sixty years maybe) of whatever that is to have an effect as big as the gap. But do these data show anything about the future? Hardly. A median years-in-school for African Americans of about eighteen, half again as much, while holding the whites at a median of around twelve is not likely to be our future.

To see the trouble here, and why it is a trouble in public discourse, I will go back to my argument (Stinchcombe 1997) that Charles Tilly has taught us to study historical changes as "a sequence of futures." Social forces produce a vision of the future that makes some ways of affecting the future (e.g., in Tilly, petitioning Parliament) seem real. That changes what is rational politics, and so changes politics. That is, for more or less rational people and corporate groups to act, they must have a view of the future and of how that future might rationally be changed. But the main lesson of history, "It was different in the old days," is a consequence of people having had a different picture of the future. Since that picture changed over time and was different between places, so the course of history was different between times and places. To change our future in light of the facts above, we have to know in considerable causal detail how the change in scores came about, and how the racial gap in achievements came about.

For example, Barbara Heyns (1978; for similar but not identical recent results, see Alexander, Entwisle, and Olson 2001) many years ago satisfied me that most of the gap in achievement scores did not develop during the school year but instead before children entered school (this seems, from other evidence, to be much less true if they participated in Head Start) and during the summers after they entered. Rich and poor children learn at about the same speed as members of the other group in the year that they had started with the same score. For example, if a student starts grade ten at a reading level of the average eighth grader, he or she will learn as much during the tenth grade school year as the average eighth grader did during the eighth grade school year and will be ready in the spring to start the junior year learning as a ninth grader. (Note that, as Alfred Binet already knew, the standard deviation of achievement within both races as measured in year-equivalents increases with year in school, which undermines many statistical treatments.) But poor and African American students will then, on the average, unlearn a part of that (or, in the recent results, not learn any more) over the summer, while the richer and whiter students will gain some. So the key differences are where a student starts the year, and whether he or she drops back, stabilizes, or keeps learning over the summer.

The argument is complex, even more complex than mine about how to run socialist steel plants. And no one, it seems, has been able to imagine a future in which summers were a different thing or in which students went to school more hours per day, or more days in the year, or more years, or one that distributed the extra time differently among the races and social classes. So there has been lack of interest in the results, very little more research along the same lines, and no theorizing among public intellectuals, sociological or not, about how to explore alternative futures.

This lack of an imaginable future means we still do not know whether the causes involved are during school or outside of school, though the preliminary evidence is that causes outside school, before starting school and during summers, are likely to be the main explanation. Imagining a future of homes and neighborhoods where poor and African American children will learn academic skills as fast as rich children learn from their homes and neighborhoods is difficult. Our future does not hold homes and neighborhoods for the poor with bigger and more subtle and abstract words, more paragraphs rather than short answers, and more useful mathematical reasoning. And that, I argue, is because we rely on participants in public discourse to sustain interest, so collectively we do not get interested in anything that is not in our imagined future. It is some comfort that during the most recent years citations to Heyns's early work have been increasing.

My argument is that if we do not value the idle curiosity of our Heynses, our Stinchcombes, and our Burawoys, and stick them in ivory towers with tenure and without questions on the bottom line (at least not too often), we will never know. The phenomenology of the discourse differences between the rich and poor (the theory of what may lie between poverty and low outside-school learning of abstract knowledge) is probably along the lines laid out by Basil Bernstein (1971–74 and 1991). He emphasizes the difference between abstract ("context free") and concrete ("context dependent") discourse, suggesting that the middle classes and teachers use more abstract forms than the poor, and so their teaching *and home life* expose children to more abstractions, rarer words, more subordinate clauses and topic sentences, more arithmetic and quantitative reasoning. Nothing is more context free than a multiple choice standardized test question. (A theory of why a modern economy or government may need people competent in abstract discourse is tentatively developed in my work on formality [Stinchcombe 2001].)

The application of such a theory to summers was diverted by Bernstein becoming a public sociologist before we knew the causes of class differences in patterns of discourse, or why the middle classes made money on it. What research there was assumed, because of the firmness of our belief in a future where schools are responsible for teaching abstraction, that the remedy to poor people's failure to learn would be found in schools, not in summers. It did not encourage educational sociology to learn about the intellectual effect of the other four-fifths of students' waking hours (my rough estimate for the United States) outside school.

I of course do not know whether this line of work would pay off in new knowledge nor whether my speculations about the line of theorizing that might work to figure it out would actually say anything about possible futures. I certainly could not sell it now as an essay to *Atlantic Monthly,* nor to the National Science Foundation as a grant proposal—it would require too much ruminating first. And it is even more problematic whether it would lead to building cultures of abstract discourse in the housing projects for poor single mothers to make part of their mother tongue.

My point here is that the puzzle I have outlined above has been there in the literature since the 1970s, with a lot of evidence in its favor. But unless we have a strong belief in idle curiosity about well-established puzzles, and an ivory tower to protect us, we will not have any truth about what causes social gaps in test scores to contribute to public discourse. And in this case, I would argue, a more powerful tradition of scholarly public intellectualism in Britain provided an alternative career for Bernstein and an alternative to solving the puzzle that he did so much to locate. The long gap before volume 4 of his *Class, Codes, and Control* (Bernstein 1991) shows some of that. Burawoy is trying to promote such alternative careers for sociologists.

Now let us look briefly and very sketchily at possible remedies, suggested by the above puzzle. Let us suppose that the figure of about half again as much teaching time (in some sort of social structure), at least for the poor and the African American population, would be required for whatever turns out to be the real problem. One place to look for money to pay for overtime teaching is at that being wasted on the crazy military policy of the United States. It is now arming so as to fight a strategic war in space against a very advanced and massive military engine elsewhere, that is, to fight the next Cold War, wherever and whenever it appears.